D1296435

Humanistic Management

In a world facing multiple crises, our foundational institutions are failing to offer effective solutions. Drawing on the emerging consilience of knowledge, Michael Pirson debunks the fundamental yet outdated assumptions of human nature that guide twentieth-century management theory and practice – as captured in the "economistic" paradigm – and instead provides an urgently needed conceptual and practical "humanistic" framework, based on the protection of human dignity and the promotion of well-being. By outlining the science-based pillars of this innovative system, Pirson provides a new model for the responsible twenty-first-century leader seeking sustainable ways to organize in a world of crisis. Highlighting relevant applications for research, practice, teaching, and policy, this book is ideal for graduate students and professionals seeking to develop their understanding of responsible business, business ethics, and corporate responsibility.

MICHAEL PIRSON is Associate Professor of Management, Global Sustainability, and Social Entrepreneurship, and Director of the Center for Humanistic Management at Fordham University. He cofounded the Humanistic Management Network and serves as Editor of the *Humanistic Management Journal*. He has won numerous awards, including from the Academy of Management, and has published extensively on humanistic management, philosophy, and business ethics.

Advance Praise

This book is an absolute must read to any business school student and leader of any type of organization, from profit to non-profit, small to large, business to political!

Christopher Arbet Engels, Chief Medical Officer *Poxelpharma*,
former VP at *Biogen*, **Boston Massachusetts**

In *Humanistic Management*, Michael Pirson argues for a significant shift in how we all – companies and individuals alike – need to conceive the practice of managing today and most importantly tomorrow, putting the old "economistic" paradigm behind us and moving rapidly towards a more humanistic paradigm for managing organizations and our economic institutions. Read this important, accessible, and beautifully-developed book. You will be glad you did!

Sandra Waddock, Boston College

As a 30-year veteran of Wall Street, I lived through many of the examples cited by Dr. Michael Pirson in exposing the shortcomings of Economistic leadership. His is a well-researched and compelling case for the critical importance of empathy, dignity and collaboration in the success of 21st century enterprises.

Ron D. Cordes, Co-founder of *AssetMark* **and the Cordes Foundation**

Humankind looks over the edge of a precipitous cliff, reflected in business scandals and public mistrust. The path we have taken stops at the edge. In *Humanistic Management* Michael Pirson points to another path, one away from the cliff, toward a future where dignity counts as much as maximization.

Thomas Donaldson, The Wharton School University of Pennsylvania

Finally! Here is a book that explains what "humanistic management" is all about. Pirson's work is an important step towards a change of paradigm in the way we think, teach, practice business.

Claus Dierksmeier, Director of the Weltethos-Institut

This is an important book. It explains how the narrative of business is changing, and why we should adopt this more human understanding of business. Read it more than once. We can and should make business better.

R. Edward Freeman, University of Virginia, The Darden School

This book is a revelation! So many people in senior management positions today feel a huge disconnect between their personal values and those of their businesses and the wider economy. They long for a new story-a new way of doing business. This brilliant book not only explains why they feel as they do but shows how to construct an economy that reflects who we truly are as people.

Stewart Wallis, Visiting Professor, Lancaster University and previously Director, New Economics Foundation

Michael Pirson provides a sterling upgrade to the inadequate business economic theories that currently shape democratic capitalism. With this brilliant book, Pirson helps readers see a path toward better theory, which has the potential of spurring better practice and a more meritorious future for us all.

Roger Martin, Institute Director of the Martin Prosperity Institute and the Michael Lee-Chin Family Institute for Corporate Citizenship, Rotman School of Management

Michael Pirson re-introduces humanity into problems of economic organizing. His book is both a masterpiece of interdisciplinary scholarship and an easy-to-read appeal to common sense in how we live and work. If you are struggling to find purpose and meaning in these turbulent times, read *Humanistic Management*. It offers a clear, accessible, dignity-centered bridge to an economy in service to life.

Chris Laszlo, Weatherhead School of Management and Case Western Reserve University

An important book, it provides critical foundations for a new narrative of an economy in service to life.

L. Hunter Lovins, President, *Natural Capitalism Solutions*

Managers and policy makers who want to improve business and society of tomorrow should read Pirson's thoughtful analysis. Shifting business strategy towards dignity and wellbeing can benefit not only employees but society at large.

Douglas Frantz, Pulitzer Prize winner and Deputy Secretary General, OECD

This is an excellent book which expounds on the basics for stakeholder responsibility: protection of dignity and contribution to wellbeing.

Klaus Schwab, Executive Chairman of the World Economic Forum

Michael Pirson provides a much needed humanistic perspective on management given the pervasive mindlessness of current business practices.

Ellen J. Langer, Harvard University

In *Humanistic Management*, Michael Pirson questions decades of teachings about what motivates people and makes them happy. We humans are complicated beings, seeking not only stuff and security, but also connection and meaning. Pirson makes the case that with a deeper understanding of human motivation, we can design better economies and companies, which of course are made up of people. Backed by deep academic research and credibility, Pirson takes us on an important and highly readable trip toward a new theory of management.

Andrew Winston, bestselling author, *Green to Gold* and *The Big Pivot*

Very few people have the intellectual breadth to accomplish what Michael Pirson did in this remarkable book. Weaving together insights from a variety of disciplines, he has shown us what lies at the core of our shared humanity –our desire to be treated with dignity– and how crucial it is to develop a paradigm for business that recognizes his fundamental truth.

Donna Hicks, Harvard University

Humanistic Management is a much needed and timely articulation of humanistic perspectives on organizations. For researchers, managers, policy makers and teachers alike this book is a wakeup call to take humanistic perspectives seriously. However, beyond waking us up through research, examples, and arguments, the book provides direction and inspiration about how to move down the pathways toward greater well-being and human dignity.

Jane E. Dutton, Robert L. Kahn Distinguished University Professor of Business Administration and Psychology

Pirson's *Humanistic Management* frames key questions, and provides good tools, for cultivating businesses that affirm rather than violate human dignity and further rather than thwart the advance of well-being for our own species and for nature as a whole.

Vincent Stanley, Yale University, Visiting Fellow at INSEAD, and co-author of *The Responsible Company* with Yvon Chouinard

Michael Pirson provides the long overdue reembedding of economic theory and managerial practice into its scientific and real-life contexts: from ethics to democracy, from psychology to ecology. Something that got completely separated and fragmented is being healed and becoming whole again. *Humanistic Management* transforms an impoverished chrematistic ideology back into what it ought and originally was thought to be: an economy serving the common good.

Christian Felber, Vienna University of Economics and Business, initiator of the international *Economy for the Common Good* movement

We are living in a time where old understandings of politics, economic organization and management are collapsing under their own weight. The pernicious idea that corporations exist to create shareholder value has reached the end of its useful life. What would organizations look like in an economy organized around the creation of well-being? *Humanistic Management* provides a solid and grounded framework for creating these new ways of management.

Jerry Davis, Michigan Ross School of Business, and author of *The Vanishing American Corporation*

An insightful book for the 99% – and the 1% who think that they run the world should take a close look, too.

John Elkington, Chairman & Chief Pollinator, Volans; co-founder of *Environmental Data Services (ENDS)* and *SustainAbility*; and co-author with Jochen Zeitz of *The Breakthrough Challenge*

We are facing a crisis decades in the making; a crisis created by the belief that economic growth would –on its own– deliver human dignity. With a powerful combination of age-old wisdom and modern scientific evidence, Michael Pirson shows why this was not and what can we do to find our way out.

Camilo A. Azcarate, Manager, The World Bank Group

In this book Michael Pirson takes us on an intriguing journey of tracing the sources and foundations of an emerging paradigm that can inspire the next generation of management research, management practice, and leadership capacity building.

Otto Scharmer, MIT Sloan School of Management; Founder, Presencing Institute; Author, *Theory U*

Michael Pirson draws upon a wide-ranging and rich set of inputs –from economics, psychology, sociology, management theory, neuroscience, sociobiology, history– to craft nothing short of a compelling and inclusive new narrative for human activity. In this relatively short book, given the breadth of its agenda, Pirson manages to define and defend just the sort of "new story" that our world so desperately needs and in so doing, he provides the "scripts" and arguments required for us to voice its case.

Mary C. Gentile, PhD, Creator/Director of *Giving Voice To Values* and Professor of Practice, University of Virginia Darden School of Business

This is a critically important book in a time where the world is confronted daily with the limitations of the current economic system. It's a comprehensive, well-researched and practical guide to an inclusive and sustainable global economy.

Patrick Struebi, Founder and CEO, *Fairtrasa Group, Ashoka Global* fellow and *Schwab Foundation* fellow

In *Humanistic Management: Protecting Dignity and Promoting Well-Being*, Michael Pirson provides a much-needed update of flawed assumptions about human motivations that have distorted policies and practices, showing how caring and humane organizations are essential for better lives, businesses, and societies. This excellent book is an important contribution to the growing leadership and management literature paving the way for a more partnership-oriented way of living and making a living.

Riane Eisler, author of *The Real Wealth of Nations: Creating a Caring Economics* and President, Center for Partnership Studies

The influence of business and how business is done is now pervasive in our lives. Unfortunately, most of business has become dehumanized – people are treated as merely functions or objects in the pursuit of maximum profits. Michael Pirson shows us how we can restore human beings to the center, where they rightly belong. This book is a landmark contribution to our understanding of how to make this happen in practice and in our research and teaching.

Raj Sisodia, Babson College; Co-founder & Chairman Emeritus, *Conscious Capitalism Inc.*

Humanistic Management

Protecting Dignity and Promoting Well-Being

MICHAEL PIRSON
Fordham University, New York

CAMBRIDGE
UNIVERSITY PRESS

CAMBRIDGE
UNIVERSITY PRESS

University Printing House, Cambridge CB2 8BS, United Kingdom

One Liberty Plaza, 20th Floor, New York, NY 10006, USA

477 Williamstown Road, Port Melbourne, VIC 3207, Australia

4843/24, 2nd Floor, Ansari Road, Daryaganj, Delhi – 110002, India

79 Anson Road, #06–04/06, Singapore 079906

Cambridge University Press is part of the University of Cambridge.

It furthers the University's mission by disseminating knowledge in the pursuit of education, learning, and research at the highest international levels of excellence.

www.cambridge.org
Information on this title: www.cambridge.org/9781107160729
DOI: 10.1017/9781316675946

First published 2017

Printed in the United Kingdom by Clays, St Ives plc

A catalogue record for this publication is available from the British Library.

Library of Congress Cataloging-in-Publication Data
Names: Pirson, Michael, author.
Title: Humanistic management : protecting dignity and promoting well-being / Michael Pirson, Fordham University, New York.
Description: Cambridge ; New York, NY : Cambridge University Press, 2017.
Identifiers: LCCN 2017008344| ISBN 9781107160729 (hardback) | ISBN 9781316613719 (pbk.)
Subjects: LCSH: Management–Social aspects. | Organizational sociology.
Classification: LCC HD30.19 .P57 2017 | DDC 658.4/08–dc23
LC record available at https://lccn.loc.gov/2017008344

ISBN 978-1-107-16072-9 Hardback
ISBN 978-1-316-61371-9 Paperback

Dedicated to
Marina,
Maximilian,
Leonard, and
Lucas
with appreciation, gratitude, and love.

Contents

Preface

Dear Reader,

   While traveling the world to talk about the concept of Humanistic Management, I have frequently been asked to recommend books providing a short overview. My answer has always been: "There are none." Then I would slowly add: "Yet."

   This book is the result of various efforts, including numerous collaborations within the Humanistic Management Network. Together with Shiban Khan, Ernst von Kimakowitz, Heiko Spitzeck, Wolfgang Amann, Claus Dierksmeier, Consuelo Garcia de la Torre, Osmar Arandia, and many others, I was one of the cofounders of the Humanistic Management Network some twelve years ago. Since then, more than twenty national interest groups and chapters of the network have been established across the globe. We have organized numerous global conferences and events to discuss the role of management in a world fraught with problems. In addition, we have published more than fifteen books and several special issues in academic peer-reviewed journals. This book is one of the first attempts to provide an overview of Humanistic Management as an alternative paradigm for Management. It cannot, of course, be definitive in any way – the field is still emerging. The point of this book is thus to introduce the basic paradigmatic ideas that have emerged from the collaborations of different groups from various academic disciplines, including practice and public policy, over a little more than a decade.

   The main purpose of this overview is therefore to inform and stimulate further discussions around the two questions that I consider fundamental: Who are we as people? And how can we organize to create a world that works for all, or as we say, a life-conducive economic system?

There may be a plurality of approaches toward more humanistic management. In the following pages, I will present one approach. It is intended to be broad and inclusive, yet naturally limited by my personal perspective. I want to thank Christian Felber, Donna Hicks, Hunter Lovins, Roger Martin, Paula Parish, and Sandra Waddock for their helpful comments on prior versions of the book. I acknowledge the remaining limitations and am responsible for all persisting errors.

This rather massive undertaking would not have been possible without the wonderful partnerships with my colleagues within the Humanistic Management Network across the globe; the rich collaboration with the Global Ethic (Weltethos) Institute in Tuebingen, Germany, the inspiring partners at the Leading for Well-Being consortium, especially Hunter Lovins, Chris Laszlo, David Levine, James Stoner, and Andrew Winston; as well as my colleagues at the Academy of Management. I am equally appreciative of the support I have received from Fordham University and its Center for Humanistic Management in New York.

Finally, my heartfelt thanks to my wife Marina and my kids Max, Leo, and Lucas, who would have preferred their daddy play soccer with them rather than write a book.

Introduction

THE NEED FOR A NEW PARADIGM IN MANAGEMENT

As you can witness almost daily, we live in tumultuous times. We face an array of global crises, ranging from increasing inequality and poverty, to fundamentalist terrorism and war, to mass migration and environmental destruction, all of them amplified by climate change. These crises require a fundamental rethinking of how we organize at the global political level, the societal level, the economic level, and the organizational level. The economic system has become increasingly dominant, and the current roadblocks toward progress challenge the way we organize, think about, and do "business."

Einstein famously stated: "We can't solve problems by using the same kind of thinking we used when we created them."[1] Nevertheless, mainstream business practitioners, as well as business school educators, seem to lack an alternative way of thinking. William Allen, the former chancellor of the Delaware Court of Chancery, notes that "[o]ne of the marks of a truly dominant intellectual paradigm is the difficulty people have in even imagining an alternative view."[2]

The Humanistic Management Network has worked on conceptualizing this much-needed alternative paradigm for business – a humanistic paradigm, one based on the protection of dignity and the promotion of well-being rather than mere wealth. This book starts by describing the dominant narrative of the current worldview – an economistic paradigm focused on wealth acquisition. The basic argument is that our understanding of "who we are as people" fundamentally influences the way we organize individually, in groups, in organizations, and in society.

1

In the following pages, I present both narratives in business: the dominant model representing "homo economicus," which accurately describes only about 1 percent of the population; and the alternative "homo sapiens" model, which represents the remaining 99 percent of us. While there is scientific evidence to support the latter perspective, the economics and management disciplines have memetically adopted an understanding based on inaccurate, axiomatic assumptions. This homo economicus worldview of human beings as uncaring and narrowly self-interested has influenced the way business structures are set up (limited liability, focus on profit maximization). The homo sapiens perspective allows us to understand the importance of care, the notion of human dignity, and the evolutionary reasons for humans only surviving when organizing for the common good. By adopting this perspective we can envision organizations as caring communities that converge to produce for the benefit of the common good.

In collaboration with the Humanistic Management Network and beyond, scholars have chronicled numerous organizations that follow the humanistic paradigm, which succeed because they focus on the protection of human dignity and the promotion of societal well-being. Some of these organizations are highlighted in Chapter 8. The fact that many such organizations are run successfully, and often more profitably over time, proves that there are alternatives to the current economistic understanding of how best to organize human endeavors.

Humanistic management scholars focus on human dignity, described by Kant as that which escapes all price mechanism and which is valued intrinsically (freedom, love, care, responsibility, character, ethics). This, they argue, has superior theoretical accuracy to the current paradigm. In addition, if the end goal of organizing were expanded to include well-being or common good, scholars can demonstrate how business might play an active role in solving current global problems.

In the first part of the book, the basic conceptual foundations of humanistic management are presented.[3] In the second part of the book, the applications of the humanistic management perspective are outlined for research, practice, pedagogy, and policy. In the first chapters, the notion of humanistic management as an organizing principle for the protection of human dignity and the promotion of human flourishing within the carrying capacity of the planet are introduced. This notion is becoming increasingly relevant given the multitude of problems humanity faces. In addition, the dysfunctionality of the existing, dominant paradigm is demonstrated by showing that it violates human dignity and undermines human flourishing, while constantly disregarding the planetary boundaries. A humanistic perspective of human nature is presented, outlining the consequences of this perspective for groups, organizations, and society. The basic pillars of the humanistic management paradigm present a framework for differing organizing archetypes. The book suggests that these archetypes can help guide a transition toward more humanistic management practice, pedagogy, and management-related public policy. It examines the research implications and specific applications by means of selected examples. Moreover, the book suggests that a humanistic paradigm is critical for academic thought leaders, business leaders, civic leaders, political leaders, as well as anybody concerned with the future of humanity.

Chapter 1 outlines the basic concept of humanistic management and contrasts it with the mainstream view of business. Chapter 2 examines the differing assumptions about and insights into human nature. Chapter 3 presents a humanistic understanding of human nature, which can serve as a cornerstone of management research, practice, pedagogy, and policy. Chapter 4 presents the consequences of such a humanistic perspective on organizing, providing examples, among others, for business strategy, governance, leadership, and motivation. In Chapter 5, the basic pillars of humanistic management, human dignity, and human well-being are outlined in greater depth. Based on these pillars, Chapter 6 suggests different archetypes for thinking about management, which inform research, teaching, practice, and policy making.[4] Chapter 7 explores how these archetypes can support a transition toward more humanistic management *research*.[5] Conversely, Chapter 8 investigates how these archetypes can support a transition toward more humanistic management *practice*. Thereafter, Chapter 9 explores how these archetypes can support a transition toward more humanistic management *pedagogy*, and Chapter 10 how they can support a transition toward more humanistic management *policy*. The concluding chapter presents a summary and outlines pathways toward a collaborative approach to a more human-centered economy.

The book is meant to be a stepping-stone to facilitate further, rich conversation and collaboration.

NOTES

1 Albert Einstein. BrainyQuote.com, Xplore Inc, 2016. www.brainyquote .com/quotes/quotes/a/alberteins121993.html, accessed June 27, 2016.

2 Allen, W. T. (1993). "Contracts and communities in corporation law." *Washington & Lee Law Review*, 50, 1395–1407. (Cited from Page 1401).

3 Readers interested in a more thorough philosophical treatment of the humanistic management paradigm should check out Claus Dierksmeier's book: *Reframing Economic Ethics- Philosophical Foundations of Humanistic Management*. www.springer.com/us/book/9783319322995

4 Some readers may want to skim or skip Chapter 6, as it may be too conceptual for them. The following chapters build on the framework presented in Chapter 6 yet present mostly case studies that can be understood without the conceptual framework.

5 Friendly reviewers also suggested that those readers who are not members of the Academy of Management might do better skimming the research chapter, as it might distract from the more digestible chapters that follow.

PART I Foundations of Humanistic Management

1 Two Narratives for Business

A FAILING NARRATIVE

Meet Elisabeth, my neighbor. Elisabeth did all she was told to succeed in life. After earning an MBA at a reputable school, she chose to work for a hospital. She wanted to stay true to her desire to serve others and thought the health care industry would allow her to do so.

One afternoon, we run into each other as she is walking her dog. I ask her how she likes her work and she confesses, "It is awful – so stressful . . . I never really wanted to be in a competitive, business type of environment, but it seems the hospital is just as corporate and mean-spirited as everything else."

Meet Richard, formerly a successful Wall Street banker. He joined the world of banking because he admired its service orientation, but quit the industry in what he later described as a midlife crisis. The more he thought about the type of work his bank was doing and the people with whom it was working, the more depressed he became. He had an especially hard time reconciling what he heard in church on Sunday with the values that surrounded him in the financial industry. The banking and service culture that he admired had turned into something of which he wanted no part. He decided to get out.

Meet Tiffany, a former student, who never wanted to be in business, which she believed was an arid field, devoid of human touch and care. She did not feel attracted to the private sector and wanted to be a "good person." She chose a low-paying public policy career and worked for nongovernmental entities to stay true to her personal philosophy.

Elisabeth, Richard, and Tiffany have the luxury of many choices. In many ways they are privileged. These real-life stories highlight a shared unhappiness about business despite privilege. While one could easily dismiss such unhappiness as a minority view, research shows that, despite unprecedented levels of material wealth, people are increasingly alienated from their work[1] and want to redefine the meaning of success.[2] On the flipside, an increasing number of people wish to engage in more meaningful activities at work and beyond, and long to be part of the solutions to the many problems that humanity faces (climate change, terrorism, social inequality, poverty).[3]

Mainstream thinking about the business world has become associated with the fictional character Gordon Gekko and his motto: "Greed is good." Money and power are portrayed as the ultimate motives of human ambition, and disagreeing with this is sheer naivety. The dominant narrative is that people are greedy, money-hungry maximizers, or *homo economicus*.

Nevertheless, there seems to be something wrong with the larger cultural narrative about what human beings value first and foremost. The economist Richard Layard has mentioned that there is something wrong when we have unprecedented material wealth and economic growth but stagnating levels of human well-being.[4] The famous Easterlin Paradox[5] states that happiness is not significantly associated with income. As such, the dominant narrative is failing.[6]

At the core of the three life stories above lies a narrative about business that has failed to deliver the "good life," as many people perceive it. The wish to change the narrative is the crux of a concerted effort to rethink how people have come to understand life and their role within the economic system. The position advocated here is that a change in the narrative can contribute to a better life *and* a better economy.

CRISIS SIGNALS — THREE CHALLENGES TO THE CURRENT SYSTEM

Our current societal setup is largely driven by an understanding of the economic system as the central driver of progress. This notion is arguably more relevant in developed regions of the world. However, some observers, including Nobel Laureate Joseph Stiglitz, bemoan the increasing spread of the "Washington Consensus" around the globe.[7] As a consequence, the economistic logic, according to which markets provide the ultimate rationale for what is valuable, is increasingly a globally shared cultural narrative. This narrative is, however, increasingly challenged.[8] We are experiencing what scientific historian Thomas Kuhn called a paradigmatic crisis.[9]

Individual-Level Challenges

On the individual level, scholars observe an interesting anomaly.[10] While the current system is credited with creating more wealth for many, the average life satisfaction level has not increased.[11] Gross domestic product (GDP) growth and growth in well-being have decoupled.[12] Factors that contribute to well-being have a relatively low correlation with material wealth once a certain wealth level has been achieved.[13] From a systemic perspective, a government's quality in terms of democratic and human rights, the level of corruption, the system's stability, high social capital, and a strong economy with low rates of unemployment and inflation all contribute to subjective well-being. On an individual level, the quality of social relationships, good physical and mental health, and a generally positive attitude toward life are central drivers of well-being.[14] As an attitude, materialism, for example, is toxic for well-being.[15] Many studies show that a personal quest for more money or consumer goods decreases people's sense of personal well-being.[16] George Monbiot highlights that:

> This is the dreadful mistake we are making: allowing ourselves to believe that having more money and more stuff enhances our wellbeing, a belief possessed not only by those poor deluded people in the pictures, but by almost every member of almost every government. Worldly ambition, material aspiration, perpetual growth: these are a formula for mass unhappiness.[17]

The current system is built on increases in consumption that may lead to economic growth, yet make many people less happy with their lives. The advertising industry, for example, exists to create artificial material wants and is considered successful when more people try to feed their wants with more consumption, which drives up raw material use and creates many related environmental and social problems. For societies that pride themselves on freedom of choice and democratic values, such unreflected practices undermine their very essence.[18]

Organizational-Level Challenges

Business practices are increasingly being challenged at the organizational level. The recent collapse of the factory building at Rana Plaza in Bangladesh, which highlighted the working conditions of textile workers; the corruption and cheating at Volkswagen; and the usage of legal loopholes to evade taxes (e.g., Google, Facebook, Pfizer) challenge the legitimacy of business as a societal institution. Over the past decades, corporations have lost their reputations and stakeholder trust has declined.[19] Trust is, however, commonly viewed as the key enabler of cooperation, motivation, and innovation, all of which organizations require for peak performance and success.[20] Surveys indicate that stakeholder trust in businesses is decreasing dramatically, specifically trust in large global companies bent on shareholder value maximization. Research finds that the decline in trust is strongly correlated with a lack of value congruency between the stakeholders and the organization.[21] People perceive profit maximization goals as inherently opportunistic, making it ever more difficult for the business community to reestablish trust.[22]

Observers have long noted that many organizations (especially corporations) face a decreasing level of employee commitment, which is indicative of the increasing lack of mutual commitment. The Hay Group, for example, finds that 43 percent of American employees are either neutral or negative toward their workplace.[23] According to several Gallup studies, around 70 percent of US employees are either not engaged or actively disengaged, showing an alarming inner with-drawal rate.[24] Management scholar Michael Jensen argues that the goal of profit maximization is partially responsible. He posits as self-evident that:

> Creating value takes more than acceptance of value maximization as the organizational objective. As a statement of corporate purpose or vision, value maximization is not likely to tap into the energy and enthusiasm of employees and managers to create value.[25]

Hence, shareholder value-maximizing organizations are under-utilizing their employees' potential.[26]

Systemic Challenges

Environmental destruction is one of the most obvious problems of our current economic system. Humanity is using the productive capacity of more than 1.5 planets to satisfy its desires.[27] If everybody on this planet were to consume natural resources at the rate of an average American, five planets would be required.[28] The current economy uses more resources than can be replenished, leading to unsustainable growth and even more economic bubbles. In financial terms, human-ity is living off its planetary capital and not off the interest it gener-ates, which is very poor management of resources. However, the logic of our current system supports this lack of sustainability. Shareholder capitalism is short-term-oriented and, when applied rigorously, rewards plundering rather than preserving.[29] According to ecological economist Robert Costanza, economics does not value the future.[30]

The current levels of poverty and inequality had pricked the conscience of many people long before the publication of Thomas Piketty's *Capital in the Twenty-First Century* in 2015.[31] The Occupy Wall Street protests and their global spinoffs, together with various political movements (Syriza in Greece, Podemos in Spain, the Brexit movement in the United Kingdom, the electoral campaigns of Bernie Sanders and Donald Trump in the United States), showcase the widespread dissatisfaction with current levels of inequality. Such dissatisfaction is a threat to the political system's stability, which the growing fundamentalist terrorism also suggests. One-sixth of the world's population lives in extreme poverty. Current globalization trends have led to a world in which the rich get richer and the poor get disproportionately poorer.[32] Absolute poverty may have decreased in recent years, but relative poverty has increased significantly. Inequalities feed political unrest, collectivization, and terrorism, which in turn require significant investments to preserve the status quo (e.g., through higher defense spending). Research increasingly shows the deleterious effects of inequality on human well-being, especially health.[33] Shareholder capitalism is mostly blind to these consequences and has not yet provided satisfactory answers to deal with these issues.[34] Sustainability scholars Paul Hawken, Amory Lovins, and Hunter Lovins have argued that economics does not value social relationships.[35]

CHALLENGES TO THEORY, PRACTICE, PEDAGOGY, AND POLICY

Economic and business theory is under attack in fundamental ways. The basic assumption that material wealth will lead to better lives is, in many parts of the world, no longer true. A lot of research shows that the assumptions that human beings are greedy and narrowly self-interested are problematic and function like self-fulfilling prophecies.[36] The genesis and development of this narrative are discussed in more detail in Chapter 2.

From a theoretical perspective, these assumptions lead scholars to understand only a very small part of human organizing practice. Just like the drunken man who lost his key in the middle of the street but is searching for them at the end of the street where the streetlight is, many academics misplace their scholarly attention. Despite the richness of the material (discussed in Chapter 2), findings that challenge the assumptions of homo economicus have been assigned to marginal "boxes" and labeled as deviant. The reductionist approach to economic and management theory is legitimate to a degree but has become a paradigmatic prison.

Many scholars have suggested that the current paradigm is not only problematic for theoretical and scholarly purposes, but leads to bad management practice.[37] W. Edwards Deming, the father of quality management and a contributor to Japan's postwar resurgence, observed that many successful business owners rarely hire MBAs because they believe they lack the mindset required for successful organizing.[38] Studies on business teaching's current effects reveal that many socially undesired traits are perpetuated when business teaching is based on purely economistic assumptions.[39] Scholars find that the rate of cheating increases, care for others is reduced, and egotistical behavior is rewarded. In fact, during the 2008 crises, leading business schools were singled out as having contributed to the global financial crisis with their teaching.[40]

In addition, the assumption model of homo economicus increases policy support for GDP growth at the societal level, income growth at the individual level, and profit maximization at the organizational level – all measures that aim to deliver material wealth, not well-being. As such, in the US context, the Securities and Exchange Commission (SEC) guidelines make it harder for organizations that propose providing equitable returns and not maximizing shareholder value to enter public financial markets. The founders of AES, a US energy company, recall that their investment bankers had refused to support a "caring approach" toward employees, claiming that this would violate SEC standards.[41]

Scholars argue that we need another Enlightenment to challenge the hegemony of homo economicus. The Enlightenment, a European movement in the late seventeenth and eighteenth centuries, challenged the dominance of religious orthodoxy. It shifted fundamental assumptions about human nature by focusing on reason, not religious dogma, as the primary source of authority and legitimacy. As a result, it empowered people to start thinking for themselves and to advance ideals such as liberty, progress, tolerance, fraternity, constitutional government, and the separation of church and state.[42] Currently, the Enlightenment needs to empower people like Elisabeth, Richard, and Tiffany to forge pathways that lead to a better life. Biologist Andreas Weber calls it *Enlivenment*.[43]

THE ECONOMISTIC PARADIGM

The experiences of Elisabeth, Richard, and Tiffany showcase the reality that the background narrative we label "economistic" causes. Because the economistic narrative is based on axiomatic notions of who we are as people, it is worth exploring if those assumptions are correct. In fact, it turns out that this narrative is not based on scientific insights, but on assumptions most often reflected in fictional characters, such as Ebenezer Scrooge or Gordon Gekko, and some real-life characters portrayed by *The Wolf of Wall Street* or villains such as Bernie Madoff. The narrative holds that people are fundamentally self-serving and looking for material wealth as an indicator of success. The narrative is therefore amoral in the sense that any behavior is acceptable as long as it helps create more money. Other people are treated as a means to personal gain, and trickster behavior is considered sly, smart, and legitimate. These assumptions are simple, and therefore very powerful.

In more scientific terms, these assumptions refer to humans as individuals driven by rational interests aimed at maximizing utility (homo economicus). As measurable entities or preferences, wealth and income have, however, gradually supplanted utility as a broad concept of what brings happiness. Rational interests are those that can be negotiated in an exchange setting: More of x utility should therefore trump less of the same. The *quantity* of options supersedes the *quality* of options. There is now a vast literature both criticizing and defending homo economicus, yet the main argument here is that beyond legitimate reductions for theoretical purposes in economics, homo economicus assumptions have become performative in ways beyond mere theoretical prescriptions, especially in the domain of business and management.

The simplicity of homo economicus assumptions follows what is also known as Occam's razor, or the law of parsimony. This law states that the hypothesis with the fewest assumptions should be selected from all the competing hypotheses. Although other, more complicated solutions may ultimately prove correct, in the absence of certainty, the fewer assumptions made, the better.[44] Applied to market-based behavior questions, these assumptions seem to accurately describe common motivations. However, when uncoupled from their original purpose, they become misguided. When studying how most people will behave in a *market* setting where the price mechanism regulates the supply of and demand for a product, the homo economicus model is useful. When human relationships are, however, studied in *organizational* contexts, such a lens will fail to capture human complexity.

Whereas parsimony in itself is valuable for theoretical purposes, it had an additional effect on economics by making it more mathematics-based. Outsiders started viewing economics as scientifically more rigorous. Rakesh Khurana, a former Harvard Business School professor turned Harvard College dean, suggests that, in general, management research and business schools adopted the methodological tool box of economics, along with its underlying assumptions, to turn a practice-based trade school into what would be seen as a science-based university school.[45] This shift was undertaken to enhance the visibility and reputational status of a newly emerging class of businessmen and professional managers, who could not otherwise compete in terms of societal status with doctors, lawyers, and priests.

Khurana argues that in order to acquire a reputational status, business and management had to become a profession that would require a university degree. Until the late 1800s, there was almost no business education, while trade schools would teach accounting, bakery, butchery, etc. Business and management research turned to the axiomatic notion of people as homo economicus to justify itself as scientific and rigorous. This enabled business schools to claim to be legitimate professional schools with affiliation to a "serious, reputable" university. Rather than seeing the irony of its unscientific basis, management theory has used "economic man" as its ticket to become a respected "science."[46]

This argument is not novel: Karl Marx and John Maynard Keynes also used it. Keynes states: "Economists, like other scientists, have chosen the hypothesis from which they set out, and which they offer to beginners because it is the simplest, and not because it is the nearest to the facts."[47]

In his essay on the Church of Economism, Richard Norgaard suggests that leading economists are aware of the quasi-religious nature of economics:

> Economists themselves have acknowledged the ultimately religious nature of their discipline. In 1932, Frank Knight, the most scholarly and broad-thinking of the founders of the influential market-oriented Chicago School of Economics, literally argued that economics, at a fundamental level, had to be a religion, the basic tenets of which must be hidden from all but a few:

> The point is that the "principles" – by which a society or a group lives in tolerable harmony are essentially religious. The essential nature of a religious principle is that not merely is it immoral to oppose it, but to ask what it is, is morally identical with denial and attack.

> There must be ultimates, and they must be religious, in economics as anywhere else, if one has anything to say touching conduct or social policy in a practical way. Man is a believing animal and to few, if any, is it given to criticize the foundations of belief 'intelligently.' To inquire into the ultimates behind accepted group values is obscene and sacrilegious: objective inquiry is an attempt to uncover the nakedness of man, his soul as well as his body, his deeds, his culture, and his very gods. Certainly the large general [economics] courses should be prevented from raising any question about objectivity, but should assume the objectivity of the slogans they inculcate, as a sacred feature of the system.[48]

The argument is that business theory and management "science" have unconsciously, memetically, uncritically, and unreflectedly adopted the precepts of the Church of Economism (for a number of reasons, including status orientation, "physics envy," or the authentic quest for scientific rigor).[49] One of the core foundations of this quasi-religious business theory is the assumption that profit maximization is a signal of effectiveness, and that the main concern of organizing should be related to efficiency.[50] Such unquestioned concerns for efficiency are mostly presented in the "objective" form. Management scientists, for example, study quantitative decision-making based on utilitarian cost/benefit assessments. Within this framework, people become resources as in "human resources" or "human capital." To be seen as objective, researchers' moral concerns have to be eliminated, and qualitative judgments replaced with fact-based evidence. The evidence, for which management science is looking, is the rational behavior that leads to an organization's greater profitability. Frederic Taylor heralded such a perspective, and Henry Ford most famously adopted it. Their successes practically legitimized what seemed theoretically expedient.

The perceived connection of economics with the theory of all theories, Darwinian evolution, was another cultural force that helped establish economics-based management theory. Many observers have noted that the Herbert Spencer's popularization of Darwin's insights gave scientific backing to an amoral kind of behavior that would favor the strongest over the weak. According to Spencer's *Social* Darwinism, natural selection favored the ruthless over the caring, the competitive over the collaborative, and, as an extension of this, the unethical over the ethical. While a careful reading of Darwin would immediately refute such a perspective, at the time, such Spencerian accounts lent credibility to homo economicus assumptions about human nature. These assumptions resonated with Adam Smith's perspective of humans as driven by self-interest, while ignoring his observations that what people really desire is to be beloved and to belong.[51]

Keynes argues that the confluence of these two perspectives took the individualist perspective of the modern era to a logical extreme:

> The parallelism between economic laissez-faire and Darwinianism, ... is now seen, as Herbert Spencer was foremost to recognise, to be very close indeed. Darwin invoked sexual love, acting through sexual selection, as an adjutant to natural selection by competition, to direct evolution along lines which should be desirable as well as effective, so the individualist invokes the love of money, acting through the pursuit of profit, as an adjutant to natural selection, to bring about the production on the greatest possible scale of what is most strongly desired as measured by exchange value.

> The beauty and the simplicity of such a theory are so great that it is easy to forget that it follows not from the actual facts, but from an incomplete hypothesis introduced for the sake of simplicity. Apart from other objections to be mentioned later, the conclusion that individuals acting independently for their own advantage will produce the greatest aggregate of wealth, depends on a variety of unreal assumptions to the effect that the processes of production and consumption are in no way organic, that there exists a sufficient foreknowledge of conditions and requirements, and that there are adequate opportunities of obtaining this foreknowledge. For economists generally reserve for a later stage of their argument the complications which arise - (1) when the efficient units of production are large relatively to the units of consumption, (2) when overhead costs or joint costs are present, (3) when internal economies tend to the aggregation of production, (4) when the time required for adjustments is long, (5) when ignorance prevails over knowledge and (6) when monopolies and combinations interfere with equality in bargaining - they reserve, that is to say, for a later stage their analysis of the actual facts. Moreover, many of those who recognise that the simplified hypothesis does not accurately correspond to fact conclude nevertheless that it does represent

what is "natural" and therefore ideal. They regard the simplified hypothesis as health, and the further complications as disease.[52]

The economistic narrative has led to problems on multiple levels, because the misrepresentation of individuals has logical consequences for groups, organizations, and society. The current perspective has led to many negative consequences (diseases, as Keynes states above), yet, owing to its dominance, a majority of educated observers consider the "quasi-religious" narrative of economics and management to be scientific and healthy.

The American sociologist Paul Lawrence suggests that the Spencerian version of social Darwinism perverted the meaning of survival of the fittest to mean the survival of the toughest, strongest, and most ruthless species, not the survival of the most adaptive species.[53] Lawrence argues that true Darwinian theory could indeed provide vital insights into human nature. He suggests that an accurate scientific understanding can help overcome quasi-religious assumptions that hinder the quest for better organizing practices. He, along with other researchers, argues that evolutionary theory can provide a truly scientific basis for economics and for management. Researchers such as E.O. Wilson, as well as David Sloan Wilson, claim that evolutionary insights can help bridge cultural divides and provide a deeper understanding of humanities' shared ambitions.[54]

THE HUMANISTIC PARADIGM

E.O. Wilson, the great biologist, argues that a renewed convergence of the humanities and sciences is helping us better understand human beings as social animals endowed with reason, which Aristotle stated so succinctly several thousand years ago. From the philosophical work of Aristotle to Adam Smith to Darwin, to the newly emerging fields of evolutionary psychology, neuroscience, and sociobiology, evidence is mounting that humans are hard-wired for empathy and collaboration, and that that sociality is fundamental to survival. The human tendency to be social, kind, and moral is no longer seen as a deviation and a bug, but as a feature. Wilson suggests that the humanities and social sciences can draw on the latest findings in natural science to project a better story for humanity – a humanistic paradigm.

Evolutionary theory concludes that humans are fundamentally caring and social, and that they are fundamentally moral. One can make more sense of this by looking at daily experience in which humans find that they care about each other (in family, work, and friendship circles) and about society at large (reading the news, checking in with "friends" on social media, etc.). A life devoid of care leads to misery in many ways. Humans have long determined that isolation is the most cruel punishment, whether physical isolation on a remote island (exiled like Napoleon), in a solitary confinement cell, or psychologically isolated through feelings of shame. Being alone is considered a tragedy and leads many to depression, dysfunction, or even suicide, rendering isolation crueller than death.

Expanding on the social nature of human beings, Darwin suggests that morality must have developed to manage the manifold social relations.[55] This insight into the relevance of morality, values, and care for our common good is normally buried by a story of business propagating greed, a psychopathic lack of care, and destruction of life. The alternative, humanistic narrative acknowledges human beings as highly social and moral. Humans become humane when they are involved in dynamic, relational communities that supersede the mere coordination of markets.

To capture this insight, the humanistic narrative employs the term *dignity*, which serves as a philosophical category for things that escape the market mechanism: those things and events that do not have a price and cannot be exchanged. To see how relevant dignity-related, non-market concerns are to human life, consider one of the most successful advertising campaigns of the early twenty-first century. For more than seventeen years, MasterCard's slogan was: "There are things in life that are priceless, for everything else there is MasterCard." The campaign was successful because it spoke to an authentic human experience. It demonstrated that while markets are important, the most important things in life transcend the market logic. The humanistic paradigm captures this essential truth about human nature and suggests that human beings require dignity to flourish. Elisabeth, Richard, and Tiffany longed for qualities in life that cannot be bought, such as integrity, love, community, and respect. Such qualities, along with empathy, compassion, and care, are key enablers of human flourishing.

In the humanistic perspective, then, humans not only desire autonomy and independence but crave for affiliation and one-ness. They are thus not independent, but interdependent. While the market is a useful coordination mechanism, it cannot fully meet our human and organizational needs. Social groups and communities are critical elements for a functioning society, and only those communities that help human beings protect their dignity can support human flourishing. Practices that allow for the protection of dignity and the promotion of well-being are part and parcel of humanistic management.

CONCLUDING REMARKS

There is a clear need for a better story of who we are as human beings. Many people experience cognitive dissonance between what they think business is and what life should be about.[56] The stories of Elisabeth, Richard, and Tiffany highlight the intense wish to flourish beyond material wealth. To achieve parsimony, economics-based management "science" has adopted a flawed paradigmatic set of assumptions about human nature. Increasing evidence from across the sciences highlights the downsides of the economistic perspective. The emerging consilience of knowledge is a starting point for more accurate theorizing and better management practice – a humanistic paradigm.

NOTES

1 www.gallup.com/poll/188144/employee-engagement-stagnant-2015.aspx
2 www.gallup.com/businessjournal/188033/worldwide-employee-engagement-crisis.aspx
3 www.forbes.com/sites/karlmoore/2014/10/02/millennials-work-for-purpose-not-paycheck/#47348b35a225

4 Layard, R. (2005). *Happiness – Lessons From a New Science*, London, Penguin Press.

5 The Easterlin Paradox describes that despite GDP growth in developed nations, happiness levels have largely remained constant since World War II.

6 It may be worth noting that more recent empirical research by Nobel Laureates Daniel Kahneman and Angus Deaton have shown a slight correlation of wealth with health and happiness, putting the overall claim of Easterlin in perspective. Nevertheless, the mere focus on GDP growth as political goal is questioned by them as well. See, e.g., Deaton, A. (2013). *The Great Escape: Health, Wealth, and the Origins of Inequality.* Princeton University Press.

7 Stiglitz, J. (2013). *The Price of Inequality.* New York, W.W. Norton.

8 I use the words "paradigm" and "narrative" interchangeably here; to be more precise, the paradigm is the base example on which thinking is based (such as homo economicus), and the narrative is the story that extends that example to make it culturally appealing.

9 Kuhn, T. (1996). *The Structure of Scientific Revolutions.* University of Chicago Press.

10 Pirson, M., et al. (2009). "Introduction to humanism in business." *Humanism in Business.* The Humanistic Management Network. Cambridge, Cambridge University Press.

11 Easterlin, R. (2001). "Income and happiness: towards a unified theory." *Economic Journal*, **111**(July), 465–484.

12 Costanza, R., I. Kubiszewski, E. Giovannini, H. Lovins, J. McGlade, K. E. Pickett, K. V. Ragnarsdóttir, D. Roberts, R. De Vogli, and R. Wilkinson. (2014). "Development." *Nature*, **505**(7483), 283–285.

13 Diener, E. and M. E. P. Seligman (2004). "Beyond money: toward and economy of well-being." *Psychological Science in the Public Interest*, **5**, 1–31.

14 Diener and Seligman. "Beyond money," 1–31.

15 Kasser, T. and A. C. Ahuvia (2002). "Materialistic values and well-being in business students." *European Journal of Social Psychology*, **32**, 137–146.

16 www.theguardian.com/commentisfree/2013/dec/09/materialism-system-eats-us-from-inside-out

17 Ibid.

18 Pirson. "Introduction to humanism in business."

19 www.theguardian.com/sustainable-business/2015/jan/21/public-trust-global-business-government-low-decline

20 Pirson, M. and D. Malhotra (2011). "Foundations of organizational trust: what matters to different stakeholders?" *Organization Science*, 22(4), 1087–1104.

21 Pirson, M. (2007). *Facing the Trust Gap: How Organizations Can Measure and Manage Stakeholder Trust*. St. Gallen, University of St. Gallen.

22 Pirson, M., et al. (2012). "Public trust in business and its determinants." *Public Trust*, eds. E. Freeman and A. C. Wicks. Simons, T. (2002). "The high cost of lost trust." *Harvard Business Review*, September, 1–3.

23 The Hay Group (2002). Engage Employees and Boost Performance. www.haygroup.com/us/downloads/details.aspx?id=7343 (accessed June 21, 2016)

24 For example: www.gallup.com/poll/188144/employee-engagement-stagnant-2015.aspx www.gallup.com/businessjournal/188033/worldwide-employee-engagement-crisis.aspx (accessed June 22, 2016)

25 Jensen, M. C. (2001). "Value maximisation, stakeholder theory, and the corporate objective function." *European Financial Management*, 7(3), 297 (citation from page 278)

26 Pirson et al., "Introduction to humanism in business."

27 www.bbc.com/news/magazine-33133712 (accessed June 21, 2016)

28 Boyle, D., et al. (2006). Are you happy? new economics past, present and future. NEF.

29 Pirson et al., "Introduction to humanism in business."

30 Costanza, R. (1992). *Ecological Economics: The Science and Management of Sustainability*. Columbia University Press. See also Chichilnisky, G. (1996). "An axiomatic approach to sustainable development." *Social Choice and Welfare*, 13(2), 231–257.

31 Piketty, T. (2014). *Capital in the 21st century*. Cambridge, MA, Harvard University Press.

32 Sachs, J. (2005). *The End of Poverty: Economic Possibilities for Our Time*. New York, Penguin Group.

33 Wilkinson, R. G., and K. E. Pickett. (2009) "Income Inequality and Social Dysfunction." *Annual Review of Sociology*, 35, 493–511.

34 Pirson et al., "Introduction to humanism in business."

35   Hawken, P., Lovins, A. B., and Lovins, L. H. (2013). *Natural Capitalism: The Next Industrial Revolution.* New York, Routledge. See also Chichilnisky, G. (1996). "An axiomatic approach to sustainable development." *Social Choice and Welfare,* 13(2), 231–257.

36   Argyris, C. (1973). "Organization man: Rational and self-actualizing." *Public Administration Review,* 33(July/August), 354–357; Ghoshal, S. (2005). "Bad management theories are destroying good management practices." *Academy of Management Learning and Education,* 4(1), 75–91; Ferraro, F., J. Pfeffer and R. I. Sutton (2005). "Economics language and assumptions: How theories can become self-fulfilling." *Academy of Management Review,* 30(1), 8–24.

37   Ibid.

38   Gabor, A. (2010), remarks delivered at Deming Memorial Conference on the future of business and business education, at Fordham University, May 11.

39   Dierksmeier, C. (2011). "Reorienting management education: from homo oeconomicus to human dignity." *Business Schools under Fire.* H. M. Network. New York, Palgrave McMillan.

40   Holland, K. (2009). Is it Time to Retrain Business Schools? *New York Times.* March 12.

41   Bakke, D. (2005). *Joy at Work.* Seattle, WA, PVG.

42   Zafirovski, M. (2010), *The Enlightenment and Its Effects on Modern Society.* New York, Springer. 144.

43   Weber, A. (2013) Enlivenment. *Towards A Fundamental Shift In The Concepts Of Nature, Culture And Politics.* Berlin, Heinrich-Böll-Stiftung.

44   http://radiopaedia.org/articles/occams-razor (last accessed May 23, 2016)

45   Khurana, R. (2007). *From Higher Aims to Hired Hands: The Social Transformation of American Business Schools and The Unfulfilled Promise of Management As a Profession.* Princeton University Press.

46   Khurana. *From Higher Aims to Hired Hands: The Social Transformation of American Business Schools and the Unfulfilled Promise of Management as a Profession.*

47   www.panarchy.org/keynes/laissezfaire.1926.html (last accessed April 12, 2016)

48   www.countercurrents.org/norgaard301215.htm (last accessed March 28, 2016)

49 For example: Dierksmeier, C. (2011). "The freedom-responsibility nexus in management philosophy and business ethics." *Journal of Business Ethics*, **101**(2), 263–283, or Khurana, *From Higher Aims To Hired Hands*.

50 Nadeau, R. (2012). *Rebirth of the Sacred: Science, Religion, and the New Environmental Ethos*. Oxford University Press.

51 Smith, A. (2010). *The Theory of Moral Sentiments*. New York, Penguin. Or Hansen, M (www.natcapsolutions.org/Presidio/Articles/ Globalization/Note_on_Adam_Smith_as_Theorist_of_Sustainability_ MHANSEN.pdf) Relevant Quotes: "Human happiness depends primarily upon "composure and tranquility of mind" which is based on feelings of "gratitude and love" (TMS49). Or "the chief part of happiness arises from the consciousness of being beloved..." (TMS56).

52 www.panarchy.org/keynes/laissezfaire.1926.html

53 Lawrence, P. (2007). *Being Human – A Renewed Darwinian Theory of Human Behavior*. www.prlawrence.com. Cambridge, MA and Lawrence, P. R., and M. Pirson (2015). "Economistic and humanistic narratives of leadership in the age of globality: Toward a renewed Darwinian theory of leadership." *Journal of Business Ethics*, **128**(2), 383–394.

54 Wilson, E. O. (2012). *On Human Nature*. Cambridge, MA, Harvard University Press. Wilson, E. O. (2012). *The Social Conquest of Earth*. New York, W. W. Norton & Company; Wilson, D. S. (2015). *Does Altruism Exist?: Culture, Genes, and the Welfare of Others*. New Haven, CT, Yale University Press.

55 Darwin, C. (1909). *The Descent of Man and Selection in Relation to Sex*. New York, Appleton and Company.

56 Tetlock, P., et al. (2000). "The psychology of the unthinkable: taboo trade-offs, forbidden base rates, and heretical counterfactuals." *Journal of Personality and Social Psychology*, **78**(5), 853–870; Baron, J. and M. Spranca (1997). "Protected values." *Organizational Behavior and Human Decision Processes*, **70**(1), 1–16.

2 Understanding Human Nature

One of the critical stepping-stones to better management theory and practice is a better and more accurate understanding of who we are as people. The economistic narrative is based on assumptions that lead to a reductionist model, which, in many ways, only describes deficient human beings, such as psychopaths, sociopaths, or free-riders – men and women without morals. In this chapter, the economistic understanding of human nature will be analyzed in greater depth and compared to current scientific insights. The chapter draws on several sources of knowledge and insight to provide a more accurate understanding and to build a humanistic perspective of human nature. In the following pages, insights from the natural sciences, the humanities, and the social sciences are presented. While one could draw on many other sources, the hope is to showcase the increasing consilience of knowledge, the convergence of our understanding across disciplines of who we are as human beings.

THE REM MODEL

The most prominent articulation of human nature according to the economistic paradigm is that set forth by Michael Jensen and William Meckling, two of the most prominent and oft-cited management scholars. Whereas many researchers have memetically and unreflectedly adopted an economistic perspective, these scholars specified their understanding of human nature.

In their 1994 paper titled "The Nature of Man," they presented a novel take on homo economicus.[1] They both largely agree that, in the traditional economistic sense, homo economicus is a useless vehicle for good science. In their words,

In [t]he economic model ... the individual is an evaluator and maximizer, but has only one want: money income. He or she is a short-run money maximizer who does not care for others, art, morality, love, respect, honesty, etc. In its simplest form, the economic model characterizes people as unwilling to trade current money income for future money income, no matter what return they could earn. The economic model is, of course, not very interesting as a model of human behavior. People do not behave this way. In most cases use of this model reflects economists' desire for simplicity in modeling; the exclusive pursuit of wealth or money income is easier to model than the complexity of the actual preferences of individuals. As a consequence, however, non-economists often use this model as a foil to discredit economics – that is, to argue that economics is of limited use because economists focus only on a single characteristic of behavior – and one of the least attractive at that, the selfish desire for money.

They also postulate that understanding human behavior is fundamental to understanding how organizations function, whether they are profit-making firms, nonprofit enterprises, or government agencies. They argue that their model, REMM – the Resourceful, Evaluative, Maximizing Model – is superior. They suggest that REMM describes actual human behavior better than does any other existing model of human behavior, including homo economicus. The REMM specification of human nature is the foundation of agency theory. Jensen and Meckling state that

[REMM] serves as the foundation for the agency model of financial, organizational, and governance structure of firms. The growing body of social science research on human behavior has a common message: Whether they are politicians, managers, academics, professionals, philanthropists, or factory workers, individuals are resourceful, evaluative maximizers.[2]

In turn, agency theory is hailed as a grand theory in the social sciences, influencing economics, management, sociology, and political science.[3] As such, REMM holds sway over a much larger part of social science than its design intended. The famed economist Harold Demsetz[4] argued that economistic theoretical models should be used to study human behavior in the marketplace.[5] They are therefore useful to help us understand the possibility of spontaneous order in the marketplace, but should not be seen as prescriptive tools with regard to other institutions, such as organizations or societies.[6]

Nevertheless, Jensen and Meckling improved upon homo economicus by proposing REMM and had an enormous impact not only on management theory but also on management practice. Based on their research on the theory of the firm, corporate governance was redesigned, motivational schemes were developed, and stock options created. Harvard University's Rakesh Khurana describes an event in the early 1980s, in which corporate raiders linked to T. Boone Pickens provided regulators with copies of Jensen and Meckling's papers when they had to convince them that his proposed takeovers would be the best way to deliver shareholder value maximization.[7] As such, REMM thinking took a firm hold on practice. REMM also became a cultural phenomenon when movie director Oliver Stone portrayed corporate raiders in his movie *Wall Street*, and his main character Gordon Gekko uttered the famous line: "Greed, for lack of a better word, is good." It is therefore difficult to understate the impact of Jensen and Meckling's perspective on human nature, as it percolates tacitly throughout the social sciences and business culture.

REMM Revisited

It may be helpful to examine REMM and its intellectual arguments more closely. Jensen and Meckling suggested that REMM was the product of more than 200 years of research and debate in economics, the other social sciences, and philosophy. They provided a number of postulates that served as a "bare bones summary of the concept."

Examining these postulates more closely is enlightening.

Postulate I

Every individual cares; he or she is an evaluator. (a) The individual cares about almost everything: knowledge, independence, the plight of others, the environment, honor, interpersonal relationships, status, peer approval, group norms, culture, wealth, rules of conduct, the weather, music, art, and so on. (b) REMM is always willing to make trade-offs and substitutions. Each individual is always willing to give up some sufficiently small amount of any particular good (oranges, water, air, housing, honesty, or safety) for some sufficiently large quantity of other goods. Furthermore, valuation is relative in the sense that the value of a unit of any particular good decreases as the individual enjoys more of it relative to other goods. (c) Individual preferences are transitive—that is, if A is preferred to B, and B is preferred to C, then A is preferred to C.[8]

While it is arguably true that everyone cares, it does not necessarily logically follow that humans are inevitably evaluators. To be an evaluator, you need to have an inherent ability to judge and assess, which a computer does routinely, but human beings less often. Psychological research suggests that we cannot process all the information required to constantly evaluate.[9] Therefore, many occurrences in life happen without evaluation, often as a result of unevaluated routines or traditions. Evaluation is essential if we are to make trade-offs, but some things in life escape quantitative evaluation. For example, most parents refuse to evaluate their love for one child over another. Similarly, psychologists find that constant evaluation is a source of stress, and most people avoid it if they can.[10] Indeed, much of mindfulness practice teaches people to NOT evaluate. While REMM is based on an assumption that people are in constant evaluation, other people practice meditation to become nonjudgmental. Increasing research indicates that when humans behave in nonjudgmental ways, they – unlike what REMM believes – are happier.[11]

In addition, some – and perhaps many – of the most important elements of life have an intrinsic value and cannot be evaluated quantitatively to allow for (b): trade-offs and substitutions. Kant offers dignity as a category to describe all the life elements that cannot be exchanged. The assumption that we are *always* willing to make trade-offs is thus false. To argue that we are always willing to make substitutions *only* makes sense in the context of markets in which substitutions are desired. Postulate I does not allow for commitments, such as marriage vows, relationships, or friendships, whose nature is not subject to barter or quid pro quo; while healthy community life, in which people support each other without taking potential payback into account (e.g., care for children, the elderly, and even dead ancestors), is unimaginable.

Jensen and Meckling extend Postulate I by adding I(b): there are no human *needs* as such, which cannot be exchanged, but only *wants* which can be exchanged:

> REMM implies that there is no such thing as a need, a proposition that arouses considerable resistance. The fallacy of the notion of need follows from Postulate I-b, the proposition that the individual is always willing to make trade-offs. That proposition means individuals are always willing to substitute—that is, they are always willing to give up a sufficiently small amount of any good for a sufficiently large amount of other goods. Failure to take account of substitution is one of the most frequent mistakes in the analysis of human behavior. George Bernard Shaw, the famous playwright and social thinker, reportedly once claimed that while on an ocean voyage he asked a celebrated actress on deck one evening whether she would be willing to sleep with him for a million dollars. She was agreeable. He followed with a counterproposal: "What about ten dollars?" "What do you think I am?" she responded indignantly. He replied, "We've already established that – now we're just haggling over price." Like it or not, individuals are willing to sacrifice a little of almost anything

we care to name, even reputation or morality, for a sufficiently large quantity of other desired things; and these things do not have to be money or even material goods.[12]

Clearly, in the example provided above, the authors imply, as Henry Mintzberg paraphrases, that humans are "whores," selling anything and everything and honoring nothing.[13] This is factually inaccurate, even though it may arise in certain situations.[14] Research increasingly finds that moral judgments and value-based commitments are intrinsic elements of human sociality.[15] While the above postulate is certainly entertaining, the mere claim that humans have no needs does not make it so. From an evolutionary perspective, humans have developed basic needs that they cannot trade off if they are to survive. Needs exist to the degree that they *must* be fulfilled, like eating or drinking, because without these, survival is impossible. According to REMM assumptions, small babies would trade off their need for food to gain fame, for example. While eating is a need, fame is a want, and it is hard to credit that babies would prefer fame over food. While there are clearly extreme situations, for example, when people trade off their personal integrity for personal survival by prostituting themselves, those situations do not represent normal human behavior.

Jensen and Meckling build on this notion of wants in Postulate II:

Postulate II
Each individual's wants are unlimited. (a) If we designate those things that REMM values positively as "goods," then he or she prefers more goods to less. Goods can be anything from art objects to ethical norms. (b) REMM cannot be satiated. He or she always wants more of some things, be they material goods such as art, sculpture, castles, and pyramids; or non-material goods such as solitude, companionship, honesty, respect, love, fame, and immortality.[16]

In this postulate, REMM shows its deep connection with the homo economicus model. REMM must have unlimited wants, otherwise the maximization of utility cannot make sense. While Jensen and

Meckling attempt to broaden the realm of "goods" from the purely material to the ideal, REMM is simply homo economicus reborn and attempting to maximize.

Psychology and neuroscience research challenges the belief that the human urge to satisfy wants is unlimited.[17] Increasing evidence shows that wanting less can be healthy,[18] and that an increasing number of young people reject the notion that more is better.[19] Pursuing unlimited wants may be burdening and troublesome. "Affluenza," the description of the consistent pursuit of more, is considered a modern disease.[20] According to REMM, affluenza should not exist; given that humans inherently want more, there can be no satiation. Not only does recent psychological evidence contradict this assumption, but the global religious traditions have long suggested that wisdom starts with the recognition that there is such a thing as "enough."[21]

Similarly, psychology finds that people are happiest if they commit to a limited number of choices.[22] For example, people with one spouse and who are able to grow in that relationship are happier than those who are promiscuous. Evolutionary biology, which finds that most humans desire to have a nuclear family, supports the finding. While not always practically possible, a stable relationship increases the survival chances of healthy offspring.[23] If people acted according to REMM, they would always desire an unlimited number of partners.

Jensen and Meckling build on the notion of unlimited *wants* with Postulate III.

Postulate III
Each individual is a maximizer. He or she acts so as to enjoy the highest level of value possible. Individuals are always constrained in satisfying their wants. Wealth, time, and the physical laws of nature are examples of important constraints that affect the opportunities available to any individual. Individuals are also constrained by the limits of their own knowledge about various

goods and opportunities; their choices of goods or courses of action will reflect the costs of acquiring the knowledge or information necessary to evaluate those choices. The notion of an opportunity set provides the limit on the level of value attainable by any individual. The opportunity set is usually regarded as something that is given and when one takes into account information costs, much behavior that appears to be suboptimal "satisficing" can be explained as attempts to maximize subject to such costs external to the individual. Economists usually represent it as a wealth or income constraint and a set of prices at which the individual can buy goods. But the notion of an individual's opportunity set can be generalized to include the set of activities he or she can perform during a 24-hour day – or in a lifetime.[24]

In this attempt to refurbish homo economicus, constraints are accepted, but the old maximization assumption still holds sway.

Optimization and satisfaction of wants certainly occur in the real world. But research has shown that it is almost impossible for real humans to accurately predict a 24-hour day of constraints, let alone a lifetime set of constraints, or satisfaction opportunities. People are bad at predicting the future.[25] While there may be *some* individuals who routinely try to maximize choice options, they are hardly representative. Research finds that *most* people tend to reduce choice options and decide to choose what is "good enough," rather than the best, simply because their brain forces them to do so.[26] Psychologists routinely find that people who balance choice options and satisfice are happier. In contrast, psychologist Barry Schwartz and colleagues report that "maximizers" are less optimistic, have less self-esteem, experience less life satisfaction, are more susceptible to social pressure, and are often more depressed.[27]

Jensen and Meckling seemingly try to solve two problems with the notion of opportunity sets. The first problem is that of theoretical accuracy, and the second that of parsimony. As they stated before, the simple linear utility maximization assumption that homo economicus represents is inaccurate and, in their opinion, reflects the economist's desire for simplicity in modeling. By contrast, the opportunity sets notion suggests that humans engage a wider spectrum of options, within which they maximize, for example, honor, knowledge, independence, or culture. This makes REMM more realistic. On the other hand, opportunity sets can still be parsimonious enough to be modeled using higher forms of mathematics supported by computing power, which should render REMM appealing to those who want to keep modeling.

While some researchers agree that opportunity sets are helpful, others suggest that if anything can become part of an opportunity set, the theory becomes vacuous and modeling impossible.[28] If Postulate III were true, it would be reasonable, for example, to assume that, for some people, character development, personal integrity, and mindful consumption are part of an opportunity set. Still, it is difficult to understand how a human being would maximize these opportunities. For example, the mindful reduction of consumption cannot logically be maximized without starvation. It is equally difficult to fathom the maximization of personal integrity or character development. If some of human beings' aspirations cannot be maximized, but only satisfied or balanced, Postulate III cannot hold.

Jensen and Meckling not only posit general static opportunity sets but also suggest that people can learn and change these opportunity sets. In Postulate IV, they state:

> The individual is resourceful. Individuals are creative. They are able
> to conceive of changes in their environment, foresee the
> consequences thereof, and respond by creating new opportunities.
> Although an individual's opportunity set is limited at any instant in
> time by his or her knowledge and the state of the world, that
> limitation is not immutable. Human beings are not only capable of
> learning about new opportunities, they also engage in resourceful,
> creative activities that expand their opportunities in various
> ways. The kind of highly mechanical behavior posited by

economists – that is, assigning probabilities and expected values to various actions and choosing the action with the highest expected value – is formally consistent with the evaluating, maximizing model defined in Postulates I through III. But such behavior falls short of the human capabilities posited by REMM; it says nothing about the individual's ingenuity and creativity.[29]

Postulate IV presents an important insight that will be critical for a humanistic perspective on human development and flourishing. However, the mechanical perspective Jensen and Meckling criticize appears in their rather mechanical postulates I–III. It is conceivable, for example, that human creativity could be employed to maximize insatiable wants, but they ignore the possibility that the same human creativity could be used to mindfully *balance* basic human needs. To take their perspective to its logical conclusion, let's consider the example of Elisabeth, who was introduced in Chapter 1. Elisabeth is a mother of two kids, married to a man who travels often for his work. She works in hospital administration and also needs to take care of her mother who lives in the area. Her wish to be successful at her job, have a good relationship with her spouse, provide a good education for her kids, and take care of her mother's needs defines her opportunity set. The REMM-type Elisabeth could use her ingenuity to create a life situation in which she decides to maximize all of these ambitions. Wanting to be successful at her job, she would need to spend more time and energy at the hospital. Because she hardly sees her husband, she decides (knowing no commitments and willing to substitute anything) to divorce her husband and marry her boss. At the hospital, they can spend more time together, while increasing her income. The additional income could be used to pay a tutor for her kids, allowing her to outsource their education. Spending that much time at work, she ingeniously suggests to her mother that she should (pretend to) become ill, which will mean that she too can be at the hospital. While such behavior may be ingenious and creative, it is also rather absurd. It is far more likely that Elisabeth will simply decide to spend just enough time at the hospital to ensure she does not lose her job, spend quality time with her current husband and not get divorced, take care of her kids when she can in order to personally provide educational experiences, and look after her mother in her home when she is able to. In the latter case, Elisabeth is balancing creatively rather than ingeniously maximizing options within her opportunity set.

It is important to note that Jensen and Meckling never strive for an accurate model, but simply for a better model than that of homo economicus. Many of their assumptions are partially true, and they spend much energy in demonstrating their postulations' validity in and beyond economics and management literature. The philosopher Karl Popper would, however, call many of these efforts "verification-ism," which he describes as the tendency to explain reality with the set of assumptions we create.[30] Consequently, when studying human organizing practices, researchers tend to make reality fit their assumptions, rather than the inverse.

ALTERNATIVE PERSPECTIVES ON HUMAN NATURE

It is important to acknowledge that every model of human behavior will have to trade off parsimony for accuracy. REMM loosens many restrictive assumptions about homo economicus to gain accuracy, but it was never designed to be perfect. Given this, there may be alternative ways to better conceptualize human nature that provide superior accuracy. Others endeavoring to understand human nature provide a counterpoint to REMM. The famed biologist E.O. Wilson suggests that there seems to be a consilience of knowledge in which core insights from the sciences overlap with those of the humanities.[31] These insights can help us understand human nature better. This increasing consilience of knowledge can serve as a stepping-stone to better theorizing and, it is hoped, better practice.

Human Nature: The View of the Sciences

A growing number of scholars criticize the current overemphasis on methodological individualism in the social sciences and management studies.[32] Stemming from the individualist traditions of the

Enlightenment, which emerged in opposition to the pervasive collectivism of the times, individualism had the unintended consequence of misinterpreting human nature as isolationist, needing no social embeddedness, and driven by exchangeable wants. Marx ridiculed this intellectual tendency in the nineteenth century's liberal economics domain as "Robinsonades."[33] Keynes similarly criticized the atomistic perspective of human nature as dangerous.[34]

The critics of mainstream economics increasingly advocate the use of evolutionary theory to help put economics (and management) on a sounder footing.[35] E.O. Wilson argues that perspectives from the natural sciences, and especially biology, shed light on human nature.[36] Biology, and in particular evolutionary biology, labels human beings as "eusocial" – truly social. In *The Social Conquest of Earth* (2012), Wilson writes that this true sociality, the interconnectedness of human beings, has been the key to survival.[37] He and many other scholars argue that the dominant species that inhabited our planet prior to the emergence of the human species were eusocial. He draws comparisons between vertebrates' and invertebrates' two different ways of achieving conquest of the earth, arguing that both came about through eusociality's main feature: collaboration. According to this theory, group and tribe formation is a fundamental human trait and is based on basic emotions that are hard-wired decision-making tools. As a consequence of this sociality, human beings have developed emotions that drive basic decision-making, allowing us to guide our emotions toward cooperative outcomes (called morality) and to behave in a genuinely altruistic way in order to benefit the group (as a result of group selection mechanisms). These insights and propositions largely contradict the REMM propositions that underpin mainstream economics and business theorizing.

Sociality

E.O Wilson makes a bold statement:

> Perhaps most people, including many scholars, would like to keep human nature at least partly in the dark. It is the monster in the

fever swamp of public discourse. Its perception is distorted by idiosyncratic personal self-regard and expectation. Economists have by and large steered around it, while philosophers bold enough to search for it always lost their way. Theologians tend to give up, attributing different parts to God and the devil. Political ideologues ranging from anarchists to fascists have defined it to their selfish advantage.[38]

Referring to biology and evolutionary theory, Wilson argues that inherited regularities in the mental development common to our species define human nature. Nevertheless, he suggests that our "epigenetic rules," which have evolved through the interaction of individual and group selection mechanisms, define us. *Homo sapiens* is therefore a result of an interplay between a genetic and a cultural evolution that occurred over a long period and started in deep prehistory. Wilson specifies that the hard-wired epigenetic rules are the core of human nature. These epigenetic rules create the resulting behaviors common to *Homo sapiens*. That means that the behaviors are "prepared" and ready to be developed, but need to be learned. That is why education and socialization are critical for human survival.[39]

Supporting this proposition, George Murdock (1945) combed through human behaviors that many hundreds of societies, which anthropologists studied in the past, share.[40] Murdock attempted to highlight cultural practices that are almost universal. A selection of these practices featuring human nature's eusocial character includes community organization, cooperative labor, courtship, dancing, decorative art, division of labor, education, ethics, faith healing, family feasting, food taboos, funeral rites, games, gift giving, government, hospitality, incest taboos, inheritance rules, joking, kin groups, kin nomenclature, marriage, mealtimes, postnatal care, property rights, religious ritual, sexual restriction, soul concepts, status differentiation, and the list goes on.

Other thought games also bear witness to our eusocial nature. Why would inventions like the internet, cell phones, or Facebook make any sense, or have any commercial value, if we were not fundamentally social? The fundamental need – Paul Lawrence calls it the "drive to bond" – is hard-wired; it serves an evolutionary purpose, which is the survival of the species rather than individual utility maximization.[41]

Morality

If we are fundamentally social, this may mean that we are also fundamentally moral. Charles Darwin observed

> that any animal whatever, endowed with well-marked social instincts, the parental and filial affections being here included, would inevitably acquire a moral sense or conscience, as soon as its intellectual powers had become as well, or nearly as well developed, as in man. For, firstly, the social instincts lead an animal to take pleasure in the society of its fellows, to feel a certain amount of sympathy with them, and to perform various services for them.[42]

Joshua Greene, a noted scholar whose work bridges various disciplines in a true humanist fashion, writes: "Under ordinary circumstances, we shudder at the thought of behaving violently toward innocent people, even total strangers, and this most likely is a crucial feature of our moral brains."[43] Greene says that, in sum, we are a caring species, albeit in a limited way, and we probably inherited at least some of our caring capacity from our primate ancestors, if not our more distant ancestors. We care most of all about our relatives and friends, but we also care about acquaintances and strangers.

Robert Wright argues in the same vein and suggests that humans are moral animals. Both Wright and Greene suggest that we have a moral machinery in our brain originating from our hypersocial nature.[44] Joshua Greene writes:

> From simple cells to supersocial animals like us, the story of life on Earth is the story of increasingly complex cooperation. Cooperation is why we are here, and yet at the same time, maintaining

cooperation is our greatest challenge. Morality is the human brain's answer to this challenge. Such morality is derived from emotional baseline responses, and Greene argues that for each cooperative strategy, our moral brains have a corresponding set of emotional dispositions that execute this strategy. Such strategies include concern for others, direct and indirect reciprocity, commitment to threats and promises, and reputation.[45]

All of this psychological machinery is perfectly designed to promote cooperation among otherwise selfish individuals, implementing strategies that can be formalized in abstract mathematical terms. The additional insight that Greene and his collaborators present is that human morality and, as a result, cooperation are typically intuitive, not calculated or rational. They conducted experiments in which they timed responses that required moral decision-making and cooperation choices. Their results demonstrated that cooperative choices were made so fast that they had to be intuitive.

E.O. Wilson writes that morality, conformity, religious fervor, and fighting ability, combined with imagination and memory, produced *Homo sapiens* as a winner in terms of survival.[46]

Empathy and Emotionality

Frans de Waal, a leading primatologist, writes that empathy is hardwired, and that the emotional basis of empathy is critical for our sociality. We cannot live peacefully in families, communities, and tribes without having the tools to do so.[47] Contrary to the Hobbesian, Spencerian, and Randian notion of human nature, *Homo sapiens* is alive today because we care. De Waal and others find that empathy is, in many ways, a key lever to collaboration and can turn self-interest into mutual interest. In fact, Eric Liu and Nick Hanauer state that, through empathy, humans experience "true self-interest as mutual interest."[48]

De Waal and others argue that humans are not even that special in terms of empathetic abilities, but that animals of all kinds are capable of empathy and collaboration. Charles Darwin early on suggested that hard-wired emotions representing the core of human nature drive such empathy. In *The Expression of the Emotions in Man and Animals*, Darwin suggests that empathetic instincts must have evolved from natural selection.[49] E.O. Wilson argues that humans are fundamentally emotional beings, because these emotions aided survival and reproduction.[50] David Matsumoto writes that

> emotions humans experience today emerged (or were naturally selected) in our evolutionary history as rapid information processing systems that helped us deal with the environment and events that occurred. That is, emotions evolved to help us cope with events and situations that had consequences for our immediate welfare. If humans didn't have emotions, we wouldn't know when to attack, defend, flee, care for others, reject food, or approach something useful, all of which were helpful in our evolutionary histories (as they are today). If we didn't feel disgusted at spoilt food, we would eat it. If we weren't outraged when rivals stole our food, resources, or mates, we wouldn't defend them strongly. If we didn't feel the joy in caring for a child, or the compassion in caring for a loved one, we wouldn't enjoy the social bonds that make human cultures and relationships unique.[51]

Joshua Greene and others suggest that empathy and our collaborative tendencies are instinctive and emotion based. Frans de Waal calls it the "feeling brain,"[52] arguing that the basis of our emotional sensors is hard-coded in our brains. As observed before about the human tendency to be social, kind, and moral, emotions are a feature, not a bug. Emotions help us deal with the complexity of our eusocial life.

Basic emotions that can be witnessed across different cultures, and thus hint at their universality, include anger, contempt, disgust, fear, enjoyment, sadness, and surprise. These emotions are called basic, because they are shared across a number of species, including our primate ancestors. This fundamental emotionality questions the uniquely rational focus of Jensen and Meckling's REMM propositions.

Emotions also call theories of human behavior that are purely based on rationality, such as rational choice and decision-making, into questions.

Altruism

Eusociality and its derivatives – morality and baseline empathy supported by emotions – lead to human behavior that further questions REMM's basic assumptions regarding the maximization of self-interest.

The role of fairness and the development of altruistic punishment to uphold the tribe's moral rules have been documented in various studies.[53] Altruism has been actively studied in fields as varied as biology, economics, sociology, and game theory. It differs from cooperation, as altruism requires no direct benefit or reciprocity. Emerging research suggests that altruism is a behavior common to the human species, because group selection favored those groups with altruists over those without.[54] Altruism can be understood as an individual's behavior that benefits other individuals, even though these actions may negatively impact the individual's chances of survival. A well-known example is that of individuals who watch out for a predator and signal danger to the group, thus potentially drawing the predator's attention to themselves.[55] Studies show that *without* the emergence of altruism, populations go extinct.[56]

David Sloan Wilson summarizes the research as: "Selfishness beats altruism within groups. Altruistic groups beat selfish groups. Everything else is commentary."[57] Selfish behavior is found to undermine communities and leads to trouble for the group. For communities that survive, E.O. Wilson argues, the countervailing forces of altruism evolve through group selection, not just through individual selection.[58] It appears that a group-based selection mechanism screens for altruism. As such, altruism is now viewed as a key feature of functioning human groups.[59]

Taken together, the findings from the natural sciences concerning human nature provide a clearer perspective on who we are as human beings. A number of elements long considered bugs in our system have now been identified as features, including sociality, morality, emotionality, and altruism. These insights challenge REMM's claims about the nature of man that underlie a larger, dominant theoretical framework in management sciences.

Human Nature: A View from the Humanities

Many of the insights that now have increasing scientific backing were developed over time in the humanities. As early as Aristotle, philosophers suggested that human beings are social animals endowed with reason.[60] In *The Human Condition*, Hanna Arendt writes that, basically, we are Aristotelian, political, social animals who crave meaning, and that this craving is often channeled into work and action as manifestations of our existence.[61] The sociality of human beings has rarely been called into question, even though the special role of human freedom and individual uniqueness has become more pronounced in modern Western thought. During the Enlightenment, philosophers established a convincing argument that although tribal, human nature requires special respect. The notion of human rights was born with the Kantian notion of the unconditional dignity of human nature.[62] These human rights are sometimes viewed as commitments that are not negotiable. As such, they should escape the economistic exchange logic (at least in theory and as an aspiration). The economistic argument that they do not, should thus be viewed with skepticism in light of the much longer philosophical tradition.

In line with Darwin's observation that morality must have developed as a survival mechanism for humanity, scholars of religion and ethics have identified the principles of such shared morality, or ethics, in order to develop a global, universal ethos that can help build bridges between religions and secular people. The noted psychologist Steven Pinker suggests:

> This foundation of morality may be seen in the many versions of
> the Golden Rule that have been discovered by the world's major

religions, and also in Spinoza's Viewpoint of Eternity, Kant's Categorical Imperative, Hobbes' and Rousseau's Social Contract, and Locke and Jefferson's self-evident truth that all people are created equal.[63]

The Swiss theologian Hans Kueng and his collaborators studied the leading global religious and secular groups' narratives[64] and suggested that we can find insights into our shared, universal human nature in the respective sacred texts' aspirational statements. Many religions have clear guiding principles in terms of how human beings should behave; some sort of universalist *ultima ratio*, which even holds against all human instincts of self-preservation, supports these principles. Many anthropologists make the case that religion and creation narratives, which include rules for altruistic acts, are crucial for building a functioning society. An example of this is the narrative of Jesus Christ. While any one such narrative may be dismissed, their universality indicates that they seem to have spoken to humans throughout the ages. As such, they may give a glimpse into true and persisting human needs and human nature.

Hans Kueng and his team suggest that secular and religious narratives have many elements in common. First, in the face of self-interest, they all assume that anyone who truly believes [in God, reincarnation, etc.] should in "practice consistently be concerned with human well-being."[65] Kueng mentions the "twofold Jewish commandment to love God and one's neighbor and its radicalization, Jesus' Sermon on the Mount along with the incessant demand of the Qu'ran for justice, truth and good works; [. . .] the Buddhist doctrine of overcoming human suffering, the Hindu striving to fulfill 'dharma' and Confucius' requirement to preserve cosmic order and thus the humanum." These all highlight the religious depth of human dignity as a basic principle and indicate human well-being as the goal of a human ethics.[66]

Furthermore, Kueng argues that despite their particularisms, all the great religions call for particular "non-negotiable standards, basic ethical norms and maxims to ensure basic humanity."

Kueng presents five universally shared commandments across all the great world religions:[67]

1. Do not kill.
2. Do not lie.
3. Do not steal.
4. Do not practice immorality.
5. Respect parents and love children.

He argues that such norms were possibly conceived as protection against unprincipled libertinism, which prioritizes personal advantage in the short run. In this sense, it could be argued that the great religions share principles that protect humanity from REMM-style behavior fixated on wants that can be exchanged at liberty.

On the other hand, Kueng makes the argument that, ultimately, in order to promote human well-being, the great world religions straddle the extremes of libertinism and legalism, offering individuals a middle way (the commandments are guides for human behavior, not binding laws). In this sense, the Golden Rule emerges as a guide for humans to live a "good life."[68] Kueng provides evidence that long before Kant specified his categorical imperative, Confucius (551–489 BCE) had written: "What you yourself do not want, do not do to another person"; Rabbi Hillel (60 BCE–10 CE) similarly wrote: "Do not do to others what you would not want them to do to you"; while the Christian Bible specifies: "Whatever you want people to do to you do also to them" (Matthew 7.12; Luke 6.31).[69]

Such moral motivations and guidelines are presented in the context of the lives of real people, be they prophets, saints, or spiritual leaders such as the Buddha, Confucius, Lao-tze, Jesus Christ, Mohammed, and not in the abstract. The religious stories that are told are cultural narratives that provide practical guidance and, above all, meaning. In his book *Antifragile*, Nassim Taleb suggests that religious institutions are pretty stable.[70] This means that they can tell us what has mattered to human beings throughout their existence. The shared principles of the global religions could therefore provide significant insights into human nature over time. These insights are a substantial challenge to REMM.

Human Nature: A View from the Social Sciences

The various domains of the social sciences have seen a number of developments rooted in a more humanistic, all-encompassing understanding of human nature. For example, Amartya Sen and his philosopher colleague Martha Nussbaum have provided a framework for a humanistic interpretation of economics. Their capability approach is based on the assumptions of human dignity as unconditional, and the presupposition that economic affairs ought to be managed to expand freedom and the capabilities of individuals to achieve a higher level of well-being.[71] Other noted economists have defied economistic orthodoxy and expanded our view of human nature. Daniel Kahneman earned his Nobel Prize in economics by debunking the foundations of homo economicus. He calls the assumptions of economic theory a "non-starter."[72] Elinor Ostrom received her Nobel Prize for defying homo economicus assumptions of pure self-interest. Ostrom is known to have not worked from theory, but from studying practice, which suggests that what works for practice should work for theory.

Ostrom's eight design principles of stable, local, common-pool resource management suggest that communities can manage the commons effectively and sustainably to advance the common good by means of:[73]

1. Clearly defined boundaries (a clear definition of the contents of the common-pool resource and effective exclusion of external unentitled parties);
2. Rules regarding the appropriation and provision of common resources adapted to local conditions;
3. Collective-choice arrangements that allow most resource appropriators to participate in the decision-making process;
4. Effective monitoring by monitors who are part of, or accountable to, the appropriators;

5. A scale of graduated sanctions for resource appropriators who violate community rules;
6. Conflict-resolution mechanisms that are cheap and easy to access;
7. Higher-level authorities who acknowledge the community's self-determination; and
8. Organization in the form of multiple layers of nested enterprises, with small local common-pool resources (CPRs) at the base level, in the case of larger CPRs.[74]

A group of researchers associated with David Sloan Wilson studied the work of anthropologists to suggest that almost all hunter-gatherer societies that still exist, or which anthropologists described prior to their assimilation into larger societies, exhibit teamwork enforced by the suppression of disruptive self-serving behaviors.[75] Bullying is not tolerated. The group as a whole has the power to thwart those who try to impose their will by creating counter-dominant coalitions. Status must be earned, and reputation is based on how much one contributes to the group. Decision-making is typically done by means of consensus, or by other processes that the group recognizes as fair. It is easy to monitor agreed-upon behaviors, because people are almost always in the presence of others. Mild sanctions, such as gossip, are usually sufficient to keep people in solid citizen mode, but these are backed up by harsher sanctions, such as exclusion and execution. Conflicts of interest are usually managed in a way that all the parties recognize as fair.[76]

In a similar way, Wilson and colleagues studied the emergence and resilience of 1,400 business corporations.[77] They found that the same principles hold. Human beings in these organizations constantly defy REMM's basic assumptions, leading the researchers to conclude:

> A theory is only as good as its assumptions and orthodox economic theory is a case of "garbage in, garbage out." Homo economicus and its imaginary social environment are such a far cry from Homo sapiens and real social environments that there is no theoretical justification for the orthodox school of thought. The argument that

the predictions of a theory can be right even though its assumptions are wrong, which was advanced by Milton Friedman in the 1950s, sounds silly after the failure of orthodox economics to predict or cope with the economic crises facing us today. Very simply, the orthodox school of economics is an emperor with no clothes and the sooner this is widely appreciated the better.[78]

Referring to the vast literature in sociology, Wilson et al. conclude that our species is genetically adapted to implement the core design principles in small groups, confirming the thoughts of nineteenth-century French social theorist Alexis de Tocqueville: "The village or township is the only association which is so perfectly natural that, wherever a number of men are collected, it seems to constitute itself."[79]

In psychology, a number of scholars have explored the elements of human dignity and the notion of human flourishing. Primarily based on the work of Carl Rogers, humanist psychologists such as Frederick Herzberg and Abraham Maslow built on an expanded notion of human nature, inspiring what is currently labeled "positive psychology." This branch of psychology, which has recently spun off positive organizational behavior and positive organizational scholarship as correlates to the organizational sciences, also challenges REMM's baseline assumptions. Jonathan Haidt, for example, has even suggested that psychologists should reject pervasive methodological individualism and study what he calls "hive psychology."[80] As such, the social sciences as a whole could benefit from a more accurate perspective that reflects the eusocial nature of human beings.

Insights from psychology are also important for an understanding of the darker side of human nature. Clearly, as E.O. Wilson suggests, the epigenetic makeup of human nature balances the outcomes of individual and group selection. In many functioning groups, disruptive self-serving behaviors and their underlying psychological impulses are only suppressed, not eliminated, and are ready to surface whenever opportunities allow. David Sloan Wilson likens humans to

Dr. Jekyll and Mr. Hyde, combined in a single person.[81] To some extent, REMM exists in all humans, but culture, civilization, and education are designed to counter REMM-style characteristics and produce the eusocial part that allowed the survival of the species. Only the economistic model's recent ascendency has elevated mankind's antisocial tendencies to a virtue.

Psychopathy

An interesting finding is that REMM actually does seem to have some basis in reality, and is not completely unfounded. Whereas most *Homo sapiens* arguably share the ability to be social and have empathy, enabling them to act morally, psychologists argue that there appears to be a minor, but important, exception. Paul Lawrence, for example, argues that across the history of human survival, some people did not develop what he calls the independent drive to bond.[82] These people were asocial and usually outcasts in society. Throughout evolution, they had been marginalized, but never completely eradicated, because they coexisted as parasites. In fact, it is estimated that about 1 percent of the population lacks an independent drive to bond, causing what is otherwise known as "psychopathy."[83] Psychologist Robert Hare, a leading researcher on psychopathy for more than 30 years, describes psychopaths as:

> social predators who charm, manipulate, and ruthlessly plow their way through life, leaving a broad trail of broken hearts, shattered expectations, and empty wallets. Completely lacking in conscience and in feelings for others, they selfishly take what they want and do as they please, violating social norms and expectations without the slightest sense of guilt or regret.[84]

They have "an insatiable appetite for power and control,"[85] combined with "a deeply disturbing inability to care about the pain and suffering experienced by others – in short, a complete lack of empathy."[86] Researchers have identified psychopaths (whom biologists and economists call "free-riders" and whom sociologists and some psychologists tend to call "sociopaths") as people with a genetic defect.[87] They are incapable of empathy, and have no skill set of conscience or morality. Their jaw-dropping selfishness and lack of empathy do not come from exaggerated drives to acquire and defend; these drives are normal – which means they are innate, unconscious, independent, and insatiable – but are not checked and balanced by a drive to have trusting and caring relationships with others.[88] Lawrence describes them as wild animals – motivated mainly by the two universal animal drives – but with all the advantages of a human drive to comprehend.[89]

Hare estimates – conservatively, he insists – that "there are at least 2 million psychopaths in North America; the citizens of New York City have as many as 100,000 psychopaths among them."[90] Hare and Babiak even argue that many of these psychopaths gain influence and power, and that the current corporate environment allows them to do so effectively.[91] In fact, recent research indicates that psychopaths are overrepresented in current business institutions, including Wall Street; estimates range from 6 percent to 10 percent psychopaths in leadership functions.[92] Historians have made the argument that, across history, many examples of bad leadership can be traced to psychopathic personalities, including Hitler, Stalin, and even Napoleon.[93]

CONCLUDING REMARKS

While this is a very selective set of findings, and many more disciplines could be drawn on to present a fuller picture of human nature, the main point is to highlight the consilience of scientific insights that now exists, and the extent to which it contradicts the prevalently held view of human nature. Human beings have survived because they are truly social beings, for better or worse. As such, they have developed a way to keep their basic emotions in check by developing their brain (i.e., prefrontal cortex) and developed morality as a set of guidelines for general survival in communities and societies. These moral guidelines require commitments beyond libertine pleasure-seeking in the moment. They allow human beings to foresee conflicts and build lasting relationships. To build environments where human beings can flourish, a dignity threshold (meeting basic needs) needs to be established. When humans can build capabilities to develop themselves and their communities to achieve higher levels of well-being, they create the conditions for flourishing.

These various insights allow us to recalibrate claims that economists made and which have been widely adopted in management science. The currently dominant narrative of homo economicus, or its successor REMM, overlooks important qualities of human nature that need to be revisited in a number of ways to enhance theorizing:

- First, humans are fundamentally social (eusocial).
- Second, they are fundamentally emotionally driven, which enhances survival.
- Third, reason and rationality act as a guide, but are not exclusively in charge of decision-making.
- Fourth, morality and ethical standards/commitments are crucial for eusocial beings.
- Fifth, altruistic behavior makes sense in the context of group survival norms that interplay with individual survival norms.
- Sixth, commitments such as unconditional respect for human dignity and the aspiration to promote human well-being are critical for good communities (eusocial beings).

Humans have needs – emotional needs, social needs, individual needs – in order to live a life in dignity. We also have needs and, quite clearly, wants, which allow us to flourish. Moral and ethical commitments are critical for survival and are not just part of a trade or exchange. These insights allow us to present a solid theoretical alternative to REMM, which will be described in the following chapter.

NOTES

1 Jensen, M. C. and W. H. Meckling (1994). "The nature of man." *The Journal of Applied Corporate Finance*, **Summer**, 4–19.
2 Ibid.
3 Eisenhardt, K. (1989). "Agency theory: an assessment and review." *Academy of Management Review*, **14**(1), 57–74.

4 Harold Demsetz was also the director of the influential Mont Pelerin Society.

5 Demsetz, H. (2011). *From Economic Man to Economic System: Essays on Human Behavior and the Institutions of Capitalism.* Cambridge University Press.

6 Ibid.

7 Khurana, R. (2007). *From Higher Aims to Hired Hands: The Social Transformation of American Business Schools and the Unfulfilled Promise of Management as a Profession.* Princeton, Princeton University Press.

8 Jensen and Meckling. "The nature of man." 4–19.

9 Kahneman, D. (2011). *Thinking Fast and Slow.* New York, Farrar, Straus and Giroux.

10 Gilbert, D. (2009). *Stumbling on Happiness.* Vintage Canada; Lama, Dalai and H. C. Cutler (2003). *The Art of Happiness at Work.* New York, Riverhead Books; Lyubomirsky, S. (2007). *The How of Happiness: A Scientific Approach to Getting the Life You Want.* New York, Penguin Press.

11 Gilbert. *Stumbling on Happiness.*

12 Jensen and Meckling. "The nature of man." 4–19.

13 Mintzberg, H. (2004). *Managers Not MBAs: A Hard Look at the Soft Practice of Managing and Management Development.* London; New York, Financial Times Prentice Hall.

14 Tetlock, P. E. (2003). "Thinking the unthinkable: Sacred values and taboo cognitions." *Trends in Cognitive Sciences,* 7(7), 320–324; Graham, J., et al. (2009). "Liberals and conservatives rely on different sets of moral foundations." *Journal of Personality and Social Psychology,* 96(5), 1029–1046; Haidt, J. (2007). "The new synthesis in moral psychology." *Science,* 316(5827), 998–1002.

15 Haidt. "The new synthesis in moral psychology." 998–1002.

16 Jensen and Meckling. "The nature of man." 4–19.

17 Seligman, M. (2002). *Authentic Happiness. Using the New Positive Psychology to Realize Your Potential to Lasting Fulfillment.* New York, The Free Press; Gilbert. *Stumbling on Happiness;* Lyubomirsky. *The How of Happiness.*

18 Kasser, T. and A. C. Ahuvia (2002). "Materialistic values and well-being in business students." *European Journal of Social Psychology,* 32, 137–146.

19 http://elitedaily.com/life/culture/millennials-minimalists/1256085/
    (accessed May 23, 2016)

20 See, for example, www.psychologytoday.com/blog/feeling-our-way/
    201602/the-affluenza-defense

21 See, for example, Peck, M. S. (2003). *Abounding Happiness: A Treasury of
    Wisdom*. Kansas City, MO, Andrews McMeel.

22 Gilbert. *Stumbling on Happiness*; Lama and Cutler. *The Art of Happiness
    at Work*; Lyubomirsky. *The How of Happiness*.

23 Wrangham, R. W. (2009). *Catching Fire: How Cooking Made Us Human*.
    New York, Basic Books.

24 Jensen and Meckling. "The nature of man." 4–19.

25 Gilbert. *Stumbling on Happiness*.

26 Simon, H. A. (1979). "Rational decision making in business
    organizations." *The American Economic Review*, **69**(4), 493–513;
    Lawrence, P. R. and N. Nohria (2002). "Driven how human nature shapes
    our choices." *Warren Bennis Signature Series*. San Francisco, Jossey-Bass.

27 Schwartz, B., A. Ward, J. Monterosso, S. Lyubomirsky, K. White, and D. R.
    Lehman (2002). "Maximizing versus satisficing: Happiness is a matter of
    choice." *Journal of Personality and Social Psychology*, **83**(5), 1178.

28 See for similar criticism: Simon. "Theories of decision-making in
    economics and behavioral science." 253–283; Kirchgässner, G. (2008).
    *Homo Oeconomicus: The Economic Model of Behaviour and Its
    Applications in Economics and Other Social Sciences* (Vol. 6). New York,
    Springer Science & Business Media.

29 Jensen and Meckling. "The nature of man." 4–19.

30 Popper, K. (2005). *The Logic of Scientific Discovery*. London, Routledge.

31 Wilson, E. O. (1998). *Consilience: The Unity of Knowledge*. New York,
    Knopf, Distributed by Random House. Steven Pinker suggests that
    scholars and society at large have been reticent to consider human nature
    as such, in part because of the perceived abuse of some of Darwin's
    insights during the first half of the twentieth century. This reticence may
    have allowed unscientific, assumption-based notions of human nature to
    be unchecked for a long time, with arguably tremendous consequences.

32 Wilson, D. S., M. Van Vugt, and R. O'Gorman (2008). "Multilevel
    selection theory and major evolutionary transitions implications for
    psychological science." *Current Directions in Psychological Science*,
    17(1), 6–9; Graham, J., and J. Haidt (2010). "Beyond beliefs: Religions bind

individuals into moral communities." *Personality and Social Psychology Review*, **14**(1), 140–150; Granovetter, M. (1985). "Economic action and social structure: The problem of embeddedness." *The American Journal of Sociology*, **91**(3), 481–510.

33 Marx, K. (1993). *Grundrisse*. London, Penguin.

34 www.panarchy.org/keynes/laissezfaire.1926.html; Mehmood, A. (2010). "On the history and potentials of evolutionary metaphors in urban planning." *Planning Theory*, **9**(1), 63–87.

35 Sober, E. and D. S. Wilson (1998). *Unto Others: The Evolution and Psychology of Unselfish Behavior*. Cambridge, MA, Harvard University Press.

36 Wilson, E. O. (2004). *On Human Nature*. Cambridge, MA, Harvard University Press.

37 Wilson, E. O. (2012). *The Social Conquest of Earth*. New York, WW Norton & Company.

38 Wilson. *On Human Nature*.

39 Wilson. *On Human Nature*; Wilson. *The Social Conquest of Earth*.

40 Murdock, G. P., (1945). "The common denominator of culture." *Science of Man in the World Crisis*. R. Linton, ed. New York, Columbia University Press, pp. 123–142.

41 Lawrence, P. R. (2010). *Driven to Lead: Good, Bad, and Misguided Leadership* (Vol. 168). New York, John Wiley & Sons.

42 Darwin, C. (1909). *The Descent of Man and Selection in Relation to Sex*. New York, Appleton and Company. Page 101.

43 Greene, J. (2014). *Moral Tribes: Emotion, Reason and the Gap between Us and Them*. New York, Penguin Press.

44 Wright, R. (2010). *The Moral Animal: Why We Are, The Way We Are: The New Science of Evolutionary Psychology*. New York, Vintage.

45 Greene, J. (2014). *Moral Tribes: Emotion, Reason and the Gap between Us and Them*. Chicago, IL, Atlantic Books Ltd.

46 Wilson. *The Social Conquest of Earth*.

47 Waal, F. B. M. d. (2009). *The Age of Empathy: Nature's Lessons for a Kinder Society*. New York, Harmony Books.

48 http://evonomics.com/traditional-economics-failed-heres-a-new-blueprint/

49 Darwin, C. (1965). *The Expression of the Emotions in Man and Animals* (Vol. 526). Chicago, University of Chicago Press.

50 Wilson. *The Social Conquest of Earth.*

51 http://davidmatsumoto.com/content/NG%20Spain%20Article_2_.pdf

52 Waal. *The Age of Empathy.*

53 Batson, C. D. (1998). "The psychology of helping and altruism: Problems and puzzles." *Contemporary Psychology*, **43**(2), 108–109; Waal, F. B. M. d. (2008). "Putting the altruism back into altruism: The evolution of empathy." *Annual Review of Psychology*, **59**(1), 279–300; Fehr, E., and Gächter, S. (2002). "Altruistic punishment in humans." *Nature*, **415** (6868), 137–140.

54 Wilson. *The Social Conquest of Earth;* Wilson, D. S. (2015). *Does Altruism Exist?: Culture, Genes, and the Welfare of Others.* New Haven, Yale University Press.

55 Lehmann, L., and L. Keller (2006). "The evolution of cooperation and altruism—a general framework and a classification of models." *Journal of Evolutionary Biology*, **19**(5), 1365–1376.

56 Wilson. *Does Altruism Exist?*

57 Wilson, D. S., and E. O. Wilson (2007). "Rethinking the theoretical foundation of sociobiology." *The Quarterly Review of Biology*, **82**(4), 327–348.

58 Wilson. *On Human Nature.*

59 Wilson. *Does Altruism Exist?*

60 Dierksmeier, C. and M. Pirson (2009). "Oikonomia versus chrematistike: Learning from Aristotle about the future orientation of business management." *Journal of Business Ethics*, **88**(3), 417–430.

61 Arendt, H. (2013). *The Human Condition.* Chicago, University of Chicago Press.

62 Dierksmeier, C. (2011). "Reorienting management education: From homo oeconomicus to human dignity." *Business Schools under Fire.* H. M. Network. New York, Palgrave McMillan.

63 www.nybooks.com/articles/2016/04/07/moral-psychology-an-exchange/

64 Kueng, H., and K. J. Kuschel (Eds.). (1993). *Global Ethic: The Declaration of the Parliament of the World's Religions.* London, Bloomsbury Publishing; Kung, H. (2004). *Global Responsibility: In Search of a New World Ethic.* New York, Wipf and Stock Publishers.

65 Kueng and Kuschel. *Global Ethic;* Kung. *Global Responsibility.*

66 Ibid.

67 Ibid.

68 Ibid.

69 Ibid.

70 Taleb, N. N. (2012). *Antifragile: Things That Gain from Disorder* (Vol. 3). New York, Random House.

71 Sen, A. (2001). *Development as Freedom*. Oxford; New York, Oxford University Press.

72 Kahneman, D. (2007). "Judgment and intuition." 2008 Distinguished Lecture Series sponsored by Harvard's Mind/Brain/Behavior (MBB) Interfaculty Initiative (MBB).

73 Wilson, D. S., E. Ostrom, and M. E. Cox (2013). "Generalizing the core design principles for the efficacy of groups." *Journal of Economic Behavior & Organization*, **90**: S21–S32.

74 Ostrom, E. (2009). "Design principles of robust property-rights institutions: what have we learned?" *Property Rights and Land Policies*. K. Gregory Ingram, Yu-Hung Hong, eds. Cambridge, MA, Lincoln Institute of Land Policy, 25–51.

75 As described in Boehm, C. (2012). *Moral Origins: The Evolution of Virtue, Altruism, and Shame*. New York, Basic Books.

76 Wilson, D. S. et al. *Doing Well by Doing Good—An Evolution Institute Report on Socially Responsible Businesses*. https://evolution-institute.org/

77 Wilson et al. *Doing Well by Doing Good*.

78 Ibid.

79 De Tocqueville, A. (2003). *Democracy in America* (Vol. 10). Washington, DC, Regnery Publishing; Wilson et al. *Doing Well by Doing Good*.

80 Haidt, J., J. P. Seder, and S. Kesebir (2008). "Hive psychology, happiness, and public policy." *The Journal of Legal Studies*, **37**(S2), S133–S156.

81 Wilson et al. *Doing Well by Doing Good*.

82 Lawrence. *Driven to Lead*.

83 Hare, R. D. (1999). *Without Conscience: The Disturbing World of the Psychopaths among Us*. New York, Guilford Press; Neumann, C. S. and R. D. Hare (2008). "Psychopathic traits in a large community sample: links to violence, alcohol use, and intelligence." *Journal of Consulting and Clinical Psychology*, **76**(5), 893–899.

84 Ibid. XI.

85 Ibid. 281.

86 Ibid. 6.

87 Neumann and Hare. "Psychopathic traits in a large community sample."
    893–899; Weber, S., et al. (2008). "Structural brain abnormalities in
    psychopaths-a review." *Behavioral Sciences & the Law*, **26**(7), 7–28.
88 Buckholtz, J. W., et al. (2010). "Mesolimbic dopamine reward system
    hypersensitivity in individuals with psychopathic traits." *Nature
    Neuroscience*, **13**(4), 419–421.
89 Lawrence. *Driven to Lead*.
90 Hare. *Without Conscience*. 1–2.
91 Babiak, P. and R. D. Hare (2006). *Snakes in Suits: When Psychopaths Go to
    Work*. New York, Regan Books.
92 Babiak and Hare. *Snakes in Suits*; Lawrence. *Driven to Lead*; Boddy, C. R.
    (2011). "The corporate psychopaths theory of the global financial crisis."
    Journal of Business Ethics, **102**(2), 255–259.
93 Neumayr, A. (1995). *Dictators in the Mirror of Medicine: Napoleon,
    Hitler, Stalin*. Bloomington, IL, Medi-Ed Press.

3   A New Humanistic Model

Harold Demsetz, the famed Chicago School economist, begins his book on homo economicus by introducing Ebenezer Scrooge, the focal character in the Charles Dickens novella *A Christmas Carol*.[1] He suggests that Ebenezer Scrooge represents the quintessential homo economicus: miserly, misanthropic, cold-hearted, and greedy. Ebenezer Scrooge was the inspiration for Walt Disney's character Scrooge McDuck, the money-counting uncle without kids. If Ebenezer Scrooge and Scrooge McDuck are the model men for economics, and, as consequence, for a large part of management science, what other model is out there?

At the beginning of Chapter 1, we met Elisabeth, Richard, and Tiffany, each disillusioned by their encounters with contemporary organizational life. Is there a model that can explain the unhappiness of such otherwise successful human beings? According to psychologist Art Markman, you cannot replace something with nothing.[2] The challenge for the many critics of homo economicus and REMM has been to propose an alternative theoretical model. Theoretical models are helpful because they reduce complexity and distill the essence of a phenomenon. The power of homo economicus and his intellectual grandchild, REMM, is the model's relative parsimony. Theorists can use it to explain and predict behavior (however inaccurate these predictions turn out to be), as well as propose alternative approaches. As stated before, theories vary in terms of their accuracy and parsimony, but the principle of Occam's razor pushes theorists toward parsimony. To paraphrase once more,

> [A]mong competing hypotheses, the one with the fewest
> assumptions should be selected. Other, more complicated solutions

may ultimately prove correct, but – in the absence of certainty – the fewer assumptions that are made, the better.[3]

Occam's razor directs theorists to adopt models containing the fewest assumptions. However, once those assumptions are falsified, models should shift to include other assumptions that can be tested. The inaccuracies of homo economicus and REMM have long been visible, and many Nobel Prizes have been awarded for doing so. For example, Herbert Simon, Daniel Kahneman, Elinor Ostrom, and Amartya Sen have received the highest distinction for economic research that challenges traditional economistic thinking. Nevertheless, academics have left the base line assumptions largely unchanged, at least in those parts of the social sciences that agency theory influences, which include management science.[4] New disciplines have emerged that reject purely economistic assumptions, such as behavioral economics, psychological economics, evolutionary economics, behavioral finance, positive management, and positive organizational behavior, but these have stayed at the margin of their respective fields. It is true that REMM yields novel insights in a number of fields, including political economy, psychology, and public policy. However, given the vast challenges and theoretical mismatches, we are probably experiencing what Kuhn calls a "pre-paradigm shift phase."[5] In this phase, the dominant models fail visibly, and new models compete for a higher level of accuracy. It is impossible to be modest about the task of formulating such alternative paradigms, yet we believe that the humanist perspective can provide valuable insights.[6] It is up to you to judge if it is the alternative model the world needs.

Many scholars, including Daniel Kahneman, Henry Mintzberg, Amartya Sen, Elinor Ostrom, and Sumantra Ghoshal, have criticized homo economicus and REMM for being inaccurate, yet the challenge has been to provide a model of similar parsimony but higher accuracy. In the following section, insights from evolutionary biology and neuroscience will form the basis of a proposed new humanistic model. The work of Lawrence and Nohria, as well as the collaborative work of Lawrence and Pirson, form the cornerstones of this proposition. Building on their work, this books seeks to integrate additional insights from the humanities and social sciences to build a model of human behavior that reflects the emerging consilience of knowledge. The proposed model is based on four innate human drives that need to be balanced to achieve dignity and well-being. The proposed model is only one of many possibilities, of course. The attempt here, though, is to present a model that is based on scientific insights rather than mere assumptions. It draws on the emerging insights into why Homo sapiens have survived.

Compared to REMM, the power of such a humanistic model is arguably twofold: it increases accuracy and it remains equally parsimonious. It also explains behavior that REM models explain, but goes beyond this.[7] It is not a naïve rejection of evil in human nature; rather it presents a comprehensive perspective that can explain good, collaborative, moral, and empathetic behavior, as well as evil, psychopathic, immoral behavior. It is thus more realistic. We believe it will also turn out to be more accurate.

BASIC CONSIDERATIONS

Before detailing the model, it is important to situate the emergence of this novel humanistic perspective. Whereas economistic and humanistic conceptions have been presented as competing, it is critical to understand that they share a common origin. The German philosopher and former Minister for Culture, Julian Nida-Ruemelin, argues that humanistic and economistic perspectives both build on the assumption of human freedom, and take the human individual as its starting point.[8] Both perspectives are therefore equally hostile to any form of imposed collectivism. Similarly, both traditions emphasize the human capacity for reasoning. As a result, homo economicus and REMM models can be helpful when examining market behavior based on individual reasoning.

The humanistic perspective of human nature will build on the old model but expand it significantly by integrating insights from evolutionary science and the humanities. In contrast to economism, the humanistic perspective, for example, assumes that human nature is not entirely a given, that it can be refined through education and learning.[9] Universities and public schools were established under the auspices of the humanist tradition to form citizens. Similarly, Nida-Ruemelin suggests that another distinctive feature of humanism is the normative, ethical component that attributes unalienable rights to everybody, independent of ethnicity, nationality, social status, or gender. This view is echoed by other scholars, who propose the notion of *human dignity* as a baseline concept of humanistic thought.[10] A dignity threshold is thus a universal baseline for the accordance of human rights for everyone.

Evolutionary biology increasingly supports the traditional humanistic perspective on human nature as a *zoon politikon*, a relational human being. According to the humanist perspective, people materialize their freedom through value-based social interactions. When they engage well with people, they do so by protecting and enhancing their respective humanity and dignity; guided by the Golden Rule, they treat each other as a means, but also as an end in themselves. This is not an idealistic vision of people as do-gooders, but is the reason Homo sapiens survived. Moral behavior allows people to build better and longer-lasting relationships that enhance mutual trust and well-being. When they thrive, they are intrinsically motivated to self-actualize and serve others through what they do. Humans do not predictably follow maximization strategies, nor do they have fixed, preconceived utility functions, but their interests, needs, and wants take shape through discourse and a continuous exchange with the outside world.[11] To thrive and be happy, such human beings balance their interests and, in accordance with general moral principles, align them with the interests of others (partners) and their community.[12] Respect for dignity and overall moral behavior are viewed as pathways to well-being and a higher common good.

To summarize, both views of human nature are based on some understanding of human agency and freedom. The economistic

Human nature	Economistic view	Humanistic view
Foundation	Wants	Drives
Goal	Maximization	Balance
Operating modes	Fixed utility curves/ Opportunity sets	Routines, Learning, Practical wisdom
Focal point	Individual	Relational
Role of dignity	Absent	Critical
Role of morality	Amoral	Moral/Immoral
Aspiration	Wealth/Status/Power/Reputation	Well -being

FIGURE 3.1: Comparative Views on Human Nature

perspective highlights wants as the foundation of human agency, and argues that the maximization of wants is a fundamental human motivation. According to the economistic perspective, fixed utility functions, or opportunity sets centered on their individual benefit above all else, guide humans. The notion of human dignity as a moral cornerstone is absent, and humans are fundamentally considered amoral (not immoral). The highest aspiration for humans is therefore to achieve wealth, power, status, and reputation (see also Figure 3.1).

In the humanistic perspective, evolutionary drives are the foundational motivation, and achieving a balance is the goal. In the humanistic perspective, humans operate according to routines, yet learn and adapt constantly. According to the humanistic perspective, the key reason for the survival of humans is their relational nature, for which dignity and morality are crucial. Their highest aspiration is to achieve a level of well-being and to flourish.

The Baseline Model

Evolutionary biology points to four independent drives of human nature, which are critical for the survival of the species. Darwin suggests we share an evolutionary background with many animals,[13] while neuroscience's insights point to deeply rooted neural mechanisms that reward us when we acquire and defend what we deem necessary for survival. Lawrence and Nohria (2002) label two basic drives that we share with all animals as (a) the drive to acquire (dA) and (b) the drive to defend (dD).[14]

The Drive to Acquire (dA)

Lawrence argues that humans, in common with all animals, have a fundamental drive to get what they need to stay alive and have progeny: food, water, warmth, sex, etc.[15] Modern neuroscience provides evidence to support the biological basis of the drive to acquire.[16] Researchers found, for example, that an area in the brain called the "nucleus accumbens" lights up with increased blood flow when people and animals experience pleasurable sensations from objects they encounter, ranging from tasty food to the sight of a beautiful face.[17] This drive is commonly acknowledged by many economic and management theorists, including Jensen and Meckling, as the basis for utility maximization.

The Drive to Defend (dD)

Lawrence and Nohria claim that in most species the drive to defend is a mirror image of the drive to acquire.[18] What needs defending is what needed to be acquired – food, water, warmth, mates, and so on. Carter and Frith present evidence that the drive to defend seems, like the other drives, to be housed in the limbic area of the brain, specifically in a module called the "amygdala."[19] Carter and Frith explain that the amygdala acts as the brain's alarm system. Depending on the situation, the amygdala may issue a feeling of panic, which translates into a flight mechanism. However, it could also stimulate excessively friendly behavior to appease the opponent. A third response could be to fight, which is increasingly inappropriate in modern civilizations. Lawrence and Nohria further argue that, in humans, the drive to defend means far more – not only the physical necessities of life and procreation but also relationships, cooperative efforts, and worldviews (see the idea of protected values).[20] Similar to the drive to acquire, humans can satisfy their drive to defend in a huge variety of ways, and often in cooperation with others.[21]

A HUMANISTIC EXTENSION

Simplified, the above two drives (drive to acquire and drive to defend) go far to explain the economistic perspective on human nature. Within this perspective, all other drives and interests are subordinate to the ambition to maximize the drive to acquire.[22] Spencer's account of Darwin's findings[23] reduced human behavior largely to a two-drive model, which subordinated all other human concerns to the impetus of acquiring and defending.

The novelty of the recent evolutionary findings and their importance lie in the addition of two important and *independent* drives, or what Lawrence and Nohria label (1) the drive to bond (dB) and (2) the drive to comprehend (dC). Based on these findings, Lawrence developed a renewed Darwinian theory (RD theory),[24] which rehabilitates Darwin's groundbreaking insights into human behavior, which are often overlooked or misunderstood.[25] In essence, RD theory explains how the human brain has developed via natural selection, as well as through sex and group selection mechanisms, to make complex decisions about all aspects of life (personal, communal, and societal). This theory posits that the two additional drives are independent of the other drives and represent critical ultimate motives that underlie all human decisions: The **drive to bond (dB)** enables long-term, mutually caring relationships with other humans, and **the drive to comprehend (dC)** allows us to make sense of the world around us in terms of its multifaceted relations with ourselves.[26] In Darwin's own words:

> The small strength and speed of man, his want of natural weapons, etc., are more than counterbalanced by his *intellectual powers*, through which he has formed himself weapons, tools, etc., and secondly by his *social qualities* which lead him to give and receive aid from his fellow-men.[27]

In the following section, the evidence for the existence of these two independent drives is presented in more detail. It is important to note that these arguments are still developing as new evidence is constantly being generated, but the theoretical basis of a four-drive model of human behavior provides propositions that can be tested. We believe it will do a better job of explaining the complexity of human behavior, and provide a better predictive theory.

The Drive to Bond (dB)

Aristotle hinted at the drive to bond when he stated that human beings are social animals (*zoon politikon*).[28] Darwin observed the drive to bond in humans when stating:

> Every one will admit that man is a social being. We see this in his dislike of solitude and in his wish for society beyond that of his own family. Solitary confinement is one of the severest punishments which can be inflicted.[29]
>
> *or*
>
> Under circumstances of extreme peril, as during a fire, when a man endeavors to save a fellow-creature without a moment's hesitation, he can hardly feel pleasure; and still less has the time to reflect on the dissatisfaction which he might subsequently experience if he did not make the attempt. Should he afterwards reflect over his own conduct, he would feel that there lies within him an impulsive power widely different from a search after pleasure or happiness; and this seems to be the deeply planted social instinct.[30]

These observations seem almost trivial, as most of us will have observed that people tend to form bonds with other people. Lawrence, however, suggests that we need to reevaluate this utterly familiar phenomenon not simply as "the way people are," or as "the innate goodness in people," but as one of four survival-oriented criteria.[31]

E.O. Wilson suggests that this sociality of human nature allowed its survival and the conquest of the Earth.[32] A number of experiments have offered evidence that there is an independent drive to bond that our brain supports. LeDoux, for example, found that when certain parts of the limbic area – the hypothalamus and anterior thalamus – are impaired, individuals have a difficult time forming any meaningful or stable social relationships.[33] Similarly, Damasio suggests that damage in certain parts of the brain leaves people lacking emotions, the ability to make rational decisions and to form new bonds.[34] In experiments that examined group bonding mechanisms, Tajfel found that a group of strangers, divided into arbitrary subgroups, forms surprisingly strong attachments to members of the same group, even if the group is completely meaningless and has no prior history.[35] Studies by Warneken and Tomasello, who found that human infants (between eighteen and twenty-four months old) show a spontaneous, unrewarded impulse to help others, even though they seem too young to have emulated this behavior from adults, provide further support for the innate and independent drive to bond.[36] In these experiments, researchers, who were strangers to the toddlers, accidentally dropped items and pretended to unsuccessfully reach for them. The children retrieved the items for the experimenter 89 percent of the time. Henrich and colleagues, who find that the value of fairness exists across cultures, and trumps the drive to acquire in what is called "the ultimatum game," provide further evidence that this impulse may not be socially learned, but inherent and universal.[37]

Searching for homo economicus, the researchers conducted experiments in fifteen countries across the globe to see how people would react when they were offered money, let's say US$100. This "ultimatum game" allows people to suggest whether and how much they would share their windfall sum. A second person has the right to accept or to reject the offered sum. If the second player rejects, no one will receive any money. The researchers found that, across the globe, players rarely behaved as homo economicus are expected to behave, i.e., either offering or accepting the smallest sum of money. Instead, they largely preferred a "fair" sharing of the cash and rejected "unfair" proposals, even to their detriment.[38] To further highlight how deeply the drive to bond affects us, Lawrence argues that all humans, except the rare psychopath, experience pain at the loss of an important long-term relationship, whether by death, divorce, downsizing, or any other causes.[39] For example, emigration is known to cause deep and lasting grief.[40] In many cases, this pain is so deep that a reductionist explanation using the drives to acquire and defend is insufficient.

The Drive to Comprehend (dC)

Aristotle observed the drive to comprehend when he qualified humans as social animals endowed with reason. Many scholars have since suggested that humans have a fundamental drive to understand themselves and their environment.[41] Gribbin and Gribbin refer to it as mankind's insatiable curiosity.[42] Darwin referred to the drive to comprehend by stating:

> As soon as the important faculties of the imagination, wonder, and
> curiosity, together with some power of reasoning, had become
> partially developed, man would naturally crave to understand what
> was passing around him, and could have vaguely speculated on his
> own existence.[43]

Lawrence argues that the drive to comprehend can be witnessed in the curiosity of children, who ask questions without knowing whether the answers will ever be of any use to them in fulfilling their other drives. Even newborns, once fed and secure, start exploring the world with their eyes and their hands. The popularity of puzzles, Sudoku, or trivia quizzes is also testimony to the independent drive to comprehend, since solving them provides immediate gratification, but only remotely serves in other terms. Another supporting argument is that anthropologists have not found a single culture that does not have a creation story, and few that do not have an afterlife story.[44] People seem to need these stories to give meaning to their lives,[45] regardless of whether or not the stories confer any advantage in acquiring, bonding, or defending. Lawrence goes as far as to suggest that religions arose in all societies primarily to help fulfill this drive. Psychologist Steven Pinker argues that the drive to comprehend has helped humans survive against stronger and faster animals by devising weaponry, building houses etc.[46] Rather than doing things by instinct, humans tend to figure things out, which in turn can prove very useful as a survival mechanism.

DEVELOPMENT TOWARD INDEPENDENCE OF DRIVES

Why is the above argument about four different, *independent* drives relevant? After all, bonding and comprehension could simply be used to acquire and defend better, thus supporting the Spencerian, economistic narrative. According to anthropologists and evolutionary psychologists, the independence of the drives to bond and comprehend from the basic drives is key to understanding human evolution. In fact, evolutionary scholars argue that humans have evolved a brain that can continually adapt to its *contemporary* environment, rather than relying on its adaptation to an *ancestral* environment.[47] Accordingly, our brain was an adaptation to a period of extreme and comparatively rapid climatic shifts, the first occurring about two million years ago, the second occurring around 150,000 years ago.[48] These two major shifts explain the development of *independent* drives to bond and to comprehend; the drive to bond emerged when human ancestors transitioned from Homo habilis to Homo erectus. The drive to comprehend emerged during the shift from Homo erectus to Homo sapiens.

The Emergence of Bonding

The first evolutionary shift occurred about two million years ago and established the human drive to bond in our neural blueprint.[49] It arguably occurred because pair-bonding proved essential to the survival of the hominid line.[50] Adam Kuper, a South African anthropologist, argues that Homo erectus proved fitter for survival than its hominid predecessor, Homo habilis, mainly because its brain supported a nuclear family structure.[51] Such a structure proved superior, because with increasing brain sizes and slower maturation, offspring needed increased protection. The family bond became a survival mechanism and was probably strengthened by the discovery of fire. Once controlled, fire supported small communities and changed their feeding patterns. Physical anthropologist Richard Wrangham and his colleagues have pointed out that cooking increased the food supply by making it possible to consume plants, such as many roots, that were otherwise toxic or too tough to chew.[52] In addition, cooking helped conserve food and allowed edibles to be stored.[53] The downside of storage was that food would be much more vulnerable to theft, particularly by larger males. According to Wrangham and colleagues, females, who most probably gathered the vegetables, therefore looked for help with guarding the food.[54] Hence, there was a clear evolutionary advantage in mating with a reliable man willing to bond with a particular woman.[55]

There is mounting evidence that the drive to bond is manifested as an independent drive in our brain. The independent status means that satiation of the drive to bond occurs independently of other drives' satiation. Nevertheless, research suggests that the brain and the human nervous system reward satiation of the drive to bond in a very similar manner as the drive to acquire and the drive to defend. For example, researchers at the National Institutes of Health scanned the brains of volunteers who had been asked to think about either donating a sum of money to charity or keeping it for themselves. When the volunteers thought about donating the money, a section of the limbic area of their brain lit up.[56] This, surprisingly, was also the nucleus accumbens, which usually lights up in response to food or sex.[57] Similar evidence suggests that bonding through, for example, donating money increases human well-being much more than acquiring, such as keeping the money for oneself.[58] Other research suggests that altruism is not necessarily a superior moral faculty for suppressing an egoistic nature, but a hard-wired element that leads to pleasure.[59] Either way, Lawrence argues the drive to bond is a full-fledged drive in its own right, and is hard-wired into the brain.[60]

Comprehension Matters

The shift from Homo erectus to Homo sapiens finally introduced the drive to comprehend as an independent drive in our neural structure.

This shift is known as the Upper Paleolithic Transition, which is believed to have occurred about 150,000 years ago.[61] According to many evolutionary scholars, Homo erectus, who probably only developed very simple tools made of stone and wood, evolved into modern Homo sapiens. With this transition, the human species developed language, sophisticated technologies, complex tribal institutions, and civilization as we know it today.[62] Steven Pinker described the dramatic transition in these terms:

> Calling it a revolution is no exaggeration. All other hominids come out of the comic strip B.C., but the Upper Paleolithic people were the Flintstones. More than 45,000 years ago they somehow crossed sixty miles of open ocean to reach Australia, where they left behind hearths, cave paintings, the world's first polished tools, and today's aborigines. Europe (home of the Cro-Magnon) and the Middle East also saw unprecedented arts and technologies, which used new materials like antler, ivory, and bone as well as stone, sometimes transported hundreds of miles. The toolkit included fine blades, needles, awls, many kinds of axes and scrapers, spear points, spear throwers, bows and arrows, fishhooks, engravers, flutes, maybe even calendars. They built shelters, and they slaughtered large animals by the thousands. They decorated everything in sight – tools, cave walls, their bodies – and carved knick-knacks in the shapes of animals and naked women, which archeologists euphemistically call "fertility symbols." They were us ... [This] first human revolution was not a cascade of changes set off by a few key inventions. Ingenuity itself was the invention, manifested in hundreds of innovations tens of thousands of miles and years apart.[63]

Pinker's observation that "ingenuity itself was the invention" suggests the emergence of what Lawrence and Nohria call an "independent drive to comprehend" in Homo sapiens; increasing empirical evidence points to its independent physical existence in the brain as well. Neuroscientists Irving Biederman and Edward Vessel found that a part of the brain that helps recognize what we see seems to be equipped with its own reward system of opiate receptors, which give a pleasurable "high" when stimulated by a new image.[64] This pleasurable "high," as described earlier, can also be experienced when getting a right answer in a trivia quiz or solving a Sudoku. In history, such emotional reactions to "getting it" have also been described as the "Eureka" effect.[65] Increasing evidence demonstrates that humans yearn for novelty, creativity, and understanding, because our brain rewards us for it. At the same time, the human brain does not reward routine and monotony, which typically lead to boredom. Biederman and Wessels found that a pleasurable response is diminished when the same image was recognized repeatedly. According to Biederman and Vessel, these opiate receptors get bored by repetition and need new stimulation, which leads us to curiosity. According to Lawrence, humans are directly rewarded with pleasure when learning something new. The human brain time and again rewards comprehending independently. Throughout evolution, the hard-wired reward for learning has had a positive side effect, in that species that learned became more adaptive than species that did not keep learning.[66]

DEVELOPING A HUMANISTIC SYNTHESIS

In summary, the new humanistic model of human nature builds on evolutionary sciences' insights. At its base it posits **four basic drives** – ultimate motives that underlie all human decisions. There are two ancient drives that all animals with some capacity to sense and evaluate their surroundings share: **the drive to acquire (dA)** life-sustaining resources, and **the drive to defend (dD)** against all life-threatening entities. In addition, there are the two newer drives, which evolved to an independent status only in humans: **the drive to bond (dB)** in order to form long-term mutually caring relationships with other humans, and **the drive to comprehend (dC)** in order to make sense of the world around us with regard to our own existence.[67]

As can be seen in Figure 3.2, the economistic model can potentially accommodate some of these drives: the drive to bond, the drive

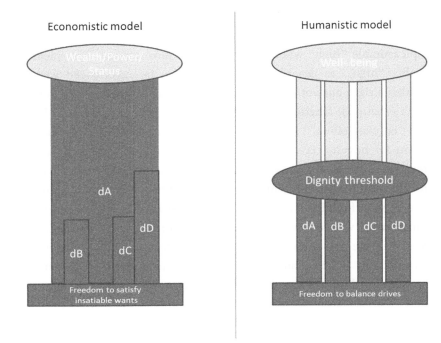

FIGURE 3.2: The Economistic versus the Humanistic Model

to comprehend, and the drive to defend all can be said to serve the drive to acquire. In contrast, the humanistic view suggests that we have four *independent* underlying natural drives that need to be continually balanced. The humanistic model presupposes that none of the drives can be maximized, but that they need to be in balance to provide a sense of dignity and well-being. In the humanistic model, the independent status of the drives to bond and comprehend means that they are treated as ends in themselves, and rewarded by the brain and nervous system in the same manner as dA or dD. The independence of the four drives thereby renders the model of human nature more complex and more accurate.

Emerging research in the field of neuroscience finds supportive evidence for the complexity of human drives, and suggests that the prefrontal cortex of the brain has been uniquely designed to handle this complexity. In the humanistic model, the drives to acquire and to defend still remain viable and important factors in determining human behavior, yet the drive to bond with fellow humans and the drive to comprehend are strong independent, competitive forces. As a result, the four independent drives are frequently in conflict with each other. In everyday life, humans struggle to decide how to behave, and how to adaptively respond to the immediate circumstances, for example, whether to treat someone with respect or to disregard this person, whether to spend time with children rather than work, or follow the news on Twitter. Lawrence suggests that this condition of drive–conflict brings the prefrontal cortex into action.[68] Its main task is to create a suitable balance when faced with drive–conflict. Neuroscience suggests that the prefrontal cortex has the capacity to call on all the resources of the rest of the cortex (long-term memory, skills, etc.) to search for a response that satisfices all four drives.[69]

Dignity as a Universal Threshold

The four-drive model of human behavior can be enhanced if we take onboard perspectives from the humanities, as outlined in Chapter 2. For example, Hans Kueng's findings suggest that there needs to be recognition of a human dignity baseline.[70] Amartya Sen points out that such dignity enables human freedom.[71] Sen argues that if people have not fulfilled their baseline drives, they cannot be considered free. In this sense, and in contrast to what Jensen and Meckling claim, these are basic needs that need to be fulfilled.

The fulfilment of human needs can be included in the four-drive model through what management researchers Thomas Donaldson and James Walsh recently called a "dignity threshold."[72] In other words, to ensure human survival at the individual level, as well as the group level, a better model of human nature needs to integrate universal dignity thresholds. The humanistic model includes a conceptual baseline that ensures basic human dignity as a matter of balance in the four drives. A dignity threshold could, for example, require minimum fulfillments of the drive to acquire (enough food), the drive to defend (basic shelter), the drive to bond (a social connection to other people), and the drive to comprehend (a basic purpose in life).

This dignity threshold represents a moral claim, but it is also a key survival mechanism. Increasing research shows, for example, that whenever dignity is violated, the human brain reacts as if it experienced physical pain.[73] Donna Hicks, an internationally renowned conflict researcher, argues that dignity violations are a pervasive source of conflict.[74] Hicks mentions that conflicts across the globe fester if those dignity violations are not addressed.[75] Introducing the notion of baseline dignity is not only helpful but essential if the model is to help explain human survival and human flourishing.

Practical Wisdom as Operating Logic

A further extension of the core four-drive model of human nature refers to how people make decisions or the operating modus. As shown in Figure 3.3, the economistic perspective suggests that humans constantly rationalize the best decisions to maximize utility, while the humanistic perspective suggests that humans draw on capabilities of learning and practical wisdom to enable the balancing necessary. These capabilities to, for example, engage with others and live a life of purpose and thriving can be further developed. In fact, Amartya Sen has argued that they *need* to be developed.[76] According to Sen, the purpose of human development in its various forms should be the development of such capabilities. Nussbaum argues that there are particular processes that demonstrate how such capabilities can be developed so that they ensure liberty and dignity. She proposes a list of elements that are core for dignified development practice.[77] Hans Kueng and others, drawing on various ancient traditions, have uncovered a number of practices designed to help guide human judgment. These are present in Buddhism, Daoism, and Christianity, which offer practical wisdom practices that can guide people to make better decisions.[78] Recently, such wisdom practices have been labeled "stakeholder engagement" or "co-creation," in which various parties allow shared responsibility and shared benefits to enable them to shape decisions together. The

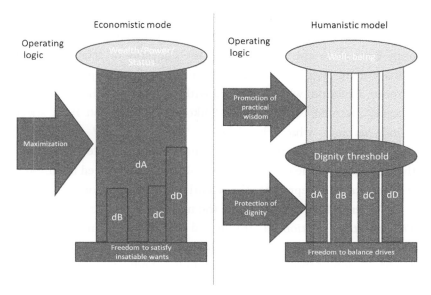

FIGURE 3.3: Operating logics of Economistic versus Humanistic perspective

development and refinement of capabilities and processes of practical wisdom are a constant learning task rather than an algorithmic process. The humanistic model embraces such practical wisdom, because it helps balance the four drives on or above the dignity threshold, thus allowing flourishing and higher levels of well-being to occur.

Well-Being as the Ultimate Objective

Another extension of the four-drive model of human nature relates to the purpose of human existence. In the reductionist, economistic model, the ultimate objective function is wealth, status, power, or anything else that can be maximized. This view has figured most prominently since technical and statistical research became the focus of economics and management studies. The work of Milton Friedman and his colleagues at the Chicago School represent this perspective best.

In the humanistic model, the ultimate purpose of human existence is the notion of flourishing and well-being. In this, the humanistic model reflects a rather consistent, albeit often forgotten, agreement between economic thinkers about the purpose of the economy. Ever since the emergence of the concepts of economics and management, there has been a debate about their respective larger purpose. Aristotle, who is credited with popularizing the term "economics," wanted to distinguish "oikonomia" early on from sheer money-making, which he labeled "chrematistike." Oikonomia should follow moral rules and ultimately enhance "eudaimonia," the well-being of the community or polis. He disapproved of chrematistike because it represents the relentless pursuit of more.[79]

When Adam Smith studied the nature and causes of wealth in *The Wealth of Nations* (1776), he did so believing that wealth is a means to a higher end, which to him was the common good.[80] More recent economic thought leaders, including Ludwig von Mises, John Maynard Keynes, and Friedrich von Hayek, similarly argue that the order of economic affairs should lead to a higher level of happiness or overall well-being. Amartya Sen picks up the Aristotelian distinction when he argues that "economic sense" is defined in one of two ways: the first includes the achievement of a good society; the second narrowly concerns itself with business profits and rewards.[81] The humanistic perspective endorses the former as the true sense of oikonomia.

Consequently, the humanistic model is oriented toward a balance of the four drives, which achieves ever higher levels of well-being and flourishing.

LEADERSHIP AND ORGANIZATIONS

The humanistic model of human nature is highly relevant to address some of the major global crises humanity faces. For example, if humans truly do care about their well-being and that of others, there should be organizing practices that allow for the formulation of solutions to problems like climate change, social inequality, and poverty. Some of these practices and the organizations that promote them will be highlighted later in the book (Chapter 8).

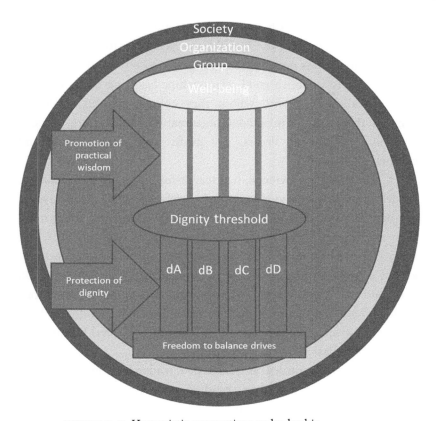

FIGURE 3.4: Humanistic perspectives on leadership

Leadership is one of the main practices that a different view of human nature can inform. As we have seen, it is an inherent ambition of the humanistic model to balance the independent four drives on or above the dignity threshold. Organizations and their leaders are responsible for ensuring these dignity thresholds and for enhancing the capabilities of the organization to achieve higher-level flourishing and the well-being of its various stakeholders.

In his book *Driven to Lead: Good, Bad, and Misguided Leadership* (2010), Paul Lawrence writes that good leaders intuitively know that they have to balance the four drives within themselves, with others, and within society (see Figure 3.4). Lawrence compares organizations to cars with four-cylinder engines. Good organizations, according to Lawrence, run on all four cylinders rather than one.[82] These organizations are able to create a purpose beyond profit (dC), and are able to establish good relationships based on trust with the various stakeholders with whom they collaborate (dB). Lawrence suggests that bad and misguided organizational leaders try to focus on only one or two drives, say profit maximization (dA) and competitiveness (dD).

According to Lawrence, bad leadership follows a psychopathic model of human behavior and solely wishes to fulfill the drive to acquire. These leaders wish to achieve status, rank, and profit more than anything. They sometimes acknowledge the other drives, but mainly to enhance the drive to acquire. The bestselling management author Jim Collins, for example, criticizes the example of the US corporate executive Albert J. Dunlap, who went into organizations to slash costs in the short term and hike up shareholder value, only to leave after a very short stint at the helm, taking several hundreds of millions of dollars as compensation with him.[83]

Examples described as misguided leadership tend to follow the economistic perspective. Leaders may very well sense, for example, that they cannot motivate employees by focusing on profit maximization; nevertheless, they try to incentivize them with stock options. Misguided leaders want to fit in with the dominant narrative of a strong leader, but do not grasp that they will only get the best out of their employees if they build authentic trust (dB), create a genuinely purposeful organization (dC), and make all stakeholders feel safe to interact with them (dD). Both Lawrence and Collins state that many leaders of publicly listed organizations fit this category.[84] In recent decades, the various attempts to discover the principles of excellence in leadership and organizations have time and again confirmed that the best organizations for people to work in, to work for, to be the customer of, and invest in are those that follow the humanistic perspective of the four-drive model.[85]

The humanistic model of human nature is not perfect, but it provides higher-level insights into successful organizing principles and decision-making than the economistic one. Guided by the humanistic model of human nature, leaders would approach their tasks differently. The humanistic perspective encourages the development of practical wisdom. Leaders can apply this wisdom in order to elevate human beings to a state of thriving, achieving this by balancing all four drives above the dignity threshold.

CONCLUDING REMARKS

Management professor Chris Laszlo argues that a change in consciousness is needed to change the quality of leadership, the quality of organizations, and the quality of our society. E.O. Wilson suggests that we need to increase our awareness of what it means to be human. The humanistic model of human nature is an opportunity for management researchers and practitioners to understand what it will take to increase such awareness.

The humanistic model of human nature provides higher levels of accuracy than the economistic model, while maintaining parsimony. The humanistic model of human nature distinguishes itself by acknowledging the four independent drives that allowed our species, Homo sapiens, to survive. The model also acknowledges that the *balance*, and not the maximization of these four drives, or any subset of them, is the goal. Furthermore, the model integrates the notion of a dignity threshold, a level that represents the fulfillment of basic needs with regard to the four drives (food, shelter, community, purpose, and safety). Finally, the model introduces well-being as an objective function.

This model can serve as a basis for leaders and managers to develop themselves, their employees, and the organizational stakeholders with whom they work. Surely people like Elisabeth, Richard, and Tiffany, who were introduced in Chapter 1, would prefer to work for leaders in organizations that address their respective four drives by, for example, paying fair wages (dA), providing opportunities for authentic care (dB), engaging in a higher purpose than profit (dC), while not threatening constant job cuts (dD).

The next chapter explores the consequences of the humanistic view of human nature for general organizing practices.

NOTES

1 Demsetz, H. (2011). *From Economic Man to Economic System: Essays on Human Behavior And The Institutions of Capitalism.* Cambridge, Cambridge University Press.

2 http://news.utexas.edu/2011/12/21/make-smarter-positive-resolutions (accessed June 28, 2016)

3 https://en.wikipedia.org/wiki/Occam%27s_razor (accessed June 23, 2016)

4 Eisenhardt, K. (1989). "Agency theory: an assessment and review." *Academy of Management Review,* **14**(1), 57–74. Eisenhardt states that Agency theory has been used by scholars in accounting (e.g., Demski & Feltham, 1978), economics (e.g., Spence & Zeckhauser, 1971), finance (e. g., Fama, 1980), marketing (e.g., Basu, Lal, Srinivasan, & Staelin, 1985), political science (e.g., Mitnick, 1986), organizational behavior (e.g., Eisenhardt, 1985, 1988; Kosnik, 1987), and sociology (e.g., Eccles, 1985; White, 1985).

5 Kuhn, T. (1996). *The Structure of Scientific Revolutions.* Chicago, University of Chicago Press.

6 This belief is shared by my colleagues at the Humanistic Management Network; the developed proposition including all its shortcomings are my personal propositions.

7 Lawrence, P. (2007). *Being Human – A Renewed Darwinian Theory of Human Behavior.* www.prlawrence.com. Cambridge, MA.

8 Nida-Ruemelin, J. (2008). "Philosophical grounds of humanism in economics." *Humanism in Business: Perspectives on the Development of a Responsible Business Society.* H. Spitzeck, M. Pirson, W. Amann, S. Khan and E. von Kimakowitz, eds. Cambridge, Cambridge University Press, 15–25.

9 Ibid.

10 See also Donaldson T. and J. P. Walsh (2015). "Toward a theory of business." *Research in Organizational Behavior,* **29**(35), 181–207.

11 Dierksmeier, C. and M. Pirson (2010). "Freedom and the modern corporation." *Philosophy of Management (formerly Reason in Practice)*, 9(3), 5–25.

12 Ibid.

13 Darwin, C. (1909). *The Descent of Man and Selection in Relation to Sex*. New York, Appleton and Company.

14 Lawrence, P. and N. Nohria (2002). *Driven: How Human Nature Shapes Our Choices*. San Francisco, Jossey-Bass.

15 Lawrence, P. (2010). *Driven to Lead: Good, Bad, and Misguided Leadership*. San Fransisco, Jossey- Bass.

16 Glimcher, P. W., et al. (2008). *Neuroeconomics: Decision Making and the Brain*. London/San Diego, Academic Press; Ridley, M. (2003). *Nature via Nurture: Genes, Experience, and What Makes Us Human*. New York, HarperCollins.

17 Lawrence, *Driven to Lead: Good, Bad, and Misguided Leadership*; Becerra, R. N., et al. (2001). "Circuitry activation by noxious thermal stimuli." *Neuron*, 323, 927–946.

18 Lawrence and Nohria. *Driven*.

19 Carter, R. and C. D. Frith (1998). *Mapping the Mind*. Berkeley, University of California Press.

20 Baron, J. and M. Spranca (1997). "Protected values." *Organizational Behavior and Human Decision Processes*, 70(1), 1–16; Haidt, J. (2012). *The Righteous Mind: Why Good People Are Divided by Politics and Religion*, New York, Pantheon.

21 Lawrence, *Driven to Lead: Good, Bad, and Misguided Leadership*; Becerra et al. "Circuitry activation by noxious thermal stimuli." 927–946.

22 Lawrence, P. (2007). *Being Human – A Renewed Darwinian Theory of Human Behavior*. www.prlawrence.com (last accessed June 21, 2016). Cambridge, MA.

23 Lawrence, P. R. and Pirson, M. (2015). "Economistic and humanistic narratives of leadership in the age of globality: Toward a renewed Darwinian theory of leadership." *Journal of Business Ethics*, 128(2), 383–394.

24 Lawrence. *Being Human*; Pirson, M. A. and P. R. Lawrence (2010). "Humanism in business – towards a paradigm shift?" *Journal of Business Ethics*, 93(4), 553–565.

25 Lawrence. *Being Human*.

26 Pirson and Lawrence. "Humanism in business – towards a paradigm shift?" 553–565.

27 Darwin, C. (1909). *The Descent of Man and Selection in Relation to Sex.* New York, Appleton and Company. 50.

28 Pirson and Lawrence. "Humanism in business – towards a paradigm shift?" 553–565.

29 Darwin. *The Descent of Man and Selection in Relation to Sex.* 110.

30 Ibid.

31 Lawrence. *Being Human.*

32 Wilson, E. O. (2012). *The Social Conquest of Earth.* New York, W. W. Norton & Company.

33 LeDoux, J. E. (1996). *The Emotional Brain: The Mysterious Underpinnings of Emotional Life.* New York, Simon & Schuster. LeDoux, J. E. (2002). *Synaptic Self : How Our Brains Become Who We Are.* New York; Viking.

34 Damasio, A. R. (1994). *Descartes' Error: Emotion, Reason, and The Human Brain.* New York, Putnam; Damasio, A. R. (2003). *Looking For Spinoza Joy, Sorrow, and The Feeling Brain.* Orlando, FL, Harcourt.

35 Tajfel, H. (2010). *Human Groups and Social Categories: Studies in Social Psychology.* Cambridge, Cambridge University Press.

36 Warneken, F. and M. Tomasello (2006). "Altruistic helping in human infants and young chimpanzees." *Science*, 311(3), 1301.

37 Henrich, J., et al. (2001). "In search of homo economicus: behavioral experiments in 15 small-scale societies." *American Economic Review*, 91(2), 73–78.

38 Ibid.

39 Lawrence. *Being Human.*

40 Lawrence. *Driven to Lead.* 34.

41 Lawrence and Nohria. *Driven*; Maslow, A. H. (1954). *Motivation and Personality.* New York, Harper & Brothers; Weick, K. E., and K. Sutcliffe (2006). "Mindfulness and the quality of organizational attention." *Organization Science*, 17(4), 514–524.

42 Gribbin, M. and J. R. Gribbin (1995). *Being Human – Putting People in an Evolutionary Perspective.* London, Phoenix.

43 Darwin, C. (1909). *The Descent of Man and Selection in Relation to Sex.* New York, Appleton and Company. 95.

44 Sproul, B. C. (1979). *Primal Myths: Creation Myths Around the World.* San Fransisco, HarperOne.

45 For example: Maslow, A. H. (1954). *Motivation and Personality.* New York, Harper & Brothers; Weick, K. E. (1995). *Sensemaking in Organizations.* Thousand Oaks, CA, Sage Publications; Wrzesniewski, A. and J. E. Dutton (2001). "Crafting a job: Revisioning employees as active crafters of their work." *Academy of Management Review,* **26**(2), 179–201.

46 Pinker, S. (2002). *The Blank Slate: The Modern Denial of Human Nature.* New York, Viking.

47 For example: Pinker, *How the Mind Works.* Diamond, J. M. (1992). *The Third Chimpanzee: The Evolution and Future of the Human Animal.* New York, HarperCollins; Wells, S. (2002). *The Journey of Man: A Genetic Odyssey.* Princeton, NJ, Princeton University Press.

48 Diamond, J. M. (2005). *Collapse: How Societies Choose to Fail or Succeed.* New York, Viking; Diamond, *The Third Chimpanzee;* Diamond, J. M. (1999). *Guns, Germs, And Steel: The Fates of Human Societies.* New York, W. W. Norton & Co; Wells. *The Journey of Man.*

49 For example: Boaz, N. T. and R. L. Ciochon (2004). *Dragon Bone Hill : An Ice-Age Saga of Homo Erectus.* Oxford, New York, Oxford University Press; Wells. *The Journey of Man.*

50 Wells. *The Journey of Man;* Lawrence. *Driven to Lead.*

51 Kuper, A. (1994). *The Chosen Primate : Human Nature and Cultural Diversity.* Cambridge, MA, Harvard University Press.

52 Wrangham, R. W. (2009). *Catching Fire: How Cooking Made Us Human.* New York, Basic Books; Wrangham, R., et al. (1999). "The raw and the stolen: Cooking and the ecology of human origins." *Current Anthropology,* **40**(5), 567–594.

53 Wrangham, R., "The raw and the stolen." 567–594.

54 Ibid.

55 Lawrence, *Being Human.*

56 Zahn, R., et al. (2009). "The neural basis of human social values: evidence from functional MRI." *Cereb Cortex,* **19**(2), 276–283.

57 LeDoux, J. E. (1996). *The Emotional Brain: The Mysterious Underpinnings of Emotional Life.* New York, Simon & Schuster.

58 Dunn, E., et al. (2008). "Spending money on others promotes happiness." *Science,* **319**(5870), 1678–1688.

59 Sober, E. and D. S. Wilson (1998). *Unto Others: The Evolution and Psychology of Unselfish Behavior*. Cambridge, MA, Harvard University Press; LeDoux, *The Emotional Brain*.

60 Lawrence, *Being Human*.

61 For example: Pinker, *How The Mind Works*; Diamond, *The Third Chimpanzee*; Wells, *The Journey of Man*; Lawrence, *Driven to Lead*.

62 Ibid.

63 Pinker, *How The Mind Works*. 202–203.

64 Biederman, I. and E. Vessel (2006). "Perceptual pleasure and the brain." *American Scientist*, **94**(3), 247–253.

65 Biederman and Vessel. "Perceptual pleasure and the brain." 247–253; Liu, J., Z. L. Lu and B. Dosher (2009). "Augmented hebbian learning accounts for the Eureka effect in perceptual learning." *Journal of Vision*, 9(8), 851.

66 Lawrence, *Driven to Lead*. Biederman and Vessel. "Perceptual pleasure and the brain." 247–253.

67 Pirson, M. A. and P. R. Lawrence (2010). "Humanism in business – towards a paradigm shift?" *Journal of Business Ethics*, **93**(4), 553–565.

68 Lawrence, *Driven to Lead*.

69 Miller, E. K. and J. D. Cohen (2001). "An integrative theory of prefrontal cortex function." *Annual Review of Neuroscience*, **24**, 167–202.

70 Kueng, H. (1998). *A Global Ethic for Global Politics and Economics*, Oxford, Oxford University Press. Kueng, H. and K. J. Kuschel (Eds.). (1993). *Global Ethic: The Declaration of the Parliament of the World's Religions, London*, Bloomsbury Publishing; Kung, H. (2004). *Global Responsibility: In Search of A New World Ethic*. Wipf and Stock Publishers.

71 Sen, A. (2001). *Development As Freedom*. Oxford; New York, Oxford University Press.

72 Donaldson T. and J. P. Walsh (2015). "Toward a theory of business." *Research in Organizational Behavior*, **29**(35), 181–207.

73 Presented by Donna Hicks at Humanistic Management Conference, Universidad de Monterey, Mexico, April 7–8, 2016.

74 Hicks, D. (2011). *Dignity – Its Essential Role in Resolving Conflict*, New Haven, CT, Yale University Press.

75 Hicks. *Dignity – Its Essential Role In Resolving Conflict*.

76 Sen. *Development As Freedom*.

77 Nussbaum, M. (2011). *Creating Capabilities – The Human Development Approach*. New York, Belknap.

78 Schwartz, B., and K. Sharpe (2011). *Practical Wisdom*. New York, Recorded Books.

79 Dierksmeier, C. and M. Pirson (2008). "Oikonomia versus chrematistike: Learning from Aristotle about the future orientation of business management." *Journal of Business Ethics*, **88**(3), 417–430.

80 As his student and first biographer Dugald Stewart puts it, Smith's interest for economic affairs was inspired by a strong concern for the "happiness and improvement of society" (Stewart 1980/1794, p. I.8). Cited in Hühn, M. P., and C. Dierksmeier (2016). "Will the real A. Smith please stand up!" *Journal of Business Ethics*, **1**: 119–136.

81 Cited from: Donaldson T. and J. P. Walsh (2015). "Toward a theory of business." *Research in Organizational Behavior*, **29**(35), 181–207.

82 Lawrence, *Driven to Lead*.

83 Collins, J. C. (2001). *Good to Great: Why Some Companies Make the Leap... And Others Don't*. New York, Random House.

84 Lawrence, *Driven to Lead*; Collins. *Good to Great*.

85 For example: Collins, J. and J. Porras (2002). *Built To Last*. New York, HarperCollins; Collins, *Good to Great*; Sisodia, R., D. Wolfe, and J. N. Sheth (2003). *Firms of Endearment: How World-Class Companies Profit from Passion and Purpose*. Upper Saddle River, NJ, Pearson Prentice Hall.

4   Economistic and Humanistic Perspectives on Organizing

The differing views of human nature can inform organizing practices. This chapter will explore how various organizational phenomena can be viewed through an economistic and humanistic lens. The central aim is to provide a comparison of economistic and humanistic perspectives on organizing, and show how a humanistic perspective can enrich our understanding of organizational practices. It considers a range of organizational practices, including strategy, leadership, corporate governance, motivation, negotiation, and engagement, as well as the creation of organizational culture and societal legitimacy. These examples are just a small subset of organizational practices, but highlight the broader relevance of the humanistic paradigm for management and organizing.*

BUSINESS STRATEGY PRACTICES

Economistic Perspective

From a purely economistic perspective, organizations are not necessary; instead, the market could coordinate individuals in their maximization of fixed-utility functions. Similarly, the economistic view of human behavior has little to say about the role of collaboration. Competition is the only relationship that matters and rational, utility-maximizing individuals need only be coordinated through the market. Only when additional assumptions are introduced, such as transaction costs and bounded rationality, can economistic theories explain collaboration in situations where the market provides suboptimal results.[1] Economist Ronald Coase famously stated that organizations emerge when transaction costs become too high and the market itself cannot provide effective and efficient solutions.[2] When these additional constraints of transaction costs and bounded rationality are included in the baseline economistic perspective, organizational arrangements make sense. When the market is suboptimal, market advocates ironically often turn to advocates of hierarchy. Hierarchical structures that use command and control mechanisms are deemed particularly superior to market-based arrangements, because they lower transaction costs.

In the economistic perspective, an organization is built on the basic assumptions of homo economicus or REMM. Since the economistic perspective on human nature assumes that individuals maximize their benefit, organizations also need to follow the maximization imperative. As a logical extension of the individual maximization hypothesis, organizations only make sense to homo economicus and REMM if they maximize their respective utility. Whereas the REMM perspective suggests that this utility could (theoretically) be any kind of objective, the orthodox interpretation says that shareholder value maximization is the firm's optimal focus. Michael Jensen, the intellectual father of REMM, argues that a business needs to maximize shareholder value. Refuting stakeholder theory, Jensen argues that there has to be a single objective for the firm, otherwise a manager could not manage it purposefully. He bases this claim on the assumptions of economic theory, which posit that maximization strategies are required in situations where there are no externalities:

> Two hundred years of work in economics and finance implies that in the absence of externalities and monopoly (and when all goods are priced), social welfare is maximized when each firm in an economy maximizes its total market value.[3]

An optimal way of ensuring utility maximization is for organizational leadership to focus on shareholder interests only. As a consequence, managerial decisions made according to the economistic paradigm aim at maximizing one overarching drive: The drive to acquire, as described in Chapter 3.

The economistic perspective presents a clear logic. Still, when one examines not only its assumptions of human nature, but also its premise regarding shareholder value maximization, important fallacies become apparent. Michael Jensen argues that "in the absence of externality and monopoly, and when all goods are priced" shareholder value is a necessary organizational strategy. In this statement, he already makes important qualifications that turn out to be rather unrealistic. Externalities, for example, are very real. The current environmental crisis, including climate change, is a prime example of negative, drastic, and persistent external costs to society. Monopolies are real, and the emergence of oligopolistic structures in such industries as consumer goods, technology, pharmaceuticals, health care, and automotive technology does not bode well for Jensen's argument. As stated before, not all goods can be priced. The philosopher Immanuel Kant famously suggested that in life there are goods that can be priced and exchanged, and there are those that have intrinsic value, which cannot. While it is theoretically possible to put a price on everything humans care about, including a stable climate and healthy environment, it is not only undignified but wildly impractical. It seems increasingly obvious, then, that the economistic paradigm, which currently functions as the operating system of our economies and societies, is suboptimal.[4]

Humanistic Perspective

The humanistic perspective suggests that organizations are better seen as communities. The perspective of organizations as communities transcends the economistic perspective of organizations as hierarchies, or a market-based set of contracts.[5] Domènec Melé, the Spanish academic argues that businesses are much more than mere sets of contracts or mechanisms for profit creation.[6] Humanism views organizations as a social phenomenon essential to the relational nature of human beings. Lawrence argues that because humans have a drive to create close friendly and cooperative relationships,[7] humanistic organizations embrace a balance of qualitatively desirable outcomes. These goals can vary, and often accommodate multiple interests. Humanistic organizations tend to involve stakeholders actively in their decision-making processes. Overall, humanistically oriented firms aim to simultaneously support independent drives for acquisition, bonding, comprehending, and defending.[8] In fact, Harvard Business School professors Nitin Nohria, Boris Groysberg, and Linda Eling-Lee find that when firms fulfil the four drives, they not only motivate their employees and other stakeholders but also produce more desirable organizational results.[9]

Rather than follow shareholder value maximization as a prede-fined goal, the humanistic perspective suggests that there are many potential organizational goals. In line with the humanistic perspective on human nature, organizations exist to enhance the common good and promote human well-being. To establish common goals, human-istically managed organizations use discourse-based social processes, rather than hierarchical command-and-control mechanisms. Their organizing practices respect the four independent drives, aim to pro-tect foundational human dignity, and promote well-being. Organiza-tions such as Gore, a family-owned industrial conglomerate best known for Goretex; Novo Nordisk, a Danish pharmaceutical; Broad Air Conditioning, a Chinese manufacturer; and many other organiza-tions around the globe implement humanistic organizing practices successfully (see Chapter 8 for more on this). These organizations have been run profitably and competitively, yet renounce the urge to maximize a single objective, such as shareholder value maximiza-tion. They have developed highly sophisticated stakeholder engage-ment processes to support collaboration, innovation, and the creation of mutually beneficial goals.[10]

The humanistic view of human nature would have business organizations balance their objectives rather than maximize any par-ticular objective. Humanism's universal ambition requires that mul-tiple objectives are integrated and harmonized. Recently, even Michael Porter, the renowned strategy professor, has accepted that businesses need to create shared value.[11] According to Porter, businesses need to do so, because they otherwise lose legitimacy and the necessary societal support. In the humanistic perspective on organizations, shared value-creation processes are not only theoretically and practically possible but imperative. Organizational strategies need to strike a balance between multiple stakeholders and between short and long-term interests. To enhance organizational legitimacy, such strategies need to balance the four independent drives of all the stakeholders involved at a level above the dignity threshold. To enhance well-being, organizations can address the societal problems that are most detrimental, and can develop value propositions that promote the common good. Chapter 8 provides examples of organizations that have done so.

LEADERSHIP PRACTICES

Economistic Perspective

Harvard Business School professor Rakesh Khurana argues that, as a relevant topic of study, leadership emerged from the paucity of economistic theorizing at the beginning of the twentieth century.[12] Economist Harold Demsetz argues that the economistic framework was built to explain human behavior in market situations.[13] Logically, there is no place for leadership in the economistic framework, because all individuals make their own independent decisions in the market; all market participants are considered equal. However, since leadership plays such an obvious role in real-life organizations, business schools merged the dominant economistic paradigm with insights from psychology in order to teach it.[14] This meant, however, that the economistic paradigm influenced a considerable part of the research and teaching on leadership.

In the more advanced economistic view, the organization is seen as a nexus of contracts that is continuously negotiated. As a consequence, the role of the leader requires being involved in a constant negotiation process. The task is to clarify goals and desired outcomes with followers. Leadership researchers Bernard Bass and

Bruce Avolio call the economistic type of leader a "transactional leader."[15] The transactional leader is primarily involved in ensuring compliance and setting incentives so that followers can deliver. Nurturing, long-term relationships are rather irrelevant and seen as a hindrance (the practice of, e.g., "hire and fire" requires leaders to be emotionally disconnected from followers). Followers are considered human resources (not human beings), and a skillful transactional leader is one that maximizes efficiency. Thus, a good leader in the economistic view is a skillful commander who can manage linearly and hierarchically to support efficiency maximization.

Borrowing from the misguided Spencerian version of Darwinism, leadership is also often understood as being the top dog in an institution. The prototypical business leader is frequently portrayed as successfully accumulating power, status, and wealth. Donald Trump represents such an economistic type of leader focusing on transactions rather than relationships. He arguably fits the Spencerian perspective of leadership of the fittest/strongest, focusing on the drive to acquire. Many psychologists maintain that he is highly narcissistic and sociopathic, personality disorders that seem to be at the core of his "success."[16]

In similar ways, Lawrence and Babiak argue that the economistic leadership model supports the rise of psychopathic individuals to the top.[17] According to their estimates, it is 6–10 times more likely that a psychopathic individual will be in a leadership position than in the general population.[18] The people pursuing "opportunism with guile," as Oliver Williamson describes them,[19] can use hierarchical institutions to rise to the top. It is therefore ironic that personality disorders may be key to successful economistic leadership. Hare argues that psychopaths and narcissists benefit from a lack of empathy and a genuine drive to bond with fellow humans, and are not hindered by moral qualms. The traits of such leaders – like Bernie Madoff – are described as cunning, smart, sly, and manipulative. Such leadership, when viewed through the lens of the four-drive theory, focuses on the drive to acquire via power, status, or rank. Very smart leaders in the economistic mold are aware of the need to satisfy their followers' other drives, but they use dC, dD, and dB to serve dA. A practical example: Networking is often sold as a way to connect with colleagues to enhance professional success. This practice instrumentalizes the drive to bond to serve the drive to acquire. Such instrumentalization often reduces people to means, thus undermining their dignity.

Humanistic Perspective

The humanistic perspective positions itself against such instrumentalization of human beings. What Bass and Avolio term "transformational leadership," fits well with a humanistic view of leadership.[20] Transformational leaders actively balance their four personal drives, and engage their followers to do so, as well. Based on moral values, transformational leaders inspire followers, stimulate them intellectually, and engage them emotionally with organizational tasks. They base their influence on the power of the argument rather than hierarchy, and demonstrate care for the individual follower and his or her personal development. Transformational, humanistic, or four-drive leaders are able to create a climate in which people understand cognitively and emotionally embrace the organization's purpose (drive to comprehend), are able to maintain very positive long-term relationships with each other (drive to bond), create financial value (drive to acquire), and can count on their collective strengths to weather the storms of competition (drive to defend).

Humanistic leaders do not draw the line at acting and influencing within their organization. Their four active drives compel them to contribute to a society that allows *all* humans to balance their four drives as well. Lawrence, therefore, argues that business leaders should play a far more active and constructive role in the public policy process, not, as is currently seen in terms of a laser focus on firm profitability (dA), but rather in terms of creating a balance in society between the four drives.[21]

The humanistic perspective on leadership gives us insights into the need for and emergence of responsible leadership. The evolutionary perspective on human nature explains good leadership as behavior that respects the dignity of all human beings and promotes human well-being by balancing the satisfaction of all four drives. Based on the humanistic view of human nature, one could view leadership as the art of building and sustaining good relationships with all the relevant stakeholders by addressing and balancing all four drives above the dignity threshold. By developing the capabilities of such practical wisdom, leaders will be able to contribute to sustainable human flourishing.

Such responsible leadership is a demanding and complex task, but, as Darwin has observed, there are certain in-built rules that can guide responsible decision-making. In his book *The Descent of Man*, Darwin states that morality developed in man so that responsible social action was possible.

He reinforced this perspective by adding:

> I fully subscribe to the judgment of those writers who maintain that of all the differences between man and the lower animals, the moral sense of conscience is by far the most important ... It is the most noble of all the attributes of man.[22]

This moral sense of conscience can serve as a guiding post for responsible leadership. Psychologists Marc Hauser presents empirical evidence of the existence of specific moral rules that hold across cultures, primarily the following:

- Help others rather than harm them.
- Tell truths, not lies – except for white lies.
- Keep promises.
- Seek fair exchanges that reflect merit differences.
- Detect and punish cheaters.[23]

Similarly, Lawrence cites the Golden Rule, which has regularly appeared in religious and philosophical teachings over the past three thousand years. He suggests that the following decision rules based on the four drives could help responsible leadership:

Moral Rules Deduced from the Golden Rule and Four Drives

dA: To support the other's drive to acquire:
- Help enhance rather than steal or destroy the other's property.
- Facilitate, do not frustrate, the other's pleasurable experiences.

dB: To support the other's drive to bond:
- Keep, rather than break, promises.
- Seek fair exchanges, no cheating.
- Return a favor with a favor.

dC: To support the other's drive to comprehend:
- Tell truths, not falsehoods.
- Share, do not withhold, useful information. Respect, do not ridicule, the other's beliefs, even when disagreeing.

dD: To support the other's drive to defend:
- Help protect, do not harm nor abandon, the other.[24]

Lawrence and others argue that when responsible leaders treat all stakeholders according to these rules, stakeholders will be engaged, because leaders will be contributing to the fulfillment of all four of the basic drives – the ultimate motives – of human beings. Supporting this claim, research conducted by Nohria, Groysberg, and Eling-Lee found that leaders' ability to meet the four fundamental drives explained, on average, about 60 percent of employee variance in motivational indicators, while previous models only explained about 30 percent. They also found that leaders can best improve employee motivation by satisfying all four drives in a balanced manner. "The whole is more than the sum of its parts. A poor showing on one drive substantially diminishes the impact of the other three drives."[25] This finding supports the humanistic view that effective, responsible leaders need to address all four drives above the dignity threshold in a balanced manner for all types of stakeholders.

CORPORATE GOVERNANCE PRACTICES

The different paradigmatic approaches have consequences not only for leadership practice but also for top-level governance structures and practices in organizations.

Economistic Perspective

Agency theory largely informs the governance notions of the economistic perspective. Agency theory builds on REMM, and assumes that people are acting opportunistically. Consequently, governance mechanisms focus on creating an environment in which opportunistic, self-serving managerial agents are held in check. The main goal of the governance structure is to control managers so they cannot harm the fulfillment of whatever goal the owners, as principals, intend to fulfill. One way to control managers is through top-down hierarchical governance structures, which unitary boards control. Unitary boards need to ensure that shareholder value is maximized. Accordingly, the organizational structure is typically centered on top-down decision-making, which maximizes efficiency.

The shadow of homo economicus looms large in the argument for unitary board structures. Two reasons why unitary boards are considered acceptable stem from the memetically adopted assumptions of complete information access and the focus on efficiency at the firm level. Board members are considered rational decision makers. Accordingly, they possess all the information needed for making optimal decisions, and follow the rational decision-making model. It is argued that they start their decision-making by identifying a problem, then defining the decision criteria, allocating weights to the criteria, developing alternatives, evaluating the alternatives, and, finally, selecting the best alternative.[26] Such a process should lead to impeccable decision-making. It would have been useful to have such board performance to manage risk so as to avoid, or mitigate the 2008 financial crisis.

Obviously, the process is not an accurate description of what actually happens in corporate boardrooms, as shareholders and stakeholders found to their enduring detriment during the financial crisis and various earlier crises. A large body of research has previously debunked this model as flawed.[27] With regard to complete information assumption, Nobel Laureate Oliver Williamson writes succinctly that human beings have a limited ability to receive, store, process, retrieve, and transmit information.[28] Other researchers suggest that these limits are rooted in physiological, neurological, and psychological mechanisms.[29] Consequently, board members have a hard time controlling command and control-based hierarchical organizations.

An alternative form of establishing control in economistic organizations is based on incentive systems. Incentive systems are considered a central structural element for aligning diverging interests, and are seen as another way to effectively deal with opportunistic agents. Economistic incentive schemes are mainly monetary in nature, and include financial bonuses or stock options. These incentives are usually targeted at the individual and mainly address the drive to acquire (dA). Such incentives are often tied to a quantitative measure that can be established in the short term. There have been some attempts to tie incentives to long-term outcomes, but, as a Danish proverb says, "It is hard to make predictions, especially about the future."[30]

Not only did the unitary board structure not help control managerial opportunism during the financial crisis, but the incentives schemes favored by proponents of economistic management also failed to support organizational excellence or shareholder value maximization. Jim Collins, who studied companies that consistently outperformed the stock market for fifteen consecutive years, finds that incentive schemes played no role in their success.[31] In fact, there are examples, like Enron, where researchers suggest that their incentive scheme propagated their downfall.[32]

Humanistic Perspective

Governance practices inspired by the humanistic paradigm support the fulfilment of stakeholders' drives above the dignity threshold. In contrast to the strong focus on the drive to acquire, humanistic governance theories, such as stewardship theory, focus on reinforcing the other-regarding, relational aspects of human nature (dB). According to governance scholars, stewardship theory assumes that higher-order needs, such as social and self-actualization needs (dB/dC), also drive intrinsically motivated human beings.[33] In the humanistic perspective, managers are not agents, but stewards guided by the intention to serve all stakeholders. They demonstrate a high level of commitment to total value creation, a focus on long-term results, and an equitable distribution of rewards to all stakeholders. As such, humanistically inspired governance mechanisms focus on strategic support for the steward, and less on hierarchical control. Economistic types of top-down control (such as time clocks, monitoring systems, etc.) are found to undermine motivation and are detrimental to the performance of stakeholders.[34]

While top-down control mechanisms are essential for the governance structure of economistic organizations (some organizational theorists call them the "remnants of feudalism"), checks and balance systems are essential in humanistic organizational structures to prevent power abuse. Lawrence argues that checks and balance arrangements parallel the function of the prefrontal cortex in the human brain.[35] That is why, he argues, checks and balance systems (such as those instituted in the US constitution) better represent all major stakeholders in strategic decisions. Akin to democratic institutions, organizations governed by humanistic principles can use different stakeholder councils (e.g., worker councils) to prevent decisions that favor one group over the other in the long term.[36] Humanistic governance scholars argue that when there are internal checks and balances, they mutually reinforce each other to serve various stakeholder needs in a balanced way.[37]

Rather than serve one group only (shareholders), humanistic governance structures include many relevant stakeholders in the governance process.[38] Rather than maximize shareholder value, humanistic governance structures support the creation of shared value. These governance structures have a higher motivational effect, because they engage the drive to bond (dB), as well as the drive to comprehend (dC). Governance scholar Shann Turnbull suggests that participatory governance structures also increase the likelihood that management will protect and, ideally, promote the various stakeholders' human dignity. As Bob Chapman and Raj Sisodia document in their book *Everybody Matters*, humanistic managers "reject the idea that employees are simply functions, to be moved around, 'managed' with carrots and sticks, or discarded at will."[39] Instead, they argue that governance and management processes need to ensure everyone's dignity. According to the authors:

> Everyone wants to do better. Trust them. Leaders are everywhere. Find them. People achieve good things, big and small, every day. Celebrate them. Some people wish things were different. Listen to them. Everybody matters. Show them.[40]

Humanistic governance structures center on building trust between stakeholders and the organization (dB). Furthermore, the structures are intended to build human capabilities. As a consequence, humanistic governance structures reduce authority levels in the organization. In humanistic organizations, decision rights are spread throughout the organization in a way that utilizes the expertise of all employees, and provides them with the opportunity to fulfill their drive to comprehend at work (dC). To extend their employees' capabilities further, humanistic organizations employ integrative mechanisms that cut across the vertical lines of control, i.e., product or project managers, task forces, matrix elements, and innovative information management systems. Such structural elements help keep the focus on overall organizational goals, but also provide employees with opportunities to make their work meaningful and fulfill their drive to comprehend (dC), and to extend their network of collaborative stakeholders (dD).

Scholars suggest that governance structures can be purposefully built to support the balance of the four drives above the dignity threshold.[41] They suggest, for example, that directors:

- dA: Use incentives of various types (monetary and non-monetary), and allow for some control of corporate resources, so that all employees have a chance to acquire financial gain, status, and a sense of personal accomplishment.

- dD: Create a transparent performance measurement system that allows for accountability, and at the same time provide an early-warning system to alert individuals and groups to threats to the achievement of their goals.
- dC. Provide all employees with a continuous learning experience, to allow for creativity, experimentation, and continuous improvement. Appoint teams and task forces that cut across organizational lines and charge them with innovating of behalf of the entire organization.
- dB. Organize by means of teams and support collaboration by building a strong organizational culture, to focus on integrity as the cornerstone of relational exchanges, and to build trusting relationships with all stakeholders.[42]

In business practice today, governance structures favor the shareholders' drive to acquire, and leaders' success is measured largely by shareholder value creation. Humanistic governance structures support the balanced fulfillment of all the relevant stakeholders' independent drives above the dignity threshold. The argument here is that this humanistic perspective can help develop new structural designs that support more responsible leadership and collaborative governance practices (such as in cooperative governance or network governance structures).

MOTIVATION AND ENGAGEMENT PRACTICES

One of the central quests in management is how to motivate and engage people.

Economistic Perspective

In the economistic model, motivation does not really pose a problem, because human wants are considered insatiable. However, in reality, people tend to be pretty content with what they have. In the economistic context, the typical approach to motivation is to focus on rewarding the drive to acquire. Built on the intellectual framework of REMM and agency theory, incentives have become the standard instrument to drive behavior change. Even at universities, for example, administrations increasingly motivate faculty by offering monetary incentives for intellectual work in the form of publications.

Incentives work, so the saying goes. The question has long not been whether they work, but how they work. Much research shows that extrinsic incentives do not work all that well. Author Daniel Pink received a lot of attention when his summary of the research findings on motivation underlined this. His main argument centers on the failure of incentives for work that demands creativity and innovation.[43] Other scholars have found that incentives actually undermine the quality of work, and crowd out intrinsic motivation.[44] In a famous study, behavioral economists found that when volunteers worked for free, they were far more productive than when they were paid.[45] The behavioral economist Bruno Frey argues that once you introduce financial rewards, volunteers' mindset shifts from a logic of gift toward a logic of exchange.[46]

Humanistic Perspective

Through the humanistic lens, it is possible to understand why incentives often do not work as intended. In fact, an extensive literature on behavioral economics has shown that extrinsic rewards (dA) crowd out intrinsic rewards, such as the pleasure of serving (dB) or learning (dC). In the humanistic perspective, such crowding out effects can be understood as the effect of price over dignity. Whenever something becomes part of an exchange, it follows a different logic than when it is intrinsically appreciated. For example, research finds that monetary incentives undermine (dA) the intrinsic motivation to help (dB). In the context of children's daycare, workers wanted to ensure that kids were picked up promptly, so they instated a late pickup penalty. However, instead of decreasing late pickups, the penalties increased late pickups. It turned out that asking parents to pay for each minute the kids overstay made them feel less guilty. Similarly, the number of volunteers for blood donations decreased significantly when they were offered cash incentives.[47] The focus on the drive to acquire undermined the focus on the drive to bond, so that people ended up caring less about others and the task, but merely saw it as a transaction.

There is another context in which the humanistic perspective can help us understand motivations: Influential economistic research has examined how people can make decisions more rationally, i.e., by enhancing their drive to acquire.[48] Through this lens, certain behaviors, such as concerns for fairness or altruistic punishment (dB), are considered irrational and basically stupid.[49] The humanistic perspective, however, allows such concerns to be part of the drive to bond, and endorse this behavior as totally reasonable.

Conflict negotiation is an area where the traditional focus on rational interests (dA) has often failed. Donna Hicks has written about the power of considering the full humanity of individuals (all four drives), rather than just rational interest.[50] She suggests that understanding the idea of a dignity threshold, and the violations thereof, can be key to successful conflict management. She writes that during a civil war situation in Central America, the dignity focus made the actual realms of concern visible, which a focus on rational interests would have completely overlooked. She states

> that the language of dignity has helped participants of conflict resolution processes to name and think about inner wounds in a way that did not make them feel ashamed or vulnerable. It legitimized their suffering. With the language of dignity, men and women are able to discuss for the first time those painful inner wounds that have never healed that hold them back from living life in full extension. Once these violations of dignity had been acknowledged a more rational discussion was possible.[51]

Hicks suggests that when one employs a humanistic perspective, it is easier to resolve conflict. By engaging in organizational practices that allow the full range of human motivations (rational and emotional) and creating a safe space (dD) to discuss serious mistreatments (dB), or incomprehensible action (dC), it is easier to make progress.[52] While such an understanding of human behavior in negotiation processes may be helpful in difficult contexts such as that of a post–civil war period, it may also provide helpful insights into intra-organizational decision-making and engagement processes.

According to the humanistic perspective, managers do well when they protect human dignity and promote well-being by focusing on a balance of the four drives. Typically, this means that in most modern-day business organizations the focus needs to shift from fulfilling the drive to acquire only and to finding ways to balance it with responses to the drive to bond, comprehend, and defend.

ORGANIZATIONAL CULTURE PRACTICES

Unsurprisingly, different paradigms also contribute to the creation of distinctive organizational cultures.

Economistic Perspective

Economistic organizations support cultures and organizational identities that are mostly oriented toward the individual.[53] These cultures are also often described as transactional in nature.[54] Consequently, economistic organizations follow rather linear, mechanistic, and closed-loop thought and interaction processes. Business ethicists Jane Collier and Rafael Esteban argue that mechanistic organizations attempt to transform the environment "adversarially and competitively rather than seek to respond to it."[55] Uncontrolled change is viewed as a threat, because it interferes with the optimal implementation of the maximization paradigm. In addition, the domination of the drives to acquire (dA) and to defend (dD) translates into a need to control the outside, and to manage and manipulate the environment, particularly government, in order to support firm profitability.[56] Economistic cultures are, at most, two-drive cultures. Paul Lawrence likens economistic companies to four-cylinder cars only driving on two cylinders.[57]

Humanistic Perspective

Conversely, organizations that follow humanistic principles support cultures that are more transformational in nature, and create organizational identities based on inter-human relations inclusive of a larger group.[58] These organizations create cultures that allow the balance of all four human drives. Humanistic organizational cultures are open, organic, circular, and constantly changing and evolving to allow this balance. Organizational practices are inclusive, participative, and values-based. Humanistic organizations thrive through exchanges with the outside, and foster constant dialog between and with their stakeholders.[59] They not only balance the four drives of internal stakeholder groups but also aim for a balance of the four drives for external stakeholders. Google, Nucor, Medtronics, and the Grameen Bank can, for all their respective faults, be seen as organizations with four-drive cultures.

PRACTICES TO MAINTAIN SOCIETAL LEGITIMACY

The different paradigms also influence the organization's view of the systemic environment and its responsibilities toward it.

Economistic Perspective

From an economistic viewpoint, the corporation's main function is to accumulate wealth, thus heeding the drive to acquire, while the main function of the state is to provide safety and cater to the drive to defend. In this division of labor, the state creates rules to coordinate organizations, and organizational leadership's main responsibility is to obey these rules while maximizing profits. These rules are, however, based on laissez faire assumptions, allowing individuals and organizations to follow their respective utility functions. Any further commitment to societal causes is incompatible with utility maximization at the individual and organizational levels. Talk of responsibilities is generally viewed as systematic interference with liberty. Calls for corporate responsibility and sustainability are only heeded when they are compulsory and part of the legal infrastructure. Voluntary engagement with societal issues, such as equity and intergenerational justice, do not fit the economistic view unless they make strategic sense in terms of increasing material wealth.[60] As Milton Friedman famously said,

> there is one and only one social responsibility of business – to use its resources and engage in activities designed to increase its profits so long as it stays within the rules of the game, which is to say, engages in open and free competition without deception or fraud.[61]

Humanistic Perspective

In the humanistic perspective, individuals, organizations, and the state all play important roles in balancing the four drives. Since there needs to be a balance on each level, there is no real division of labor in terms of fulfilling the four basic drives. Rather, there is cooperation in terms of ensuring that checks and balances enable an optimal balance on all the levels. In the humanistic view, personal morality is connected with responsibility for the systemic consequences of one's actions. Therefore, business leaders should accept and assume responsibility for the consequences of their actions, both on the systemic and the individual levels. As such, organizations engage with the outside world, and view responsibility to stakeholders (people) as elementary in terms of conducting business. Liberty is contingent on morality; individual and organizational freedom materializes through care and concern for the other. Sustainability and corporate responsibility are intrinsically relevant concerns in the humanistic view of business; attempts to alleviate social problems through business are an imperative. A balance of the four drives is only possible in the mutual responsibility for individuals, organizations, and the wider system.[62]

CONCLUDING REMARKS

In this chapter, we have seen the differences between the economistic and the humanistic perspectives on strategy, leadership, corporate governance, motivation, as well as the creation of organizational culture and societal legitimacy. This chapter explained how a humanistic perspective can enrich the understanding of organizational practices, providing a small subset of organizational practices as examples. These highlight the relevance of the humanistic paradigm for management more broadly. While the different perspectives on human nature form the cornerstone of the argument in Chapters 3 and 4, the focus in the next chapter moves onto two other important building blocks of the humanistic management perspective: dignity and well-being.

NOTES

* The thoughts in this chapter are based and adapted from Pirson, M. A., and Lawrence, P. R. (2010). Humanism in business – towards a paradigm shift?. *Journal of Business Ethics*, **93**(4), 553–565.

1 Nida-Ruemelin, J. (2008). "Philosophical grounds of humanism in economics." *Humanism in Business: Perspectives on the Development of a Responsible Business Society*. H. Spitzeck, M. Pirson, W. Amann, S. Khan and E. von Kimakowitz, eds. Cambridge, Cambridge University Press, 15–25.

2 Coase, R. H. (1937). "The nature of the firm." *Economica*, **4**(16), 386–405.

3 Jensen, M. C. (2002). "Value maximization, stakeholder theory and the corporate objective function." *Business Ethics Quarterly*, **12**(2), 235–257.

4 Many proponents of the economistic paradigm would argue that anything we care about can be maximized, so that the objective function does not have to be shareholder value or profit. While intellectually accurate, the orthodox perspective, including Michael Jensen's own writings, suggest otherwise.

5 Williamson, O. E., M. Aoki, and B. Gustafsson (Eds.). (1990). *The Firm as a Nexus of Treaties* (pp. 112–132). London, Sage.

6 Mele, D. (2009). "Current trends of humanism in business." *Humanism in Business: Perspectives on the Development of a Responsible Business Society*. H. Spitzeck, M. Pirson, W. Amann, S. Khan and E. von Kimakowitz, eds. Cambridge, Cambridge University Press, 123–139.

7 Lawrence, P. (2010). *Driven to Lead: Good, Bad, and Misguided Leadership*. San Francisco, Jossey-Bass.

8 Pirson, and Lawrence. "Humanism in business – towards a paradigm shift?" 553–565.

9 Nohria, N., et al. (2008). "Employee motivation: A powerful new model." *Harvard Business Review*, **7/8**(HBS Centennial Issue), 78–84.

10 See also Kimakowitz, E., et al. (2010). *Humanistic Management in Practice – The Humanistic Management Network*. London, Palgrave McMillan; Pirson, M., and Von Kimakowitz, E. (2014). "Towards a human-centered theory and practice of the firm: presenting the humanistic paradigm of business and management." *Journal of Management for Global Sustainability*, 2(1), 17–48.

11 Porter, M. and M. Kramer (2011). "The big idea: creating shared value." *Harvard Business Review*, January–February(1), 1–17.

12 Khurana, R. (2007). *From Higher Aims to Hired Hands: The Social Transformation of American Business Schools and the Unfulfilled Promise of Management as a Profession*. Princeton, Princeton University Press.

13 Demsetz, H. (2011). *From Economic Man to Economic System: Essays on Human Behavior and the Institutions of Capitalism*. Cambridge, Cambridge University Press.

14 Khurana, *From Higher Aims to Hired Hands*.

15 Bass, B. M. and B. J. Avolio (1994). "Transformational leadership and organizational culture." *International Journal of Public Administration*, 17(3/4), 541–554.

16 See for example: www.theatlantic.com/health/archive/2016/07/trump-and-sociopathy/491966/ (last accessed July 23, 2016).

17 Lawrence, P. (2010). *Driven to Lead: Good, Bad, and Misguided Leadership*. London; San Diego, Jossey-Bass; Babiak, P. and R. D. Hare (2006). *Snakes in Suits: When Psychopaths Go to Work*. New York, Regan Books.

18 Babiak and Hare. *Snakes in Suits*.

19 Williamson, O. E. (1975). *Markets and Hierarchies: Antitrust Analysis and Implications*. New York, The Free Press.

20 Bass and Avolio. "Transformational leadership and organizational culture." 541–554.

21 Lawrence, P. (2007). *Being Human – A Renewed Darwinian Theory of Human Behavior*. www.prlawrence.com (last accessed June 2, 2016), Cambridge, MA.

22 Darwin, C. (1909). *The Descent of Man and Selection in Relation to Sex*. New York, Appleton and Company; Lawrence, P. R., and Pirson, M. (2015). "Economistic and humanistic narratives of leadership in the age of globality: Toward a renewed darwinian theory of leadership." *Journal of Business Ethics*, 128(2), 383–394.

23 Hauser, M. D. (2006). *Moral Minds: How Nature Designed Our Universal Sense of Right and Wrong.* New York, Ecco.

24 Cited from: Lawrence. *Driven to Lead: Good, Bad, and Misguided Leadership.* 92–93.

25 Nohria, N., et al. (2008). "Employee motivation: A powerful new model." *Harvard Business Review,* 7/8 (HBS Centennial Issue), 78–84.

26 Pirson, M. and S. Turnbull (2011). "Toward a more humanistic governance model: network governance structures." *Journal of Business Ethics,* **99**(1), 101–114.

27 Kahneman, D., et al. (1986). "Fairness and the assumptions of economics." *Journal of Business Ethics,* **59**, 5285–5300; Frey, B. S. (2007). "Rewards as compensation." *European Management Review,* **2007**(4), 6–14; Osterloh, M. and B. S. Frey (2000). "Motivation, knowledge transfer, and organizational forms." *Organization Science,* **11**(5), 538–550.

28 Williamson, O. E. (1979). "Transaction cost economics: The governance of contractual relations." *Journal of Law and Economics,* October 22, 233–261.

29 Pirson, M. and S. Turnbull (2011). "Toward a more humanistic governance model." 101–114; Turnbull, S. (2002). "The science of corporate governance." *Corporate Governance: An International Review,* **10**(4), 256–272; Pirson, M. and S. Turnbull (2011). "Corporate governance, risk management, and the financial crisis: an information processing view." *Corporate Governance: An International Review,* **19**(5), 459–470.

30 http://quoteinvestigator.com/2013/10/20/no-predict/ (last accessed May 15, 2016).

31 Collins, J. C. (2001). *Good to Great: Why Some Companies Make the Leap ... and Others Don't.* New York, Random House.

32 McLean, B., and P. Elkind (2003). *The Smartest Guys in the Room: The Amazing Rise and Scandalous Fall of Enron.* New York, Portfolio.

33 Davis, J. H., et al. (1997). "Toward a stewardship theory of management." *Academy of Management Review,* **22**(1), 20–47.

34 Donaldson, L. and J. H. Davis (1991). "Stewardship theory or agency theory: CEO governance and shareholder returns." *Australian Journal of Management,* **16**(1), 49–66; Muth, M. M. and L. Donaldson (1998). "Stewardship theory and board structure: A contingency approach." *Corporate Governance: An International Review* **6**(1), 5–29.

35 Lawrence, P. (2007). *Being Human – A Renewed Darwinian Theory of Human Behavior.* www.prlawrence.com. Cambridge, MA.

36 Turnbull, S. (1997). "Stakeholder governance: A cybernetic and property rights analysis." *Corporate Governance: An International Review*, 5(1), 11–23.

37 Pirson, M. and S. Turnbull (2011). "Toward a more humanistic governance model: Network governance structures." *Journal of Business Ethics*, 99(1), 101–114; Gratton, L. (2004). *The Democratic Enterprise: Liberating your Business with Freedom, Flexibility and Commitment*. London, Financial Times.

38 Pirson and Turnbull "Toward a more humanistic governance model." 101–114.

39 Chapman, B., and R. Sisodia (2015). *Everybody Matters: The Extraordinary Power of Caring for Your People Like Family*. New York, Portfolio Trade.

40 Ibid.

41 Nohria, N., et al. (2008). "Employee motivation: a powerful new model." *Harvard Business Review*, 7/8 (HBS Centennial Issue), 78–84; Simons, R. (2005). *Levers of Organization Design: How Managers Use Accountability Systems for Greater Performance and Commitment*. Cambridge, MA, Harvard Business School Press.

42 Cited in Nohria, N., et al. (2008). "Employee motivation: A powerful new model." 78–84.

43 Pink, D. H. (2011). *Drive: The Surprising Truth About What Motivates Us*. London, Penguin.

44 Frey, B. S. (1998). *Not Just for the Money. Books*. New York, Edward Elgar Publishers.

45 Frey, B. S., and Jegen, R. (2001). "Motivation crowding theory." *Journal of Economic Surveys*, 15(5), 589–611.

46 Ibid.

47 Frey, B. S. (1997). *Not Just for the Money. Books*. London, Edward Elgar Publishers.

48 Milkman, K. L., et al. (2009). "How can decision making be improved?" *Perspectives on Psychological Science*, 4(4), 379–383; Bazerman, M. (2005). *Judgment in Managerial Decision Making*. New York, Wiley.

49 Hertz, N. (2013). *Eyes Wide Open: How to Make Smart Decisions in a Confusing World*. New York, HarperBusiness.

50 Hicks, D. (2011). *Dignity – Its Essential Role in Resolving Conflict*. New Haven, Yale University Press.

51 Ibid.

52 Ibid.

53 Brickson, S. L. (2007). "Organizational identity orientation: The genesis of the role of the firm and distinct forms of social value." *Academy of Management Review*, **32**(3), 864–888.

54 Bass, B. M. and B. J. Avolio (1994). "Transformational leadership and organizational culture." 541–554.

55 Collier, J. and R. Esteban (1999). "Governance in the participative organisation: Freedom, creativity and ethics." *Journal of Business Ethics*, **21**(2–3), 173–188.

56 Dierksmeier, C. and M. Pirson (2009). "Oikonomia versus chrematistike: Learning from Aristotle about the future orientation of business management." *Journal of Business Ethics*, **88**(3), 417–430; Dierksmeier, C. and M. Pirson (2010). "Freedom and the modern corporation." *Philosophy of Management (formerly Reason in Practice)* **9**(3), 5–25.

57 Lawrence, P. (2010). *Driven to Lead.*

58 Brickson, S. L. (2007). "Organizational identity orientation: The genesis of the role of the firm and distinct forms of social value." *Academy of Management Review*, **32**(3), 864–888.

59 Dierksmeier, C. and M. Pirson (2010). "Freedom and the modern corporation." *Philosophy of Management (formerly Reason in Practice)*, **9**(3).

60 Dierksmeier and Pirson. "Oikonomia versus chrematistike." 417–430. Dierksmeier and Pirson. "Freedom and the modern corporation." 5–25.

61 Friedman, M., "The Social Responsibility of Business is to Increase its Profits," *The New York Times Magazine*, September 13, 1970. www.colorado.edu/studentgroups/libertarians/issues/friedman-soc-resp-business.html (last accessed May 23, 2016).

62 Dierksmeier, C. and M. Pirson (2010). "Freedom and the modern corporation." *Philosophy of Management (formerly Reason in Practice)*, **9**(3); Pirson and Lawrence. "Humanism in business – towards a paradigm shift?" 553–565.

5 Dignity and Well-Being as Cornerstones of Humanistic Management

Humanistic management rests on two cornerstones drawn from the fundamentally different perspective on human nature described before. The notion of dignity and the dignity threshold form one pillar of humanistic management. The notion of well-being forms the second pillar, and is the ultimate organizing goal of humanistic management. This chapter explores both concepts.

Dignity is what distinguishes humanistic management from traditional economistic management. There are three relevant aspects of dignity: dignity as a general category encompassing that which has no price, human dignity as inherent and universal, and human dignity as conditional and earned. Despite its ambiguity, I argue that the notion of dignity can improve management research's theoretical accuracy in the future.

Similarly, the chapter describes the concept of well-being, starting from a historical perspective and its Aristotelian roots, to its utilitarian reinterpretation. This reinterpretation of well-being as utility became the foundation of modern economic thought at the end of the nineteenth century and, in turn, the basis for a large part of management theory.[1] Humanistic management suggests a return to the foundational concept of well-being as flourishing (Eudaimonia). The chapter concludes by describing how the creation of shared well-being, not wealth, is the ultimate goal of organizing practices in the humanistic perspective, and argues that this better serves individuals, companies and society.

DIGNITY AS A PILLAR OF HUMANISTIC MANAGEMENT

Dignity represents, in humanistic management, a category of everything that has an inherent value and cannot therefore be part of an exchange logic. This includes categories that are intrinsically valuable, like the dignity of character, the dignity of the environment, or the dignity of aesthetics. It, of course, includes human dignity as well, but can extend beyond the dignity of human beings to all things animate or inanimate that do not have a price but are nevertheless valuable. Importantly, however, applying this "categorical" dignity to human relationships is the crucial difference between humanistic and economistic perspectives on how best to organize groups of people.

DIGNITY AS A GENERAL CATEGORY

Hans Kueng's work on the global ethic highlights that dignity serves as a general principle of humanity, deeply rooted across global spiritual and religious traditions.[2] The legal scholar Jeremy Waldron suggests that the concept of dignity provides a principle of morality and a principle of law.[3] He argues that dignity is a constructive idea, with a foundational and explicative function much like utility; it is complex, yet foundational, in a variety of ways.[4]

Immanuel Kant (1724–1804) stated that,

> In the kingdom of ends everything has either a *price* or a *dignity*. What has a price can be replaced by something else as its *equivalent*; what on the other hand is above all price and therefore admits of no equivalent has a dignity.[5]

He specifies dignity as a category by making further comparisons:

> What is related to general human inclinations and needs has a *market price*; that which, even without presupposing a need, conforms with a certain taste, that is, with a delight in the mere purposeless play of our mental powers, has a *fancy price*; but that which constitutes the condition under which alone something can be an end in itself has not merely a relative worth, that is, a price, but an inner worth, that is, *dignity*.[6]

He continues to elaborate:

> Skill and diligence in work have a market price; wit, lively imagination and humor have a fancy price; on the other hand,

fidelity in promises and benevolence from basic principles (not from instinct) have an inner worth. Nature, as well as art, contains nothing that, lacking these, it could put in their place; for their worth does not consist in the effects arising from them, in the advantage and use they provide, but in dispositions, that is, in maxims of the will that in this way are ready to manifest themselves through actions, even if success does not favor them.[7]

In this sense, dignity is established as a category for all that which cannot be replaced and all that which has no price, including the arts or the environment. In addition, dignity can also represent the intrinsic value of a capability or virtue. Cicero (106–43 BCE) writes in *De Officiis* about the dignity of public office and the desired traits of its keeper. For him, dignity is achieved by virtuous pursuit of character development attained through study and reflection.[8] Waldron similarly views dignity as a capacity of inherent value when he writes:

Dignity has resonances of something like noble bearing ... it connotes ... self-possession and self-control; self-presentation as someone to be reckoned with; not being abject, pitiable, distressed, or overly submissive in circumstances of adversity.[9]

In this case, dignity is viewed as a virtue based on self-reflection, self-accorded, and self-developed; it requires a certain level of character or personality development. The possibility of such capability development was often the base line argument introduced to accord humans a special role in terms of living beings. The Judeo-Christian tradition gives human beings a special and dignified status in terms of the Creation, due to this capacity for morality and virtue.[10]

This understanding of dignity, however, not only extends to human beings but also represents categories of activities and other forms of life. Francis Bacon (1561–1626) writes about the dignity of scientific learning, highlighting the intrinsic value of such activity.[11] As such, the activity of learning becomes the source of dignity, and is in itself dignified.[12] In a similar vein, other activities, for example, acquiring knowledge and wisdom, or engaging others with love, trust, or forgiveness, are also called dignified. Martha Nussbaum's research enumerates the central elements of dignity, which include physical, psychological, and moral integrity.[13]

Extending the category of dignity further, political scientist Michael Rosen suggests that dignity has been accorded to certain forms of relationships, such as marriage.[14] Other scholars point out that institutions of various kinds have been ascribed with dignity such as democracy, monarchy, or the Supreme Court. In all these cases, dignity represents what St. Thomas Aquinas (1225–1274) argued was "something's goodness on account of itself."[15] This could, for example, include aesthetics, as the conservative philosopher Roger Scruton argues.[16] Similarly, it could be found in all parts of "god's creation," including animals, nature, and innate objects such as air and water.[17] Management scholar Sandra Waddock makes the case that animals and the Earth as such (*Gaia*) are endowed with dignity.[18]

HUMAN DIGNITY — UNCONDITIONAL AND CONDITIONAL ASPECTS

As a general category of all things that have inherent value, special significance is given to the meaning of human dignity.[19] For humanistic management, dignity is a critical basis, because it provides a response to the question of who we are as human beings. Are we mere tools and instruments, as the terms "human resources" or "human capital" indicate, or human beings with inherent worth and value?

While human dignity has various philosophical roots, scholars have argued for two separate, yet connected, notions across time.[20] The first notion suggests that people have a certain inherent dignity as a result of being human (unconditional). The second notion suggests that people earn dignity through their actions (conditional). Consequently, since human vulnerabilities materialize in a social context, (1) human life has an intrinsic, inherent, unconditional, and universal value that needs to be protected, and (2) an ability to establish a sense of self-worth and self-respect that needs to be promoted.[21]

Some scholars argue that these two notions of human dignity are contradictory; others suggest that the concept dynamically connects the egalitarian notion of unconditional, intrinsic value with the conditional form of differentiation.[22] Waldron offers a synthesis on which humanistic management builds. He suggests that the concept of human dignity can be understood as accepting and protecting inherent value as a baseline, while moving dynamically toward the highest common denominator as the aspiration of organizational activity.[23] As such, the protection of dignity and the promotion of dignity are two interlinked notions that can inform organizing practices of humanistic management.

Human Dignity as Unconditional

Throughout antiquity and the Middle Ages, human nature was considered dignified and special, but fundamentally vulnerable. This vulnerability was considered a shared and universal experience. Human beings and their special status in terms of all living things therefore required protection.[24]

In the earlier arguments, dignity was used to ascribe special value to human beings, emphasizing how human capabilities differ from those of other life forms. This special status was conferred in theory to *all* human beings. Stoic philosophers, for example, advocated a cosmopolitan humanism comprising a universal attribution of dignity.[25] Extending Stoic perspectives, early Christian theologians used biblical sources to argue that all human beings are created in the image of God (*imago dei*) and therefore possess dignity.[26] Emanating from this understanding, Thomas Aquinas (1225–1274) arguably built the intellectual foundation for a Christian tradition that endorses human dignity as *unconditionally* encompassing all people, independent of their worldly status.[27] Accordingly, if all human beings are creatures of God and created in his image, they deserve treatment worthy of such heritage. As a consequence, society and its organizations ought to be organized in support and defense of human dignity.[28] This argument was successfully used against slavery, for example, during the times of the Spanish conquest of Latin America.[29]

The philosopher and business ethicist Claus Dierksmeier points out the role of the Renaissance philosopher Giovanni Pico della Mirandola (1463–1494), who developed an argument for human dignity independent of religious beliefs. In his influential book on the dignity of man (*Oratio de hominis dignitate*), he defends all people's unconditional dignity, without making the typical comparison to animals or God. Instead, he argues that dignity is the core of human life, emanating from the freedom of human beings. This freedom requires a fundamental self-definition of existence. Whether humans want it or not, they are in charge of their own destiny, and this endows them with dignity.[30] Later, existentialist philosophers, such as Jean-Paul Sartre (1905–1980), developed this argument is further. Existentialists argue that human beings must ultimately define themselves who they want to be: *existence precedes essence*. This fundamental freedom is, regardless of whether a god exists or not, a universal human feature that dignifies humans unconditionally.

Others argue that, rather than existential freedom, the ability to be moral is the source of universal and unconditional dignity. They suggest that human dignity is given because humans have the capacity to define their own ends, ideally – but not always – in the pursuit of a good, i.e., moral, life.[31] Such an argument is supported by Kant's position that:

> Morality is the condition under which a rational being can be an end in itself, since only through this is it possible to be a law-giving member in the kingdom of ends. Hence morality, and humanity insofar as it is capable of morality, is that which alone has dignity.[32]

For these thinkers, human capacity for moral agency is the true source of a human being's uniqueness and dignity. It is important to note that the universal *capacity* to be moral, and not actual moral behavior, is viewed as the basis for *unconditional* dignity. The source of *conditional* dignity is therefore found in the actual ability to behave morally, i.e., act in accordance with universalizable law.[33]

Human Dignity as Conditional

Contrary to the unconditional, universal ascription of dignity to all human beings, the second overarching notion of human dignity lies in the conditional aspect of earned respect. In this perspective, dignity can be earned through the development of certain faculties.[34] Early Greek philosophers suggested that dignity is developed through a good education, which leads to moral behavior. Humans therefore had to develop personally to improve their judgment and achieve practical wisdom in order to achieve dignity. Such an education did not have to be formal, but required the formation of character. According to Plato, citizens of the polis were ideally able to form their own opinions and defend these on the basis of their deeply rooted values and convictions.[35] Aristotle suggested that dignity is achieved by those who live up to the practical ideal of excellence.[36]

According to this understanding, human dignity – while theoretically available to all – is a rather elitist concept only attained by a few.[37]

Dierksmeier writes:

> While the Stoics broadened the scope of the term [dignity] to include *principally* everyone, they agreed with Plato and Aristotle regarding its narrow *factual* application: dignity must be earned. Whereas dignity, as a potential, was considered to lie within human beings' nature as such, its actualization was thought to depend on contingent subjective achievements.[38]

Other philosophers agreed with the dichotomous nature of dignity as unconditional in principle and conditional in actuality. Kant, for example, suggested that people possess *absolute* value and *relative* value. Relative value depends on their ability and willingness to conduct themselves in praiseworthy and ethical ways.[39] Dierksmeier explains that

> Kant argued that every human being has dignity (*Würde*) in his or her ability to be moral. However, he also noted that only those who

do, in fact, lead moral lives deserve the praise of personal ethical value (*Wert*).[40]

This distinction between unconditional, universal dignity and conditional, earned dignity provides a basis for management, in that the former needs to be protected and the latter needs to be promoted.[41]

HUMAN DIGNITY IN THE HUMANITIES AND SOCIAL SCIENCES

Dignity has long been part of the scholarly conversation in various humanities and social sciences disciplines. Humanistic management draws on these insights and brings them into the context of organizing practices – it is, after all, *humanistic* management.[42] In philosophy, the concept of dignity has sparked numerous debates on the nature of human beings. Similarly, in theology, dignity is a cornerstone for understanding human freedom and responsibility. It also serves as a guide in contested debates, such as in bioethics. In historical debates, the quest for dignity is often seen as a precursor of social change, whether the abolishment of slavery, the various political revolutions, battles for human rights, or the reconstitution of states after tumultuous crises (see Germany, Ireland, South Africa).[43]

The debates on dignity have influenced various social science disciplines as well, most notably sociology. Many sociologists have studied the sources of dignity denial: Marx focused on alienation;[44] Durkheim contemplated anomie (normlessness) as the result of economic efficiency,[45] and Weber was concerned with excessive bureaucratic rationality.[46] In psychology, William James,[47] Carl Rogers,[48] Erich Fromm,[49] Abraham Maslow,[50] and Martin Seligman[51] embraced human dignity as a vehicle in order to distance themselves from the behaviorist, deficiency-oriented analysis of human behavior. In economics, the notion of human dignity – regardless of wealth or utility concerns – has gained increasing visibility due to the works of Amartya Sen[52] and Martha Nussbaum.[53]

The application of dignity-related concepts is most advanced, though, in the context of legal studies. Dignity is, for example, a core concept in the constitutions of South Africa and Germany. In these countries, it is a judicial concept that influences major constitutional decisions, including antidiscrimination issues. Dignity is also the foundational concept for scholarship on human rights. Legal scholars argue that the idea of human dignity is so important that it is a central feature in the quest for human rights, the battle for democracy, and the establishment of modern governance systems.[54]

Beyond its legal implications, the concept of dignity has had repercussions for economic development. The quest for dignity has been so relevant that economic historians argue that the accordance of dignity was *the* central success factor of economic progress in the West.[55] Economic historian Deirdre McCloskey argues that neither property rights, nor trade, nor capital investments explain the rise in affluence over the past 200 years. She maintains that the accordance of unconditional rights and the liberty to define one's own life pathways, which include entrepreneurial activity, were the main factors of economic development. She states:

> The crucial remaining antecedent, I claim, was a rhetorical change around 1700 concerning markets and innovations and the bourgeoisie, a rhetoric spread after 1800. It was merely a change in talking and thinking about *dignity* and liberty. But it was historically unique and economically powerful.[56] (italics added)

McCloskey argues that the bourgeoisie of England, Continental Europe, and the United States only started innovating, learning, and accumulating massive wealth once such human dignity was accorded *and* protected. The introduction of rights that protected the dignity of an expanded class of citizens arguably allowed more general civic activity, including economic dynamism. Members of the bourgeoisie had the autonomy to develop and determine plans for life that engaged more human capability than ever before. As such, dignity can, in

Waldron's words, be seen as a "cornerstone for the conception of humanity"[57] in law, economics, politics, and business.

DIGNITY IN MANAGEMENT RESEARCH

Whereas the notion of dignity has clearly been a central topic in the humanities and the legal profession, the management sciences have seemingly neglected it. Having said so, Domènec Melé makes the case that many influential management thinkers draw on a humanistic perspective, and intuitively view human beings as endowed with dignity. He mentions the work of Mary Parker Follet,[58] Chester Barnard,[59] Elton Mayo,[60] and Frederik Herzberg.[61] He also highlights the work of others, such as the human relations movement, which is concerned with the humanization of work and the construction of more humane organizations.

In recent years, psychology has inspired an increasing amount of work in management-related fields, resulting in a better understanding of the roles of self-esteem, autonomy, meaningful work, as well as justice and well-being.[62] However, this is only a recent trend and is mostly prevalent in the areas of organizational behavior and business ethics. Highlighting the field's indifference to human dignity, business ethicist Norman Bowie has convincingly argued that traditional management science has consistently neglected it.[63] Others argue that a Taylorian[64] and Fordian understanding of Scientific Management has supported two forms of dehumanization.[65] Psychologist Nick Haslam labels the first form "mechanistic dehumanization,"[66] which violates the unconditionality and universality principle of human dignity by treating people like machines. Haslam labels the second form "animalistic dehumanization," which violates the conditional aspects of human dignity by preventing personal and character development.

Ford's famous question, "Why is it that every time I ask for a pair of hands, they come with a brain attached?"[67] illustrates what Haslam means by mechanistic dehumanization. While scientific management's legacy has been expounded on elsewhere,[68] its tradition is visible in operations management, operations research, information systems, as well as in strategic management, organizational behavior, and marketing. Animalistic dehumanization especially occurs when people are viewed as human capital or human resources. For instance, animalistic dehumanization is invoked when human resource scholars study how improving technical knowledge can increase organizational effectiveness and efficiency.[69] They are, for example, currently researching how you can best train and develop human resources. Much like dogs that need to be trained, humans are considered resources that need to be trained, rather than have their character developed. This perspective is clearly in opposition to ancient philosophical ideals.

DRAWBACKS OF DIGNITY AS A CONCEPT

Waldron makes the case that, as a foundational concept, dignity can serve as a guiding principle for organizing practice – legal or otherwise.[70] Rosen cautions that the notion of dignity can be abused in various forms. He points out that dignity has been used as a Trojan horse for religion-inspired attacks on equality (i.e., gay marriage), or legal attacks on individual autonomy (i.e., in the "dwarf tossing" case), leading to paternalistic practices.[71] The concept of dignity therefore remains ambiguous to such a degree that some consider it impractical as a means of guiding practice.

To highlight the concept's inherent ambiguity, Donna Hicks suggests that dignity can be very useful in the context of conflict resolution. She finds the language of dignity helpful in opening up important conversations that have been blocking peace negotiations.[72] She, for example, asks people to talk about a time when they felt their dignity was violated. Through this simple question she elicits a very rich conversation that engages more of the conflicting parties' humanity. She and the Reverend Desmond Tutu view this process as cathartic, and see it as a pathway to forgiveness and resolution. Using the "dignity" approach has worked well in the context of post-apartheid South Africa and post–civil war Northern Ireland.

However, Donna Hicks notes that there is a real danger of "false dignity." In her view, false dignity represents the notion of rank, status, and "being special and different from others," which people often hijack to make claims for their benefit. She warns against the tendency to "save face" or to carve out special treatment for oneself. For example, a participant suggesting that his dignity was violated because he was not given more time than others to speak, or, in a rather absurd instance, a person arguing that she needs to possess a Prada bag to feel dignified are trading on false dignity.

Reconnecting the concept of dignity to a universal ethic or norm addresses this ambiguity. Arguments for "true dignity" support those activities and behaviors that are part of a universally applicable law or norm. If everyone needs a Prada bag to feel dignified, the status difference it signals is lost. If everyone needs more time than others to speak their thoughts, people would rarely want to get together, as a few speakers could hijack the conversation. If unchecked, such false dignity claims can therefore pose problems for organizing practice.

INCREASING THE ACCURACY OF MANAGEMENT THEORY

The concept of dignity, despite any potential downsides and ambiguities, can nevertheless advance the conversation in management by providing three benefits: (1) a baseline argument about the intrinsic value of all human beings, (2) the acknowledgment of activities and behaviors of intrinsic value outside the exchange paradigm, and (3) the aspiration to achieve the highest common denominator in terms of human development (purpose of organizing).

Regarding the first benefit, it seems rather obvious that management research could add additional insights into better organizational practices by focusing on how human dignity can be protected. The dignity perspective has the potential to broaden management science by highlighting a number of research areas that transcend human beings as human resources and human capital, relevant only for the pursuit of performance and profit. In organizational contexts, character development could be one such area; trust development and human development others (more on this in Chapters 6 and 7).

Regarding the second benefit, dignity can help broaden management theory's perspectives significantly. Some management scholars have long complained that the study of intrinsically valuable human activities, such as trust, forgiveness, love, or character development, is located outside management research's traditional parameters. When studying trust, love, or forgiveness in organizational settings, the traditional paradigm requires an instrumental focus. Despite its obvious benefits, such management research currently needs to justify itself with profitability or performance concerns;[73] an example of such reasoning: "We study the development of trust among stakeholders because it shows that it improves performance." A more humanistic approach would allow such a study without resorting to justification of its instrumental benefits.

The dignity category can also help unearth mechanisms of human sociality that extend beyond a typical market exchange. The logic of gift, for example, typically escapes an economistic perspective, but becomes more relevant in various humanistic organizational settings.[74] Business ethicist Guglielmo Faldetta argues that the logic of gift is a new and relevant conceptual lens for viewing business relationships beyond a merely contractual logic.[75] He argues that it is crucial to see the circulation of goods and personal commitments as a foundation for the development of good and ethical relationships. In a distinct yet related perspective, the philosopher Elizabeth Anderson suggests that we understand value judgments occurring in organizations not only through an economistic cost-benefit assessment but also by accepting the plurality of values at play.[76] In her work, she offers a theory of value and rationality that rejects cost-benefit analysis in organizations, and highlights how one can value the "invaluables." She provides arguments that allow for conversations and collective decision-making processes that include valuing environmental protection, equality of rights, etc. as intrinsically valuable but lacking a price.

Regarding the third benefit, the concept of dignity can provide the foundation for a different organizing goal. Waldron and others state that dignity can be regarded as the highest common denominator in terms of human development. Dignity can therefore inspire organizational practices that go beyond wealth creation. This aspiration to create well-being is the second pillar of humanistic management.

WELL-BEING AS THE ULTIMATE ORGANIZING PURPOSE

In the humanistic conception of management and organizing, the central aspiration is a contribution to the common good, or, in other words, the creation of shared well-being. This aspiration is not new, but has been marginalized in the past 200 years as far at the economic context is concerned. From Aristotle to the Utilitarians, well-being was considered the central ambition of human existence. Robert Kahn and Thomas Juster write that it is an "article of faith that the supreme criterion by which a government can be judged is the quality of life its citizens experience."[77] An increasing number of positive psychologists take it as a given that human beings wish to be well and flourish. While the goal of well-being may be uncontested for individuals, as well as governments of nation states, the humanistic management perspective suggests it can be equally relevant at the organizational level. Aristotle's theory of life and the concept of Eudaimonia offer useful perspectives that can be applied to the goal of organizational well-being.

Aristotle's thinking forms the basis of much of Western thought, and revisiting his thinking can inspire more accurate management theory. Aristotle developed a theory of life that centers on human beings' quest for happiness. As Claus Dierksmeier argues,

> Aristotle's ethics rests upon a (*teleological*) theory about life that ascribes to each living entity a certain goal (*telos*) to which it strives. Plants, for example, need specific environments (soil, water, sun, etc.) but will, given these conditions, predictably prosper and flourish

in a certain way. Therein they realize their genetic program, or what Aristotle describes as their final end. (*PA* I, 641b, 34–39)[78]

Dierksmeier and Pirson argue that Aristotle's views on ethics and political governance offer interesting propositions for the good management of organizations. Aristotle states that, in the pursuit of the human good, ethics and politics are conjoined, which elevates the domain of political science (containing the theory of economics) to a position of highest importance.[79]

> In all sciences and arts the end is a good; and the greatest good and in the highest degree a good in the most authoritative of all – this is the political science of which the good is justice, in other words, the common interest. (*Pol* III,12, 1282b, 15–19)[80]

Aristotle reflects on the common interest by asking what the ultimate goal of a universally shared human life is. Dierksmeier and Pirson write:

> According to Aristotle, one thing is clear from the beginning, "wealth is evidently not the good we are seeking" (*NE* I, 7, 1096a, 6). The answer instead has to be gleaned from the natural faculties of the human being (*NE* I, 7, 1097b, 33). Whatever our private idiosyncrasies, certain capabilities are common to us all. In our most common faculties lay natural objectives. The quest for (goods such as) food, shelter, defense, and procreation, we share with animals. In addition, human beings seek communication, education, and cultivation (*Pol* I, 2, 1253a, 10–39). Yet even these higher goods can be declared functional; they are not necessarily sufficient in themselves, and neither are they necessarily sought after universally. Happiness, however, is universally pursued, and, moreover, it is sought for its own sake. For formal reasons, it must hence be declared the ultimate good of human life (*NE* I, 7, 1097a, 28–37).[81]

But what does Aristotle mean by happiness? Was it the version that Coca-Cola invites its customers to enjoy? Aristotle does not endorse a purely hedonistic vision of happiness. In fact, Aristotle's term for happiness was *Eudaimonia*, not *Hedone* (pleasure), which connoted a purposeful, virtuous life lived in harmony with society and the environment. Scholars extrapolating management principles from Aristotle suggest that the goal of organizing should be the facilitation of such Eudaimonia or flourishing. While Aristotle did not propose concrete steps on how to achieve well-being, he suggested following time-proven concepts like customs, personal, and communal reflection, as well as constant learning (philosophy) guided by the counsel of the wise.[82]

The utilitarian reinterpretation of Aristotle's insight may have had the greatest impact on the development of modern economics and management. Originally, Utilitarianism was an ethical theory that argued that the best moral action would also maximize happiness, now labeled "utility." When utility was first used, Jeremy Bentham defined it as the aggregate of pleasures of any activity minus the suffering incurred. John Stuart Mill added that, in order to give an accurate account of utility, the quality of pleasures and suffering mattered. Similar to Aristotle, these authors argued that virtuous behavior ultimately yielded more utility, i.e., happiness. This may sound rather awkward when one is used to seeing utilitarian concerns equated with simple cost-benefit analysis. While the history of Utilitarianism is beyond the scope of this book, it is important to note that it is widely credited as the foundational theory of modern economics. From the humanistic perspective, it is critical to point out that, at its onset, utility meant well-being. Claus Dierksmeier points out that utility's meaning was changed to material wealth only recently, and for quite pragmatic reasons.[83]

While the shift toward measuring material wealth as the path to happiness may have made sense in the early phases of economic development in the nineteenth century, well-being and wealth had arguably decoupled by the middle of the twentieth century.[84] To reflect this shift, the Organization for Economic Cooperation and Development (OECD) decided in 2011 to move away from measuring economic progress as the output of gross domestic product (GDP) so that it can, once again, reflect well-being. Governments and economists are similarly returning to the roots of economic thinking and starting to measure what matters. Robert F Kennedy argued poetically for such a humanistic turn when he said:

> Even if we act to erase material poverty, there is another greater task, it is to confront the poverty of satisfaction – purpose and dignity – that afflicts us all. Too much and for too long, we seemed to have surrendered personal excellence and community values in the mere accumulation of material things. Our Gross National Product, now, is over $800 billion dollars a year, but that Gross National Product – if we judge the United States of America by that – that Gross National Product counts air pollution and cigarette advertising, and ambulances to clear our highways of carnage. It counts special locks for our doors and the jails for the people who break them. It counts the destruction of the redwood and the loss of our natural wonder in chaotic sprawl. It counts napalm and counts nuclear warheads and armored cars for the police to fight the riots in our cities. It counts Whitman's rifle and Speck's knife, and the television programs which glorify violence in order to sell toys to our children. Yet the gross national product does not allow for the health of our children, the quality of their education or the joy of their play. It does not include the beauty of our poetry or the strength of our marriages, the intelligence of our public debate or the integrity of our public officials. It measures neither our wit nor our courage, neither our wisdom nor our learning, neither our compassion nor our devotion to our country, it measures everything in short, except that which makes life worthwhile.[85]

CONCLUDING REMARKS

The humanistic management perspective reflects in many ways the inspiring words of the late US presidential candidate, and suggests that management theory also needs to refocus on the things that make life worthwhile. Humanistic management embraces dignity as a notion that represents all the things that have intrinsic value. It also espouses the aspiration to organize for higher levels of well-being. Humanistic management, should help us develop an understanding of the organizing principles that protect dignity and promote well-being, rather than performance and wealth creation.

NOTES

1 Dierksmeier, C. (2011). "The freedom–responsibility nexus in management philosophy and business ethics." *Journal of Business Ethics*, **101**(2), 263–283.

2 Kueng, H. (1998). *A Global Ethic for Global Politics and Economics*. Oxford, Oxford University Press; Kueng, H., and Kuschel, K. J. (Eds.). (1993). *Global Ethic: The Declaration of the Parliament of the World's Religions*. New York/Eugene, OR, Bloomsbury Publishing; Kung, H. (2004). *Global Responsibility: In Search of a New World Ethic*. New York, Wipf and Stock Publishers.

3 Waldron, J. (2013). Citizenship and Dignity. *Understanding Human Dignity*. C. McCrudden, ed. Oxford, Oxford University Press.

4 Waldron, J., and Dan-Cohen, M. (2012). *Dignity, Rank, And Rights*. Oxford, Oxford University Press. 82; Waldron, J. (2013). Citizenship and Dignity. *Understanding Human Dignity*. C. McCrudden, ed. Oxford, Oxford University Press.

5 Kant, I. (1998). *Groundwork of the Metaphysics of Morals*. Edited and translated by Mary J. Gregor. Cambridge, Cambridge University Press. 42 [4:434].

6 Ibid.

7 Ibid.

8 Cicero, D. O., and Keyes, C. W. (1928). "Loeb classical library." *Volume XXI, On Duties*, 1(9), 29.

9 Waldron, J., and Dan-Cohen, M. (2012). *Dignity, Rank, and Rights*. 82.

10 McCrudden, C. (2013). "In pursuit of human dignity: an introduction to current debates." *Understanding Human Dignity*. C. McCrudden, ed. Oxford, Oxford University Press. 192; Dierksmeier, C. (2011). "Reorienting management education: from homo oeconomicus to human

dignity." *Business Schools Under Fire*. H. M. Network. New York, Palgrave McMillan.

11 Rosen, C. (2012). *Dignity: Its History and Meaning*. Cambridge, MA, Harvard University Press.

12 Rosen. *Dignity: Its History and Meaning*; Bacon, F. (1828). *Of the Proficience and Advancement of Learning: Divine and Human*. London, JF Dove.

13 Nussbaum, M. (2011). *Creating Capabilities – The Human Development Approach*. New York, Belknap.

14 Rosen. *Dignity: Its History and Meaning*.

15 Cited in Rosen, *Dignity: Its History and Meaning*.

16 Scruton, R. (1999). *The Aesthetics of Music*. Oxford, Oxford University Press.

17 McCrudden, C. (2013). "In pursuit of human dignity: An introduction to current debates." 192

18 Waddock, S (2014). Presentation at Academy of Management, Words Rarely Used in Management Theory, Philadelphia, 2014.

19 This section has been largely adapted from Pirson, M. A., and C. Dierksmeier (2014, January). "Reconnecting management theory and social welfare: A humanistic perspective." *Academy of Management Proceedings*, **2014**(1), 12245. Academy of Management.

20 Hodson, R. (2001). *Dignity at Work*, Cambridge, Cambridge University Press; Meyer, M. J. and W. A. Parent (1992). *The Constitution of Rights: Human Dignity and American Values*. Ithaca, NY, Cornell University Press.

21 Pirson, M., C. Dierksmeier and K. Goodpaster (2014). "Human dignity and business." *Business Ethics Quarterly*, **24**(02), 307–309.

22 Waldron, J., and Dan-Cohen, M. (2012). *Dignity, Rank, And Rights*. Oxford, Oxford University Press. Waldron, J. (2013). "Citizenship and dignity." *Understanding Human Dignity*. C. McCrudden, ed. Oxford, Oxford University Press.

23 Ibid.

24 Pirson, Dierksmeier and Goodpaster. "Human dignity and business." 307–309; Rosen, *Dignity: Its History and Meaning*; Dierksmeier, C. (2011). "Reorienting management education: from homo oeconomicus to human dignity." *Business Schools Under Fire*. H. M. Network. New York, Palgrave McMillan.

25 Forschner, M. (2011). "Stoic humanism." *Humanistic Ethics in the Age of Globality.* C. A. Dierksmeier, W. Amann, E. Kimakowitz, H. Spitzeck, and M. Pirson, eds. London, Palgrave Macmillan; Forschner, M. (1981). *Die stoische Ethik : über den Zusammenhang von Natur-, Sprach- und Moralphilosophie im altstoischen System.* Stuttgart, Klett-Cotta. Dierksmeier, C. (2011). "Reorienting management education."

26 McCrudden, C. (2013). "In pursuit of human dignity: An introduction to current debates." *Understanding Human Dignity.* C. McCrudden, ed. Oxford, Oxford University Press. 192; Soskice, J. (2013). "Human dignity and the image of god." *Understanding Human Dignity.* C. McCrudden, ed. Oxford, Oxford University Press; Dierksmeier. "Reorienting management education."

27 Dierksmeier. "Reorienting management education."

28 Pirson, Dierksmeier and Goodpaster. "Human dignity and business." 307–309; Rosen, *Dignity: Its History and Meaning.*

29 Dierksmeier. "Reorienting management education."

30 Ibid.

31 Pirson and Dierksmeier. "Reconnecting management theory and social welfare"; Dierksmeier, "Reorienting management education."

32 Immanuel Kant (1998). *Groundwork of the Metaphysics of Morals.* Edited and translated by Mary J. Gregor. Cambridge: Cambridge University Press. 42 [4:435].

33 See also Kateb, G. (2011). *Human Dignity*, Cambridge, MA, Harvard University Press.

34 Hodson, R. (2001). *Dignity at Work.*

35 Dierksmeier. "Reorienting management education."

36 Nussbaum, M. (1998). *Plato's Republic: The Good Society and the Deformation of Desire.* Washington, DC, Library of Congress; Rosen, *Dignity: Its History and Meaning.*

37 Holloway, C. (2008). *Magnanimity and Statesmanship.* Lanham, MD, Lexington Books; Dierksmeier. "Reorienting management education."

38 Dierksmeier. "Reorienting management education."

39 See also Kateb, G. *Human Dignity.*

40 Dierksmeier, "Reorienting management education."

41 Pirson and Dierksmeier. "Reconnecting management theory and social welfare."

42 Humanistic management is largely inspired by the humanistic enlightenment that the humanities generated.

43 For more see: McCrudden, C., Ed. (2013). *Understanding Human Dignity.* Proceedings of the British Academy, Oxford, Oxford University Press.

44 Marx, K. (1906). *Capital.* New York, The Modern Library; Hodson, R. (2001). *Dignity at Work.* Cambridge, Cambridge University Press.

45 Marks, S. R. (1974). "Durkheim's theory of anomie." *American Journal of Sociology,* **80**(2), 329–363; Hodson, R. (2001). *Dignity at Work.*

46 Weber, M. and S. Andreski (1983). *Max Weber on Capitalism, Bureaucracy, and Religion: A Selection of Texts.* London; Boston, Allen & Unwin; Hodson, R. *Dignity at Work.*

47 McDermott, J. J. (1977). *The Writings of William James,* Chicago, University of Chicago Press.

48 Rogers, C. (1995). *On Becoming a Person: A Therapist's View of Psychotherapy,* Mariner Books.

49 Fromm, E. (2000). *Art of Loving.* New York, Continuum International Publishing Group; Fromm, E. (2001). *The Sane Society.* New York, Psychology Press.

50 Maslow, A. H. (1954). *Motivation and Personality.* New York, Harper & Brothers.

51 Seligman, M. and M. Csikszentmihalyi (2000). "Positive psychology: an introduction." *American Psychologist,* **55**(1), 5–14.

52 Sen, A. (2001). *Development as Freedom.* Oxford; New York, Oxford University Press; Sen, A. (2002). *Rationality and Freedom.* Cambridge, MA/ London, Harvard University Press.

53 Nussbaum, M. (2011). *Creating Capabilities – The Human Development Approach.* New York, Belknap; Nussbaum, M. (2003). "Capabilities as fundamental entitlements: Sen and social justice." *Feminist Economics,* **9** (2–3), 33–59.

54 See also Kateb, G. *Human Dignity –* McCloskey, D. (2010). *Bourgeois Dignity: Why Economics Can't Explain the Modern World,* Chicago, University of Chicago Press.

55 McCloskey, *Bourgeois Dignity.*

56 Ibid. 33.

57 Dimock, W. in J. Waldron and M. Dan-Cohen (2012). *Dignity, Rank, and Rights.* Oxford, Oxford University Press. 119.

58 For example Schilling, M. A. (2000). "Decades ahead of her time: Advancing stakeholder theory through the ideas of Mary Parker Follett." *Journal of Management History*, 6(5), 224–242.

59 Mele, D. (2009). "Current trends of humanism in business." *Humanism in Business: Perspectives on the Development of a Responsible Business Society.* H. Spitzeck, M. Pirson, W. Amann, S. Khan, and E. von Kimakowitz, eds. Cambridge, Cambridge University Press, 170–184.

60 For example: Mayo, E. (1933). *The Human Problems of an Industrial Civilization.* New York, Macmillan.

61 For example: Herzberg, F. (1976). *The Managerial Choice: To Be Efficient and to Be Human.* Homewood, Dow Jones-Irwin.

62 See for example: Cameron, K. (2003). "Organizational virtuousness and performance." *Positive Organizational Scholarship.* K. S. Cameron, J. E. Dutton, and R. E. Quinn, eds. San Francisco, Berrett-Koehler.

63 For example: Bowie, N. E. (1998). "A Kantian theory of capitalism." *Business Ethics Quarterly(Ruffin Series)*, 37–60.

64 Taylor, F. W. (1914). *The Principles of Scientific Management.* New York, Harper.

65 Haslam, N. (2006). "Dehumanization: An integrative review." *Personality and Social Psychology Review*, 10(3), 252–264.

66 Ibid.

67 Hamel, G. (2000). "Reinvent your company." *Fortune.* 141, 98–118.

68 Khurana, A. (2009). *Scientific Management: A Management Idea to Reach a Mass Audience.* New Delhi, Global India Publications Pvt Ltd.

69 For example: Hersey, P. and K. H. Blanchard (1993). *Management of Organizational Behavior: Utilizing Human Resources.* Upper Saddle River, NJ, Prentice-Hall; Wexley, K. N. and G. P. Latham (2001). *Developing and Training Human Resources in Organizations.* Upper Saddle River, NJ, Pearson.

70 Waldron, J., and M. Dan-Cohen (2012). *Dignity, Rank, and Rights.* Oxford, Oxford University Press.

71 Rosen, M. (2013). "Dignity: The case against." *Understanding Human Dignity.* C. McCrudden, ed. Oxford, Oxford University Press.

72 Hicks, D. (2011). *Dignity – Its Essential Role in Resolving Conflict.* New Haven, Yale University Press.

73 Walsh, J. P., et al. (2003). "Social issues and management: Our lost cause found." *Journal of Management*, **29**(6), 859–881.

74 Baviera, T., W. English, and M. Guillén (2016). "The 'logic of gift': Inspiring behavior in organizations beyond the limits of duty and exchange." *Business Ethics Quarterly*, **26**(02), 159–180.

75 Faldetta, G. (2011). "The logic of gift and gratuitousness in business relationships." *Journal of Business Ethics*, **100**(1), 67–77.

76 Anderson, E. (1995). *Value in Ethics and Economics*. Cambridge, MA, Harvard University Press.

77 Kahn, R. L., and F. T. Juster (2002). "Well-being: Concepts and measures." *Journal of Social Issues*, **58**(4), 627–644.

78 Dierksmeier, C. and M. Pirson (2009). "Oikonomia versus chrematistike: learning from aristotle about the future orientation of business management." *Journal of Business Ethics*, **88**(3), 417–430.

79 Ibid.

80 Ibid.

81 Ibid.

82 Ibid.

83 Dierksmeier, C. (2011). "The freedom-responsibility nexus in management philosophy and business ethics." *Journal of Business Ethics*, **101**(2), 263–283.

84 Easterlin, R. (2001). "Income and happiness: Towards a unified theory." *Economic Journal*, **111** (July), 465–484; Layard, R. (2005). *Happiness – Lessons from a New Science*, London, Penguin Press.

85 www.jfklibrary.org/Research/Research-Aids/Ready-Reference/RFK-Speeches/Remarks-of-Robert-F-Kennedy-at-the-University-of-Kansas-March-18–1968.aspx.

6 Economistic and Humanistic Archetypes of Management

Given the manifold problems of this world, we need ways to actively address them; better forms of organizing are required. I suggest that we embrace more humanistic forms of management and move away from economistic ones. This means we need to progressively learn how to be more human and how our organizations can help with that. While this is easier said than done, this chapter provides a framework that provides a perspective on how this transition can be conceptualized.

The framework represents a synthesis of the foundational work laid down in Chapters 1–5. It outlines a number of ideal types[1] that provide clarity of the parameters that influence our current reality. The framework also shows the possibility of alternative forms of organizing that outline our potentiality. The framework will guide a discussion of how we can transform research, practice, pedagogy and policy in the next section of the book.

INTRODUCTION OF FRAMEWORK

Max Weber, one of the founding fathers of sociology, suggested that social science depends on the construction of abstract, hypothetical concepts. He proposed that social scientists focus on the formation of ideal types or, as I will call them, archetypes. Weber wrote: "An ideal type is formed by the one-sided accentuation of one or more points of view and by the synthesis of a great many diffuse, discrete, more or less present and occasionally absent concrete individual phenomena, which are arranged according to those one-sidedly emphasized viewpoints into a unified analytical construct."[2]

I am therefore proposing a framework of such ideal types of organizing. As all good theories are parsimonious, I propose two dimensions along which alternative forms of organizing and management can be conceptualized. The first dimension, *the input dimension*, relates to the role dignity plays as foundational assumption regarding human nature. The second dimension, *the output dimension*, relates to the ultimate goals of organizing.[3]

Input Dimension: The Role of Dignity

The role that dignity plays within a number of different management approaches is crucial for an understanding of the input dimension. A first distinction can be drawn according to whether organizing is mainly a function of exchange, or whether non-exchange goods and activities play a role as well. A second distinction can be drawn with regard to the role of human dignity within an organization. If the foundational assumption is that humans are *unconditionally* endowed with dignity, then organizing practice should reflect that by aiming to *protect* it. If, in addition, there is a concern for the *conditional* aspects of human dignity, then organizational practices should aim to *promote* such dignity.

This distinction can be understood by the enforcement of human rights, i.e., the freedom of speech. To *protect* dignity it would be required to allow people to speak their mind, to *promote* dignity would mean to protect the right to free speech but also invest in the education toward informed speech.

As a consequence, the input dimension is represented by a spectrum according to the relevance of dignity within an organization, i.e., whether it is (1) neglected, (2) protected, or (3) promoted.

Output Dimension: The Ultimate Goal of Organizing

As discussed in Chapter 5, the output dimension can be categorized according to whether the ultimate goal of organizing is wealth or well-being. These two concepts refer to the differing notions of utility and

	Role of dignity (Input)		
Output	Neglected	Protected	Promoted
Wealth creation *Economism*	Pure economism	Bounded economism	Enlightened economism
Well-being creation *Humanism*	Bureaucratic paternalism	Bounded humanism	Pure humanism

FIGURE 6.1: Economistic vs. humanistic archetypes of management

welfare. These differences are reflected in the proposed alternative management archetypes in Figure 6.1.

As shown in Figure 6.1, these two dimensions result in six management archetypes: three economistic and three humanistic. The economistic management archetypes are all focused on wealth creation. Management practices within that economistic approach may (1) neglect dignity, as in *Pure Economism*, (2) protect dignity as in *Bounded Economism*, or (3) promote dignity as in *Enlightened Economism*. However, the humanistic management archetypes are all focused on well-being creation. Management practices within a humanistic approach may (1) neglect dignity, as in *Bureaucratic Paternalism*, (2) protect dignity as in *Bounded Humanism*, or (3) promote dignity as in *Pure Humanism*.

Following Weber's advice, I outline these archetypes to advance paradigmatic alternatives for organizing. These archetypes represent a normative stance and reflect an ideal type: a mindset through which people can engage in research, practice, pedagogy, and policy.[4] In the following pages, each archetype is outlined in turn. I attempt to illustrate their respective distinctiveness with examples from current management research, pedagogy, practice, and policy. I do this knowing that none of the examples fits neatly into one single archetype; one can reasonably argue that the above framework represents more of a fluid spectrum. Nevertheless I posit that the categorizations can be helpful in a more radical rethinking of management.

Drawing distinctions which are typically overlooked in management, I discuss:

- Assumptions of human nature
- The role of dignity
- The ultimate objective function.

Archetype 1: Pure Economism

In the *Pure Economism* archetype, human beings are viewed as homo economicus or REMM. As outlined in Chapter 2, assumptions regarding human nature center on insatiable wants. Humans in this context are considered rational when they always want more and aim to maximize their utility. Utility in this context is understood as wealth and money. In the context of *Pure Economism*, concerns for other evolutionary needs such as bonding, comprehension, or safety are moot; everything is up for exchange, there are no protected values, and commitments do not count. As Henry Mintzberg paraphrases, humans are practically whores, willing to trade anything.[5]

In *Pure Economism*, humans are seen and studied in the context of market engagement only, for example, as participants in the labor or consumer market. Considerations outside the exchange paradigm, such as love, trust, or care, are considered irrelevant. Rational behavior is based on cost-benefit calculations and any notions of fairness are considered irrational.[6]

In *Pure Economism*, organizations are treated as a nexus of contracts in which rationally maximizing agents negotiate their respective benefits, often at the expense of others. An example of this type of economistic practice can be found in the financial markets, where "exchange" is the dominant logic. At the extreme end of the scale, *Pure Economism* can be represented by psychopaths engaging with each other, such as traders in the financial markets trying to game the system for their own benefit.[7]

In *Pure Economism*, the market becomes *the* organizing mode above all other forms such as community, family, or hierarchy. The ideal society within this archetype is represented by a market society.[8] The ultimate goal of a market society is to create efficiencies and increase wealth. Developments such as the financialization and marketization of organizations, from Uber to Air B&B, to freelance websites such as Huffington Post, are a witness to the marketization logic.[9] In this organizing perspective, human dignity does not really matter and human beings are typically referred to as "human resources" or "human capital."

Research: For the purposes of management research, the *Pure Economism* archetype provides a platform for studying efficiency and effectiveness as the means of wealth creation. In this perspective, human beings are resources to be managed. The notion of dignity does not play a role and as a consequence, only those activities that contribute to wealth creation are accounted for. *Pure Economism* is dominant in the research fields of finance and accounting. Management research most influenced by those fields is often connected to strategy and corporate governance. Observers argue that much of the research conducted within the Business Policy & Strategy division of the Academy of Management would fall within this archetype.[10] A typical research question within this archetype would, for example, concern the effective use of strategic human resource practice to enhance firm performance.[11] At the extreme end of the spectrum, the study of the use of a human resource to enhance firm performance might include sweat shop labor or even slavery.[12] As previously mentioned, *Pure Economism* does not consider rights and dignity universally. It is therefore unsurprising that management theories of this archetype often deploy the same arguments used by slave owners. In her latest work, business historian Caitlin Rosenthal found that many of the advanced management techniques, i.e., regarding rewards, were already in place in the southern plantations of the United States. According to Rosenthal, slave owners started keeping records of their trade as early as 1750, and tested the effects of diet, workplace conditions, or job rotation on slaves' productivity. As in Taylor's early management studies,[13] slavers experimented with ways to increase labor productivity, including the effects of incentives on the individual and at the group level. Rosenthal notes that these accounting techniques reduced slaves to "human resources or capital," a term that, nowadays, represents the special value accorded to human resources/assets.[14]

Practice: The *Pure Economism* archetype of management can be found in a number of management practices. Clearly the use of slave labor and sweat shops denies universal human dignity, and most large corporations dealing with global supply chains seem to engage in some form of dignity violation, whether they are aware of it or not.[15] The most prominent cases of *Pure Economism* in practice are represented by the large investment banks that were in part responsible for the financial crisis of 2008. Banks, once iconic, such as Lehman Brothers, Bear Stearns, and Merrill Lynch engaged in economistic practices in the purest sense in the run up to the financial crisis. They behaved opportunistically in order to maximize short-term profits, in some cases only to be saved from the market system that would have destroyed them.

Bear Stearns, for example, developed mortgage-backed securities that focused on value extraction and monetization. It also developed several highly leveraged hedge funds trading with asset-backed securities. These products were sold to oftentimes unsuspecting customers without concern for their actual risk.[16] Lehman Brothers was similarly notorious for its fixation on profit maximization. To support their profit maximization strategy, Lehman's CEO Dick Fuld focused on high-risk investments. The bankruptcy report suggests that the internal leadership and culture of the bank were so focused on money making that they neglected the risk of their investments; poor risk management and fraud led to Lehman's downfall. Merrill Lynch followed a similar management logic.[17] Behavioral economist Hersh Shefrin comments that in 2004 "the five major Wall Street investment banks successfully petitioned the Securities and Exchange Commission (SEC) to raise leverage limits dramatically, from 12 to 40! Not all banks increased their leverage as high as 40, although one did – Merrill Lynch."[18]

Observers argue that investment banks had turned into casinos, and never particularly cared about the actual societal value of their products.[19] While not all investment banks failed, other banks such as Deutsche Bank, UBS, and JP Morgan are caught up in a litany of scandals.[20] Fraudulent behavior seems commonplace and fines are a calculated business risk. As one might expect from homo economicus, opportunism is truly part of business strategy.[21]

Pedagogy: In the United States and probably in many other parts of the world, business has become the most popular degree-level course of study. The sheer number of graduates wields great influence over actual management practice, and a (dominant) paradigm influences how students of business are taught. Finance and accounting are core topics within the business schools, and these disciplines and their intellectual foundations rest on economistic assumptions. It has long been suggested that these assumptions create self-fulfilling prophecies.[22] As many studies have shown, teaching students economics, finance, and accounting will make them less ethical,[23] less social, less empathetic, and more psychopathic.[24] Based on those insights, even economists are now worried. Luigi Zingales, a prominent representative of the Chicago School of Economics and a professor of finance wrote an article asking: Do business schools incubate criminals?[25]

> The recent scandals at Barclays Plc, JPMorgan Chase & Co., Goldman Sachs Group Inc. and other banks might give the impression that the financial sector has some serious morality problems. Unfortunately, it's worse than that: We are dealing with a drop in ethical standards throughout the business world, and our graduate schools are partly to blame.[26]

He cites an example of the impact of the economistic paradigm:

> Oddly, most economists see their subject as divorced from morality. They liken themselves to physicists, who teach how atoms do behave, not how they should behave. But physicists do not teach to atoms, and atoms do not have free will. If they did,

physicists would and should be concerned about how the atoms being instructed could change their behavior and affect the universe. Experimental evidence suggests that the teaching of economics does have an effect on students' behavior: It makes them more selfish and less concerned about the common good. This is not intentional. Most teachers are not aware of what they are doing.

My colleague Gary Becker pioneered the economic study of crime. Employing a basic utilitarian approach, he compared the benefits of a crime with the expected cost of punishment (that is, the cost of punishment times the probability of receiving that punishment). While very insightful, Becker's model, which had no intention of telling people how they should behave, had some unintended consequences. A former student of Becker's told me that he found many of his classmates to be remarkably amoral, a fact he took as a sign that they interpreted Becker's descriptive model of crime as prescriptive. They perceived any failure to commit a high-benefit crime with a low expected cost as a failure to act rationally, almost a proof of stupidity. The student's experience is consistent with the experimental findings I mentioned above.

In other words, if teachers pretend to be agnostic, they subtly encourage amoral behavior without taking any responsibility. True, economists are not moral philosophers, and we have no particular competence to determine what is ethical and what is not. We are, though, able to identify behavior that makes people better off. When a theater catches fire, the individual incentive is to rush to the exit as fast as possible. Yet if everyone in the audience rushed at once, the crowd near the door would allow fewer people to escape – indeed, many could die. Not surprisingly, there are social norms against this behavior. People who violate those norms are judged rude, egotistical, ill-behaved, or in certain cases even criminally negligent.[27]

Pedagogy of the economistic kind does not teach or focus on rules and norms, as Zingales clearly states. Very few business programs offer mandatory ethics classes. In those ethics classes that do exist, the focus lies mostly on identifying ethical dilemmas and learning various perspectives in order to discuss potential solutions (through utilitarian, deontological, and/or virtue lenses).[28] While the usefulness of such classes is in question, it is apparent that the effect they currently have is minimal. Even at their best, the ability of one ethics class to counter the dominant narrative of amoral business behavior is to be doubted.

Policy: Even though, for some, the assumed opportunism of homo economicus calls for a heavy hand and top-down regulation or control, *Pure Economism* suggests that markets in themselves provide the best form of control. As a result, in the perspective of *Pure Economism* markets are cherished as the solution to all human problems. Michael Sandel, representing the liberal spectrum,[29] and Roger Scruton,[30] representing the conservative spectrum, have challenged the "markets above all view." The financialization of public life has long been criticized, despite the dominant trend to see markets and privatization as the solution to practically any ill, be it education, public health, defense, etc. ... Critics challenge the marketization of society, and what Sandel calls the "market society" – the ideal of pure economism – where a transaction rather than a relation is the final word on everything:

> If you look at it, we have drifted over the last three decades from having a market economy, to becoming a market society. A market economy is a valuable and effective tool for organizing productive activity. But a market society is a place where everything is up for sale. It's a way of life, where market values reach into every sphere of life. That can be everything from family life in personal relations, to health, education, civic life, and civic duties.[31]

The pure economistic view pushes, for example, for vouchers in school systems, for monetary incentives for voting, or for paying students to read books. In the wider context, financialization is the desired goal, and the role of public policy is to support it. In *Pure*

Economism, the role of the government is to use markets to provide efficient management of the economy *and* society.

Archetype 2: Bounded Economism

The *Bounded Economism* archetype represents very similar ideas to the *Pure Economism* archetype, yet there is an intentional limit on the reach of marketization. Human beings are viewed in a more enlightened way, acknowledging the relevance of the basic four evolutionary drives. Equally, the commodification of human beings is bounded by legal strictures, norms, and attitudes. Human beings are viewed as human resources *with rights*. Sometimes people use the term "human capital" to denote the increased respect and value that human beings bring to the production system. Greed, as the character Gordon Gekko suggests, is viewed as a central feature of human aspiration, yet needs to be curbed and controlled. Opportunism is not wholeheartedly endorsed, and "cheating behavior" requires punishment. Dignity, as a category of intrinsically valuable traits, including trust, wisdom, or responsibility, can play a role. Yet these traits enter the fray as a means to the end of wealth creation, so that trust and wisdom enter the conversation mostly to facilitate performance. A typical statement to demonstrate *Bounded Economism* would be: "Corporate Social Responsibility is good *because* it adds to the bottom line."

Research: The research focus of the *Bounded Economism* archetype is centered on the protection of human dignity, whilst accepting the overall aim of wealth creation. Research within this archetype allows for a broader conceptualization of human beings as requiring a baseline fulfilment of the basic drives to acquire, bond, comprehend, and defend. In addition, the research involves an acceptance and focus on the relevance of the legal strictures and cultural norms which protect basic human rights. Business ethics research on human rights and human rights violations by corporations, for example, is representative of *Bounded Economism*. Still, the main focal point within this archetype is to understand the dignity-related phenomena within the

context of their connection and contribution to economic performance, rather than flourishing and well-being creation.

Bounded Economism lends itself to studying people under
market conditions with a certain enlightened approach to human
nature. Marketing research or, more specifically, consumer research
does often focus on aspects of human nature that stem from
bonding needs or comprehension needs. Similarly, research in the
field of human resource management touches on dignity-related
issues in order to explain performance outcomes. Research in this
archetype can further focus on the effects of mechanistic dehumanization on wealth creation, as is done in sociology and psychology.[32] Following Haslam's categorization, research can explore
how the absence of humaneness along the effects of inertness,
coldness, rigidity, passivity and superficiality influences organizing
practices.[33] Furthermore, this archetype also includes research on
the effects of reintroducing human nature into wealth creation via
emotional responsiveness, interpersonal warmth, cognitive openness, agency, and personal depth. Bounded Economism research
considers, for example, the impact of emotions, compassion, mindfulness, entrepreneurial activity, and character on financial
performance.

While many of the above topics are of interest in organizational behavior research, they are almost always presented in a
manner that justifies firm performance as a relevant dependent
variable. As an example of many such studies, organizational
scholars around Fred Luthans study the effects of psychological
capital on employee performance.[34] Observers suggest that organizational behavior research often adopts the angle of the dominant
search for financial performance to legitimize a human dignity-
related research focus,[35] thus fitting in the *Bounded Economism*
archetype.

Practice: The *Bounded Economism* archetype of management
is common in much of management practice, and would seem to
represent the majority of practice within Western economies. The

use of slave/child labor and sweat shops is illegal in this archetype, and laws protecting human rights, worker rights, consumer rights, etc. exist and are typically enforced. These laws and norms provide the frame for such "bounded economistic" practice, which still focuses on the goal of profit maximization. On the global level, however, such rules and legislation are difficult to enforce, so that many Western companies that behave legally within their home country do not do so overseas. Examples within the textile industry, such as the Rana Plaza incident that killed more than 1,000 workers in a building collapse,[36] showcase such problems. More enlightened practitioners understand that their legitimacy depends on protecting human dignity at some basic level. Many of these practitioners sign voluntary compacts to ensure practices that aim to protect dignity.

Among the various global initiatives, the United Nations Global Compact established in 2000 is worth highlighting. The Global Compact was co-created by business practitioners and public policy makers who understood the need to fill a void for human dignity as well as environmental protection (with dignity as a category). As the current website states, the Global Compact is

> A call to companies to align strategies and operations with
> universal principles on human rights, labor, environment and anti-
> corruption, and take actions that advance societal goals.[37]

Most global companies have signed the Global Compact, but its critics note that they often do so out of expedience rather than true ethical commitment.[38] Instances of companies such as Siemens fundamentally violating the Global Compact are common, as the compliance standards are rather low and enforcement is weak.

The rationale that companies give for joining such efforts is often couched in an economistic logic that present concerns for dignity as a benefit that contributes to the business case for earning more profit. Even the reasons given to encourage companies to join the Global Compact are couched in an economistic language of cost and benefit. Again, the website states that the Global Compact is:[39]

> A win-win for business and society. The connection between the bottom-line and a company's environmental, social, and governance practices is becoming clear:
>
> **How will I benefit?**
> **It's good for business.** Corporate and organizational success requires stable economies and healthy, skilled and educated workers, among other factors. And sustainable companies experience increased brand trust and investor support.
>
> **It's good for society – and business really *can* make a difference.** Companies offer fresh ideas and scalable solutions to society's challenges – exactly what we need to create a better world. More than 8,000 business participants and 4,000 non-business participants in the UN Global Compact are already changing the world. They're helping alleviate extreme poverty, address labor issues, reduce environmental risks around the globe, and more.

While the case for societal well-being is made, it is interesting to note that the ultimate reasoning here is the contribution of such dignity-protecting practices to the financial bottom line. The results of a study are shown prominently:

> **CEO's agree that sustainable practices matter:** 93% say it is important to the future success of their business, 80% see it as a route to competitive advantage in their industry and 78% view it as an opportunity for growth and innovation.[40]

Practice within *Bounded Economism* aims to protect dignity to ensure profitability.

Pedagogy: The educational paradigm in *Bounded Economism* focuses on teaching the basics of the "pure economistic" approach within certain limits. Rather than building on narrow homo economicus assumptions, pedagogy engages a wider anthropological framework that addresses the fundamental social (dB) and intellectual nature (dC) of human beings. Nevertheless, the educational goal remains wealth creation. Classes in marketing, consumer behavior, human resource management, and organizational behavior, along with compulsory ethics classes or business law classes reflect the principles of bounded economism. Luigi Zingales, as well as many others, view the future of business education within the framework of *Bounded Economism*. They argue that many more business schools need to reflect the value of norms, laws, and societal consequences of business transactions:

> When the economist Milton Friedman famously said the one and only responsibility of business is to increase its profits, he added "so long as it stays within the rules of the game, which is to say, engages in open and free competition without deception or fraud." That's a very big caveat, and one that is not stressed nearly enough in our business schools.[41]

Pedagogy within *Bounded Economism* aims to provide boundaries to purely economistic behavior.

Policy: Within *Bounded Economism*, public policy needs to take an active role in limiting *Pure Economism* to the degree that it ensures the protection of human dignity. It is a limited laissez faire approach with boundaries. This is an approach that, with careful reading of the original sources, was advocated by many of the so-called fathers of modern economics. As Roger Scruton argues,

> Left-wing thinkers often caricature the conservative position as one that advocates the free market at all costs, introducing competition and the profit motive even into the most sacred precincts of communal life. Adam Smith and David Hume made clear, however, that the market, which is the only known solution to the problem of economic co-ordination, itself depends upon the kind of moral order that arises from below, as people take responsibility for their lives, learn to honor their agreements and live in justice and charity with their neighbors. Our rights are also freedoms, and freedom makes sense only among people who are accountable to their neighbors for its misuse.[42]

It can similarly be argued that both Milton Friedman[43] and Friedrich von Hayek[44] called for the bounding of the markets by law, and that the government had an important role to uphold boundaries to "dog-eat dog" competition. Likewise, Michael Sandel points out that public policies within *Bounded Economism* recognize that human beings are acting not only as market participants but also as citizens. He calls for limits to markets and the financialization of societal life, such as limiting the privatization of prisons, the privatization of military activity, and other civic duties.[45] Henry Mintzberg in his latest book *Rebalancing Society* also calls for much stronger boundaries to private sector activity.[46]

Archetype 3: Enlightened Economism

In the *Enlightened Economism* archetype, human beings are viewed as endowed with dignity. In addition, the guiding assumption is that human beings wish to promote their dignity through personal development. In other terms, human beings need to achieve a minimum balance of the evolutionary drives and expect to develop a higher-level balance in order to flourish. The main distinction here is that humans not only want to satisfy their basic drives at a minimum level but also want to balance the four drives at ever higher levels. Organizations then need to facilitate that development to include a sense of accomplishment (dA), a sense of personal connection (dB), a sense of deeper purpose (dC), as well as a sense of community and safety (dD). A central focus in organizing practice rests on the development of faculties that are intrinsically valued, such as aesthetic and artistic dexterity, or wisdom, trustworthiness, and character. However, the ultimate objective is to increase performance and wealth. Melé therefore calls this archetype "Masked Economism," where protecting and promoting people's dignity serves as a means to higher financial gains.[47]

Research: In *Enlightened Economism* the notion of dignity plays a dominant role. Within this archetype, management research not only embraces the notion of human dignity but attempts to understand how it can be developed and promoted. However, such dignity promotion is examined within the organizing goals of wealth creation. As such, only those efforts to promote dignity that effectively support wealth creation are included in such theorizing. Melé suggests that such efforts are studied in more developed economies that tend to rely more on individual creativity for economic success.[48] Research that examines how animalistic dehumanization and the restoration of human uniqueness affect wealth creation, would fall into this archetype.[49] Such theorizing would involve all the different aspects that hamper dignity development, such as uncivil treatment, coarseness, amorality, a lack of self-restraint, instinct-based behavior, and personal immaturity. It would also involve all aspects that restore human uniqueness by fostering civility, refinement, moral sensibility, reason, and maturity.[50]

Research conducted within the Academy of Management that most closely resembles this archetype can be found across several divisions, including Social Issues in Management or Organizations and the Natural Environment. The overarching logic presented is that fully flourishing people and organizations will produce better business results. While there is increasing evidence for that, the overarching logic puts human dignity concerns in the service of wealth creation. For example, when examining the role of civility in the form of stakeholder management or organizational culture, some research decidedly focuses on the connection between such dignity-promoting/demoting activities and their impacts on financial performance. Organizational scholar Shawn Berman and colleagues examine how different approaches to stakeholder management (strategic and intrinsic) impact firms' financial performance.[51] Sustainability scholars Sanjay Sharma and Harrie Vredenburg highlight how the development of moral and sustainability-related capabilities in firms can support competitive advantages.[52] Diversity scholar Orlando Richard and colleagues examine how the management of diversity leads to better financial performance.[53]

Practice: The *Enlightened Economism* archetype of management can be found in an increasing number of businesses. Conscious

Business, Conscious Capitalism, or Business with Purpose are only a few of the ever more popular labels. It seems that many business practitioners have understood that human beings are not only human resources but that they are their most "important assets." For that reason, people need to be engaged, trained, and developed. Clearly the notion of human beings as assets is meant to highlight the value of human beings to the business, but also connotes that the main purpose of a human being is to service the wealth creation of the organization.

The dominant discourse for promoting practices of *Enlightened Economism* revolves around the business case. The business case for sustainability, for example, attempts to put the appreciation of the intrinsic value of a healthy environment into the language of cost-benefits.[54] Similarly, Corporate Social Responsibility is hailed as a means of boosting employee engagement.[55] Studies show that employees enjoy volunteering and appreciate a company more if it is engaging in CSR activities. The reason why many companies now do so is partly to regain lost legitimacy, but also to increase performance as well as bottom line results.

Pedagogy: Pedagogy in *Enlightened Economism* draws on a wide array of disciplines including management, but also from the liberal arts. Many of the best-known economistic companies, including investment banks and consulting agencies, prefer to hire liberal arts students rather than business students. They do so because the liberal arts provide these students with a richer educational experience and a broader perspective on life. Goldman Sachs famously is hiring their second largest cohort from students with liberal arts background. The firm is convinced, rightly or wrongly, that liberal arts majors bring, "a unique perspective and set of skills to the table."[56] They do so also to buffer against operational risk. Tim Skeet, managing director of RBS capital markets, has invested liberal arts graduates with special powers to prevent finance types from going astray: "If going through this crisis we had had a few more people who could have said – look, explain that to me in plain English ... I think we might have avoided some of the problems."[57]

While that might indicate that the liberal arts degree is regaining lost luster, business education in the *Enlightened Economism* archetype typically draws on all kinds of educational experiences to make students more marketable.

Policy: The *Enlightened Economism* archetype encompasses all policies that relate to what Henry Mintzberg calls "adjectival capitalism":

> Proposals for adjectival capitalism are springing up like
> mushrooms: we have Sustainable Capitalism, Caring Capitalism,
> Breakthrough Capitalism, Democratic Capitalism, Conscious
> Capitalism, Regenerative Capitalism, Inclusive Capitalism – and
> I have probably missed a few. Democratic Capitalism probably tells
> it best: capitalism is the noun, democracy is just the adjective.[58]

There is increasing awareness that business as usual does not work anymore. The proposals in this archetype accept that capitalism and wealth creation are the dominant goal of organizing, yet prefer to improve upon it. In *Enlightened Economism* the role of public policy is to help organizations do less or no harm and help elevate sustainable, regenerative, democratic, or conscious practices to achieve prosperity.

Archetype 4: Bureaucratic Paternalism

In the *Bureaucratic Paternalism* archetype, the organizing objective shifts toward well-being. Wealth creation can play a role in that it becomes a *means* to achieve well-being. Nevertheless, in *Bureaucratic Paternalism* well-being is achieved without particular consideration to human dignity. The freedom and autonomy needed to address the four independent drives above the dignity threshold do not figure centrally. It is thus conceivable that in the name of "well-being," individual dignity is neglected. Therefore *Bureaucratic Paternalism* provides room for authoritarian and possibly even totalitarian organizational forms. It has been argued with good reason that in the guise of welfare or well-being, human liberty and dignity can be abused.[59]

Even in its more benign forms, *Bureaucratic Paternalism* can be authoritarian and undermine respect for human dignity.

Research: In *Bureaucratic Paternalism* research, the notion of dignity does not play a role, yet some form of well-being is assumed to be the overarching goal of organizing. Economists Lee Alston and Joseph Ferrie define paternalism as an implicit contract in which workers trade faithful service for nonmarket goods (such as well-being).[60] This could be the safety of a tribe, the health of a community, or the education of group. Many such goals can be achieved through paternalistic, bureaucratic, and authoritarian rule, such as in public administrations or military units. Sociological studies of bureaucratic routines and paternalistic practices represent research in this archetype.[61] Such research suggests that paternalistic practices reduced the monitoring of labor and turnover costs in cotton cultivation in the US South until the mechanization of the cotton harvest kicked in in the 1950s.[62] Research within the *Bureaucratic Paternalism* archetype is most prevalent in welfare economics, the sociology of organizations, the field of international management, and the general study of organizing practices of the military, government, and family businesses. *Bureaucratic Paternalism* is also reflected by management scholars such as Sheila Puffer and Daniel McCarthy who examine the role of paternalistic attitudes in their study on entrepreneurship in Russia.[63] Similarly, Lane Kelley and Clayton Reeser find vestiges of paternalistic culture in American managers of Japanese descent.[64] Dirk Matten and Jeremy Moon (2008) theorize why there are different approaches toward CSR practices and suggest that paternalistic cultural legacies explain the role of explicit versus implicit CSR attitudes.[65] Scholars of leadership and mentoring present similar cultural effects.[66]

Practice: *Bureaucratic Paternalism* in practice can be found in public administrations including the military and government bureaucracies. These organizational forms use command and control structures to create well-being. The *Bureaucratic Paternalism* archetype can also be found in various organizational practices of the nineteenth and early twentieth century in Western Europe and the United States. Companies led by strong founders like Werner von Siemens, Robert Bosch, or Henry Ford were concerned for their workers' welfare, built housing for their employees, as well as entire cities. These businessmen often acted like statesmen rather than profit maximizers. The Tata Group in India is also credited with working toward the well-being of its country,[67] and is building a state within the state for its workers. *Bureaucratic Paternalism* practices are often rooted in larger cultural practice. Businesses in Latin America, Asia, and Africa are often run "like a family."[68] As a result, a "strong" leader or a benevolent dictator is an acceptable and often desirable leader, and hierarchical practices in which men more frequently than women make key decisions, are justified.

Pedagogy: Pedagogy within *Bureaucratic Paternalism* aims to educate wise and benevolent administrators. Neglecting the idea of universal dignity, education is often aimed at the elite. Various disciplines can form the basis for such elite education, including law, public administration, the classics, or the liberal arts. In France, for example, the highest level bureaucrats are mostly recruited from the Ecole Nationale d'Administration (ENA). The education provided at ENA focuses on administrative law, and equips graduates to take leadership roles within the administrative hierarchy. In the British Empire and in Imperial China, such administrative elites were prepared mostly through the study of the classics. In many countries to this day, the study of the liberal arts is still central to the formation of future leaders. In the United States, many of the leading educational institutions, such as the Ivy League schools, offer a humanities-heavy curriculum, and expect their graduates to take on various leadership positions in public and private administrations.

Pedagogy in *Bureaucratic Paternalism* is focused on creating professional administrators who ideally aim to improve the public good, yet don't necessarily have a particular concern for universal human dignity.

Policy: *Bureaucratic Paternalism* encourages policies that support administrative structures to create well-being. The welfare state is an ideal of a paternalistic policy in which individual dignity and freedom may be less relevant than the idea of giving everyone a better life. Such policies can sometimes take on autocratic or "socialistic" bents, as witnessed in Venezuela under Presidents Chavez and Maduro.

Archetype 5: Bounded Humanism

In *Bounded Humanism*, the organizing objective remains well-being, yet there is a central focus on valuing human dignity to prevent autocratic and paternalistic practices. Human beings are valued in themselves, which reflects on organizational practices in terms of decision-making, governance, and strategy. Scholars suggest that the metaphor of community and family are helpful to an understanding of organizing practices within this archetype. Yet the distinction between *Bureaucratic Paternalism* and *Bounded Humanism* rests in the accordance and protection of individual freedom and autonomy. Transcending the individual, *Bounded Humanism* embraces the practices that are intrinsically valuable for the creation of a functioning community. Such practices can relate to building and maintaining social trust, responsibility, and wisdom.

Research: In the *Bounded Humanism* archetype, management theory operates according to the assumptions that human dignity is protected and that the overall aim of organizing is well-being creation. Research is mostly focused on how organizing practices can protect dignity, not necessarily on how they can actively promote it. As such, researchers study managerial activities that will not endanger physical, psychological, or social well-being. Research following this management theory archetype accepts the relevance of legal strictures and the cultural norms protecting human rights, and examines how related phenomena affect well-being creation. The work of many members of the Critical Management Studies (CMS) division at the Academy of Management falls into this archetype. These scholars actively criticize the prior archetypes as dehumanizing.[69] Similarly, studies on the effects of workplace bullying related to well-being fall into this category.[70] When the purview of research extends to the well-being creation of external stakeholders, the areas of normative stakeholder management, nonprofit management, as well as public administration often fall into this archetype as well.

Practice: *Bounded Humanism* practice can be witnessed in many NGOs, churches, and some family-run businesses that wish to contribute to the community. For benefit corporations (B-Corps) and social enterprises similarly reflect *Bounded Humanism*, as they aim to protect human dignity while contributing to the common good. These organizations recognize the intrinsic value of human beings; that is why they are in existence. Grameen Bank, for example, is an organization that set out to decrease poverty through microloans. Starting in Bangladesh, Grameen Bank gave out small loans mainly to women so they could buy the equipment necessary to launch businesses, such as sewing machines. Prior to Grameen Bank, these women had no access to loans other than loan sharks. Grameen Bank founder Muhammad Yunus considers credit a fundamental human right and therefore worked tirelessly to ensure that that right was protected. Another example of *Bounded Humanism* in practice is an organization of lawyers in New York City which helps minorities to understand their legal rights. This organization even sponsors legal action in cases of discrimination. In both cases, organizational practices focus on protecting the dignity of minorities. Wealth creation is not the main point, even though wealth creation can be used to promote well-being, such as in the case of Grameen Bank.

Pedagogy: Within *Bounded Humanism*, pedagogy is often focused on understanding the deeper meaning of well-being. Questions such as "What does it mean to lead a good life?" are central to the educational experience. Philosophy, theology, and other disciplines clearly guide such inquiry. Equally relevant is an understanding of the rights that need to be protected, so that this type of education is often to be found in professional schools, including schools of education, social service, and law. Within the field of management, leadership is often a topic that allows for the exploration of practices within the *Bounded Humanism* archetype. Increasingly business schools offer courses in nonprofit leadership, social entrepreneurship, and community organizing. Such classes are based on the assumption of human beings as endowed with dignity, and aim to contribute to well-being rather than wealth creation.

Policy: *Bounded Humanism* is represented by policies that support the protection of human dignity, often through the vehicle of human rights. Human rights policies feature centrally within *Bounded Humanism* because it is assumed that when human rights are protected well-being is increased. The application of policies that support companies operating outside of the profit maximizing logic also fall within the category of *Bounded Humanism*. An example is the push for laws in the United States to allow companies to register as B-Corporations, which do not have to cater to shareholders primarily.

Archetype 6: Pure Humanism

In the *Pure Humanism* archetype, the organizing objective is still well-being, and dignity in its various forms is protected. The difference between *Bounded Humanism* and *Pure Humanism* is the latter's focus on promoting dignity through organizing practices. This may seem a small difference, yet it highlights an important aspirational shift. Within *Pure Humanism*, the formal protection of human dignity through the application of human rights is insufficient on its own; it is important to allow space for the co-creation of human development so that all people can flourish.

Research: Research in *Pure Humanism* is not only interested in finding out how organizing practices can advance the common good and *protect* dignity but also explores which practices can actively *promote* it. Organizational success is part and parcel of personal and stakeholder development. Within *Pure Humanism* the relevance of research is justified by explaining practices that contribute to stakeholder well-being or societal benefit, rather than traditional performance. *Pure Humanism* research is reflected in the budding fields of social entrepreneurship and social business.[71] Similarly, research that focuses on developing responsibility toward all societal stakeholders (aka people) (in addition to the protection of human rights) falls into this theoretical archetype.[72] Research that is based, for example, on Amartya Sen's capability development approach and its application within organizations is also reflective of *Pure Humanism*.[73]

Practice: *Pure Humanism* practices are reflected in some form of co-creation and self-management that advance the common good. Organizational researcher Frederic Laloux calls these humanistic practices "teal" practices.[74] Using Ken Wilber's integral theory, he suggests that some organizations achieve a higher level of consciousness that allows for organic self-organization and personal development. These organizations are organically organizing communities that are guided by a higher purpose than wealth creation. These practices reflect a higher level of consciousness, and promote the full human development of all people affected by the organization. Social enterprises, in many ways, embody such practices.

Pedagogy: In *Pure Humanism*, many of the disciplinary boundaries are blurred, and education becomes a vehicle for promoting human dignity. Education can be viewed as raising awareness and consciousness to foster character development. Pedagogical approaches can involve a combination of contemplation and action. The *Pure Humanism* educational experience does, however, need to translate such raised consciousness into meaningful practices that can affect the well-being of all involved. The organization Ashoka argues that education needs to be rethought to enable positive change-making skills. Such skills may be rooted in empathy, and expressed through an ability to co-create meaningfully. To do that successfully, students need to assimilate knowledge across disciplinary boundaries, and need to be able to formulate solutions to global problems. While most universities are not currently set up to provide such advanced pedagogy, a promising attempt is being undertaken by a number of Ashoka U Changemaker Campuses.[75] While there has been much progress in recent years, pedagogy reflective of the *Pure Humanism* archetype is still in its infancy.

Policy: Similarly, policy in *Pure Humanism* is still emerging. Bill Drayton, the founder of Ashoka, formulated the ultimate goal of social entrepreneurship for everyone to become a positive change-maker. Public policy in the *Pure Humanism* archetype can aspire to support this universalist ambition to promote well-being. For everyone to become a positive change-maker, many institutions need to change, including businesses, NGOs, universities, hospitals, government agencies, etc. The guiding principle for such policies, that still require a lot more dedicated thought, is the creation of well-being for 100 percent of humanity, by respecting and promoting their dignity.

CONCLUDING REMARKS

As we can see, there is much work to be done to fill the gaps within the *Pure Humanistic* archetype. Practices need to be formulated, tried, and improved. Pedagogical models need to be invented and reinvented. Policies need to be developed and discussed. The following chapters provide suggestions of how such a transformation, from economistic organizing toward humanistic organizing, might be achieved without falling into the "bureaucratic paternalism" trap.

NOTES

1 Using ideal types as a way to gain conceptual clarity, Weber is very aware of their fictional nature. Against the tradition of positivism that deduce from observation, he suggests to work from conceptual premises. For him the "Ideal Type" never seeks to claim its validity in terms of a reproduction of or correspondence with social reality. Its validity can be ascertained only in terms of conceptual adequacy. I argue for the sake of exploring alternative management practices, ideal types can be helpful.

2 Shils, Edward A. and H. A. Finch (trans. and ed.), (1997) *The Methodology of the Social Sciences (1903–17)*, New York, Free Press, 90.

3 According to Weber, and Ideal type is formed from characteristics and elements of the given phenomena (e.g., dignity and well-being), but it is

not meant to correspond to all of the characteristics of any one particular case. It is not meant to refer to perfect things, moral ideal, or to statistical averages, but rather to stress certain elements common to most cases of the given phenomena.

4 There has been a long discussion in the literature about science being non-normative and purely descriptive. The author subscribes to the view that even a position about management science as non-normative is a normative stance.

5 Mintzberg, H. (2004). *Managers Not MBAs: A Hard Look at the Soft Practice of Managing and Management Development*. London; New York, Financial Times; Prentice Hall.

6 Hertz, N. (2013). *Eyes Wide Open: How to Make Smart Decisions in a Confusing World*. New York, HarperBusiness.

7 Boddy, C. R. (2011). "The corporate psychopaths theory of the global financial crisis." *Journal of Business Ethics*, **102**(2), 255–259.

8 Sandel, M. J. (2012). *What Money Can't Buy: The Moral Limits Of Markets*. New York, Macmillan.

9 Davis, G. F. (2009). *Managed by the Markets: How Finance Re-Shaped America*. Oxford, Oxford University Press.

10 Walsh, J. P., et al. (2003). "Social issues and management: Our lost cause found." *Journal of Management*, **29**(6), 859–881.

11 Collins, C. J. and K. D. Clark (2003). "Strategic human resource practices, top management team social networks, and firm performance: The role of human resource practices in creating organizational competitive advantage." *Academy of Management Journal*, **46**(6), 740–751.

12 Rosenthal, C. (2014). *From Slavery to Scientific Management*. Cambridge, MA, Harvard University Press.

13 Taylor, F.W. (1914). *The Principles of Scientific Management*. New York, Harper.

14 Rosenthal. *From Slavery to Scientific Management*.

15 The global textile industry and the Rana Plaza incident can serve as an example.

16 Pirson, M., and A. Gangahar. (2016). "Humanistic and economistic approaches to banking–better banking lessons from the financial crisis?" *Business Ethics: A European Review*, **25**(4), 400–415.

17 Ibid.

18 Shefrin, H. (2009). "Ending the management illusion: Preventing another financial crisis." *Ivey Business Journal*, **73**(1), 7; Pirson and Gangahar. "Humanistic and economistic approaches to banking–better banking lessons from the financial crisis?" 400–415.

19 Taibbi, M. (2010). *Griftopia*. New York, Spiegel & Grau.

20 Zingales, L. (2015). *Does Finance Benefit Society?* (No. w20894). Cambridge, MA, National Bureau of Economic Research.

21 Zingales, L. (2015). *Does Finance Benefit Society?*

22 For example: Argyris (1973). "Some limits of rational man organizational theory." *Public Administration Review*, **33**(May/June), 253–267; Ghoshal, S. (2005). "Bad management theories are destroying good management practices." *Academy of Management Learning and Education*, **4**(1), 75–91.

23 For example: Wang, L., D. Malhotra and J. K. Murnighan (2011). "Economics education and greed." *Academy of Management Learning & Education*, **10**(4), 643–660.

24 Netimpact (2011). "Undergraduate perspectives: The business of changing the world." *Business Schools Under Fire- Humanistic Management Education as the Way Forward*. W. Amann, M. Pirson, C. Diercksmeier, E. v. Kimakowitz and H. Spitzeck, eds. New York, Palgrave McMillan; Wang, Malhotra and Murnighan. "Economics education and greed." 643–660.

25 www.bloomberg.com/view/articles/2012-07-16/do-business-schools-incubate-criminals (accessed May 28, 2016).

26 Ibid.

27 Ibid.

28 Gentile, M., (Ed.) (2011). *Giving Voice to Values – A Novel Pedagogy For Values Driven Leadership*. Business Schools under Fire. London; New York, Palgrave McMillan.

29 Sandel. *What Money Can't Buy*.

30 www.spectator.co.uk/2014/01/the-right-way/ (accessed May 21, 2016).

31 http://blogs.spectator.co.uk/2013/05/michael-sandel-interview-the-marketization-of-everything-is-undermining-democracy/ (accessed May 28, 2016).

32 Haslam, N. (2006). "Dehumanization: An integrative review." *Personality and Social Psychology Review*, **10**(3), 252–264.

33 Ibid.

34 Luthans, F., et al. (2008). "The mediating role of psychological capital in the supportive organizational climate–employee performance relationship." *Journal of Organizational Behavior*, **29**(2), 219–238.

35 Walsh, J. P., et al. (2003). "Social issues and management: Our lost cause found." *Journal of Management*, **29**(6), 859–881.

36 www.globallabourrights.org/campaigns/factory-collapse-in-bangladesh

37 www.unglobalcompact.org/what-is-gc (accessed, May 23, 2016).

38 Knight, G., and J. Smith (2008). "The global compact and its critics: Activism, power relations, and corporate social responsibility." *Discipline and Punishment in Global Politics*. New York, Palgrave Macmillan, 191–213.

39 www.unglobalcompact.org/participation/join/benefits (accessed May 23, 2016).

40 www.unglobalcompact.org/participation/join/benefits (accessed May 23, 2016).

41 www.bloomberg.com/view/articles/2012-07-16/do-business-schools-incubate-criminals (accessed May 28, 2016).

42 www.spectator.co.uk/2014/01/the-right-way/ (accessed May 21, 2016).

43 Friedman, M. (1962). *Capitalism and Freedom*. Chicago, University Of Chicago Press.

44 Hayek, F. (1970). *Constitution of Liberty*. Chicago, University of Chicago Press.

45 Sandel. *What Money Can't Buy*.

46 Mintzberg, H. (2015). *Rebalancing Society: Radical Renewal Beyond Left, Right, and Center*. Oakland, CA, Berrett-Koehler Publishers.

47 Mele, D. (2009). "Current trends of humanism in business." *Humanism in Business: Perspectives on the Development of a Responsible Business Society*. H. Spitzeck, M. Pirson, W. Amann, S. Khan and E. von Kimakowitz, eds. Cambridge, Cambridge University Press, 170–184.

48 Ibid.

49 Haslam, N. (2006). "Dehumanization: An integrative review." 252–264.

50 Ibid.

51 Berman, S. L., et al. (1999). "Does stakeholder orientation matter? The relationship between stakeholder management models and firm financial performance." *Academy of Management Journal*, **42**(5), 488–506.

52 Sharma, S., and H. Vredenburg (1998). "Proactive corporate environmental strategy and the development of competitively valuable organizational capabilities." *Strategic Management Journal*, **19**(8), 729–753.

53 Richard, O. C., et al. (2004). "Cultural diversity in management, firm performance, and the moderating role of entrepreneurial orientation dimensions." *Academy of Management Journal*, **47**(2), 255–266.

54 Dyllick, T. and K. Hockerts (2002). "Beyond the business case for corporate sustainability." *Business Strategy and the Environment*, **11**(2), 130–141.

55 www.incentivemag.com/Strategy/Ask-the-Experts/Roy-Saunderson/Top-10-Ways-to-Use-CSR-to-Motivate-Employees/ (accessed May 26, 2016)

56 http://news.efinancialcareers.com/us-en/190592/banks-like-hire-liberal-arts-graduates-redux/ (accessed May 28, 2016).

57 Ibid.

58 www.mintzberg.org/blog/getting-past-adjectival-capitalism-fix (accessed May 28, 2016).

59 Friedman, M. (1962). *Capitalism and Freedom*. Chicago, University Of Chicago Press; Hayek, F. (1970). *Constitution of Liberty*. Chicago, University of Chicago Press.

60 Alston, L. J. and J. P. Ferrie (1993). "Paternalism in agricultural labor contracts in the US South: Implications for the growth of the welfare state." *The American Economic Review*, **83**(4), 852–876.

61 For example: Pentland, B. T. and H. H. Rueter (1994). "Organizational routines as grammars of action." *Administrative Science Quarterly*, **39**, 484–510.

62 Alston, L. J., and J. P. Ferrie (1999). *Southern Paternalism and the American Welfare State: Economics, Politics, and Institutions in the South, 1865–1965*. Cambridge, Cambridge University Press, 119.

63 Puffer, S. M. and D. J. McCarthy (2001). "Navigating the hostile maze: A framework for Russian entrepreneurship. " *The Academy of Management Executive*, **15**(4), 24–36.

64 Kelley, L. and C. Reeser (1973). "The persistence of culture as a determinant of differentiated attitudes on the part of American managers of Japanese ancestry." *Academy of Management Journal*, **16**(1), 67–76.

65 Matten, D. and J. Moon (2008). "'Implicit' and 'explicit' CSR: A conceptual framework for a comparative understanding of corporate social responsibility." *Academy of Management Review*, **33**(2), 404–424.

66 Chen, M. J. and D. Miller (2010). "West meets East: Toward an ambicultural approach to management." *The Academy of Management Perspectives*, **24**(4), 17–24; Ansari, M. A., et al. (2007). "Leader-member

exchange and work outcomes: The mediating role of perceived delegation in the Malaysian business context." *Academy of Management Proceedings*, **2007**(1), 1–6; Hunt, D. M. and C. Michael (1983). "Mentorship: A career training and development tool." *Academy of Management Review* ,8(3), 475–485.

67 Sharma, R. R. and S. Mukherji (2011). "Can business and humanism go together? The case of the TATA group with a focus on nano plant." *Humanistic Management in Practice*. London; New York, Palgrave Macmillan, 247–265.

68 See, for example, Thornberry, N. E., Rangan, S. R., Wylie, D. (1999): Casa Pedro Domecq, Harvard Business School Case, HBS Publishing, BAB004-PDF-ENG

69 Aktouf, O. (1992). "Management and theories of organizations in the 1990s: Toward a critical radical humanism?" *Academy of Management Review*, **17**(3), 407–431; Raelin, J. A. (2011). "The End of Managerial Control?" *Group & Organization Management*, **36**(2), 135–160; Ghoshal, S. and P. Moran (1996). "Bad for practice: A critique of the transaction cost theory." *Academy of Management Review*, **21**(1), 13–48.

70 Barker, M. C., et al. (2005). "Bullying down under: organisational strategies to address workplace bullying." *Academy of Management Proceedings*, **2005**(1), 1; Sutton, R. I. (2007). *The No Asshole Rule : Building A Civilized Workplace and Surviving One That Isn't*. New York, Warner Business Books.

71 Bornstein, D. and S. Davis (2010). *Social Entrepreneurship: What Everyone Needs To Know*. New York, Oxford University Press; Mair, J. and I. Marti (2006). "Social entrepreneurship research: A source of explanation, prediction, and delight." *Journal of World Business*, **41**(1), 36–44.

72 Carroll, A. B. (1991). "The pyramid of corporate social responsibility: Toward the moral management of organizational stakeholders." *Business Horizons*, **34**(4), 39–48; Waddock, S. (2008). "Building a new institutional infrastructure for corporate responsibility." *Academy of Management Perspectives*, **22**(3), 87–108.

73 Bartelheimer, P. and O. Leßmann (2012). "The capability approach: A new perspective for labor market and welfare policies?" *Management Revue*, **23**(2), 93–97; Canton, C. G. (2012). "Empowering people in the business frontline: The ruggie's framework and the capability approach."

Management Revue. The International Review of Management Studies, **23**(2), 191–216.

74 Laloux, F. (2014). *Reinventing Organizations: A Guide to Creating Organizations Inspired by the Next Stage in Human Consciousness.* Brussels, Nelson Parker.

75 See www.ashokau.org (accessed May 26, 2016).

PART II Applications of Humanistic Management

If management is to play an effective role in addressing the multiple global crises facing humanity, it needs to turn from the dominant economistic perspective toward a more humanistic one. In the following chapters, the guiding framework presented in Chapter 6 is used to explore this transition toward a more humanistic perspective on management research (Chapter 7), practice (Chapter 8), pedagogy (Chapter 9), and policy (Chapter 10) in more depth.

I develop each chapter along two conceptual pathways for transition: one pathway focuses on re-embedding the notion of dignity, the other on shifting the objective function toward well-being. These pathways allow for a clearer conceptual distinction yet are mutually reinforcing in practice.

Output	Role of Dignity (Input)		
	Neglected	**Protected**	**Promoted**
Wealth creation	Reality		
Well-being creation			Possibility

The framework highlights spheres of reality and possibility. The dark gray represent forms of organizing that we witness mostly in our day-to-day reality. The light gray represent forms of organizing we often hope for and which have shown to be feasible. Still, we need to learn and apply ourselves a lot more to what Donna Hicks calls the practice of being fully human. The upcoming chapters identify examples of our possibilities for better management research, practice, pedagogy, and policy. They are not naïve dreams, but clearly an inspiration for our human potential. Much needs to be learned to make the realm of possibility our day-to-day reality.

7   Developing Humanistic
       Management Research

This chapter argues that management research should dedicate itself to understanding managerial practices that improve the world. The overarching question for humanistic management research is how organizational practices can be transformed to protect and promote human dignity and, ultimately, achieve well-being and flourishing. There are several ways to transition toward this kind of humanistic management research. These pathways are represented in Figure 7.1.

ASSESSING THE CURRENT FOCAL POINTS OF MANAGEMENT RESEARCH

Management researchers should take stock and reflect why we do not know more about organizational practices that could address the current crises. They should question whether the amount of time and effort spent on research within the *Pure Economism* archetype is contributing to finding solutions or worsening the crises. Research within *Pure Economism* can provide important insights, especially into the phenomena it was designed to explain: exchanges in the marketplace. As such, it remains useful, but society needs researchers to study organizing practices that go beyond the market. Researchers need to ask themselves whether they ask certain questions simply because they fit into the dominant paradigm, or because they provide a secure "theoretical basis" rooted in economics. Why, for example, did the study of well-being start in economics and psychology, and not in management, where it should be highly relevant? These disciplines can provide critical insights, but management research should contribute to this and pioneer its own insights.

One of the reasons for this lag seems to be that "empiricism" is the dominant form of research and statistical analysis the most

Output	Role of dignity (Input)		
	Neglected	Protected	Promoted
Wealth creation	Pure economism	Bounded economism	Enlightened economism
Well-being creation	Bureaucratic paternalism	Bounded humanism	Pure humanism

FIGURE 7.1: Pathways toward humanistic management

legitimate way of generating results. Even Friedrich von Hayek, one of the intellectual guides of *Economism*, lamented:

> [I]n the social sciences often that is treated as important which happens to be accessible to measurement. This is sometimes carried to the point where it is demanded that our theories must be formulated in such terms that they refer only to measurable magnitudes.[1]

Phenomena such as well-being, trust, fairness, and justice – no matter how relevant to the human experience – will evade, at least initially, quantitative measurement and statistical analysis. There are clear advantages to statistical analysis, and many insights have been generated through it, especially when focal outcomes such as financial performance, are clearly measurable. Nevertheless, these methods' blindness to the human experience as fundamentally moral and social have critical disadvantages. In the guise of objective science, economistic research enforces what Ed Freeman calls the "separation thesis," which separates market exchange from social embeddedness, and ethics from business.[2] Such research is ill-equipped to promote insights into organizing practices that could solve current global social problems.

In a similar manner, researchers should reconsider the amount of time and effort spent on research within the *Bureaucratic Paternalism* archetype. Such research is often based on what Michael Jensen calls the "sociological" or "social victim" model.[3] It does not accord freedom or agency, but only explains outcomes by means of social structures, i.e., bureaucracy. While this type of research may be conceptually and historically relevant, it also reinforces the "separation thesis," as most administrative practices are disconnected from human dignity. This approach rarely helps explore organizational practices that enable people to live better lives.

Researchers interested in protecting and promoting human dignity should therefore put more emphasis on research within the spectrum that runs from *Bounded Economism*, to *Enlightened Economism*, and from *Bounded Humanism*, to *Pure Humanism*. Overall, the transition toward *Bounded/Enlightened Economism* is easier, as it extends the dominant paradigm. Consequently, many of the dominant research approaches, such as empiricism, can be adapted. Ultimately, the transition toward *Bounded Humanism* and *Pure Humanism* is more urgent if management research wishes to be more relevant, accurate, applicable, and legitimate in these times of crisis.

PATHWAY I: TRANSITION TOWARD DIGNITY-BASED RESEARCH

Humanistic management brings the idea of dignity (back) into management research. Research that puts dignity at its center will enable a better exploration of organizational practices and, simultaneously, (1) increase management research's theoretical accuracy, (2) extend its applicability, and (3) increase its legitimacy.

Reinstating the notion of dignity as a category can, for example, allow management researchers to study phenomena that evade the economistic paradigm. Integrity, trust, character, virtue, and love are all critical phenomena for successful human relations, but they fit badly into exchange logic. This logic assumes that something decreases when exchanged; for example, when Person A trades gold for beer, he has less gold to spend. However, integrity, trust, character, and virtue do not decrease when people embody them. If one person exhibits high integrity, he or she may inspire others to do the same. If another person trusts someone, reciprocity usually occurs, because trust begets trust. Character can be built and consciousness can grow, leading others to share in the growth of virtuous behavior. Some of these phenomena have gained more research attention in recent years, but are conventionally sidelined, accepted as relevant only when proven to be performance-relevant.

Similarly, reintroducing dignity as *unconditional* human dignity can increase management research's theoretical accuracy. This may be a contentious statement, but research indicates that, across religious and secular cultures, most people wish to be treated with dignity. A theory of management that integrates this fundamental human concern will provide more accurate information about good organizing practices than theories which do not.

Reinstating the notion of human dignity in its *conditional* form can help organizations consider dignity advancement as a goal.[4] Research suggests that most stakeholders regard advancing human dignity and well-being as a more legitimate and trustworthy organizational goal than profit maximization.[5] This holds especially true in times of crisis. Figuring out how organizational practices can help advance human dignity can be part of the solutions the world now needs.

Understanding the Notion of Dignity

A core endeavor for humanistic management research should therefore be to produce a better understanding of the notion of dignity. As suggested in Chapter 5, there are three broad areas that could benefit from a deeper exploration of dignity, because they relate to organizational practice:

- Dignity as a category for all that which is intrinsically valuable
- Human dignity as an unconditional intrinsic value
- Human dignity as a conditional, earned value.

Management research on each of these areas is rather sparse, but this does not mean it is nonexistent. Management research inspired by positive psychology is, for example, alive and well, although more dedicated research is needed to develop more conceptual depth. Similarly, theory development and theory testing need to be strengthened in this broad field.

Shifting Toward Bounded Economism

Shifting toward *Bounded Economism* would move research from a narrow focus on how one can organize human resources to achieve maximum profit, to exploring how organizational practices can protect human dignity within the context of achieving maximum profit. The guiding research question becomes: "Which organizational practices *protect* human dignity while creating more wealth?" Researchers could investigate breaches of dignity and their consequences for productivity or performance. A different notion of human nature, based on the insights presented in Chapter 3, could guide the transition toward *Bounded Economism* research. This notion can also focus on phenomena that evade the market and exchange logic (including trust, compassion, and mindfulness). Another starting point for inquiry could be the Universal Declaration of Human Rights (especially Articles 1–4, as well as 18–24), which provides ample substance for dignity protection research.

Relevant research questions might refer to the effects of the violation of dignity on individual, group, or organizational performance. This could occur at the employee, customer, or any other stakeholder level. To do so epistemologically, it may help to use approaches that measure notions of dignity and human rights, including physical, psychological, and relational health. While the psychology field offers numerous types of assessment that have increasingly played a role in organizational behavior research, there may be new areas that have eluded systematical research. The impact of emotions, compassion, mindfulness, creativity, and character on firm performance could, for example, also receive more attention.

Example: From Agency Theory to Integrity

A reconsideration of human nature is foundational in the transition toward more humanistic management research. As previously mentioned, Michael Jensen has been one of the main proponents of the economistic paradigm. It is interesting to note that he shifted his perspective on human nature quite drastically over the past decade or so. He credits this shift to a large group awareness training program to help people realize their true potential. Owing to this program and more engagement with mindfulness and consciousness practices, he has since focused his research on the importance of integrity.

Once again, integrity is a concept that evades the market logic and is hard to measure quantitatively. Yet, as Jensen argues, it is a basic concept without which nothing works. His understanding of integrity required him to abandon his prior suggestion that everything has a price (see Chapter 3). Integrity, he says, requires firm commitments, not opportunistic advantage-seeking. In 2014 Jensen understood integrity as:

> An individual is whole and complete when their word is whole and complete, and their word is whole and complete when they honor their word. We can honor our word in one of two ways: first, by keeping our word, and on time; or second, as soon as we know that we won't keep our word, we inform all parties counting on us to keep our word and clean up any mess that we've caused in their lives. When we do this, we are honoring our word despite having not kept it, and we have maintained our integrity.[6]

In respect of the 2008 financial crisis, he views the notion of trust as critical – another concept that did not previously figure prominently in agency theory. He suggests that:

> Out-of-integrity behavior has been pervasive, both on an organizational and an individual basis. ... Putting the system back in order is deceptively simple: people have to start honoring their word. If they do, trust will materialize almost instantly. The interesting thing about it is that you actually create trust more

rapidly if you fail to keep your word but you honor it, because this is always so surprising to people. If you're straight with people – "I told you that I'd have this report done a month from now, but I know now that I'm not going to be able to and I apologize, but I'll get it to you in a month and a half. Let's have a talk about what I can do to clean up the mess I have caused for you." If I then get the report to you in a month and a half, our relationship will be strengthened; but if I simply don't keep my original word, trust will be lost.

The study of both concepts, integrity and trust, are another way to shift the focus away from *Pure Economism* more in the direction of humanistic practices.

Shifting to Enlightened Economism

The guiding research question when transitioning to *Enlightened Economism* research is: "Which organizational practices *promote* human dignity while creating more wealth?" In this area, research focuses on earned, conditional aspects of dignity, like human development and character development. In this archetype, research can employ the capability development approach promoted by Amartya Sen and Martha Nussbaum.[7] Complementing a human rights perspective with a human responsibility focus can also achieve the transition from *Bounded Economism* to *Enlightened Economism*. In the context of organizations, research is needed to establish the kind of responsibilities associated with certain human rights that produce higher levels of performance. Research can also examine how such responsibilities can be developed.

Martha Nussbaum's list of basic capabilities presents a possible conceptual and empirical starting point for such research. Her basic capability catalog includes: (1) life; (2) bodily health; (3) bodily integrity; (4) the full engagement of senses, imagination, and thought; (5) the ability to express emotions; (6) the ability to use practical reason; (7) the ability to affiliate with others; (8) being concerned about and living in harmony with animals, plants, and the natural world; (9) the ability to engage in play; and (10) the ability to exercise political and material control over one's environment.[8] These capabilities span various levels of analysis. Research that examines them can focus on capabilities at the individual, the group, and the organizational level, as well as the cultural and societal level.

Empirically, such research could be conducted in organizations that embrace conscious capitalism or long-term-oriented profit maximization. There are traces of such research in business ethics and in organizational behavior; but this is still underdeveloped and peripheral.

Example: From "Negative" To Positive Organizational Scholarship

Positive organizational scholarship represents another transition toward humanistic management research. The field emerged in the early 2000s as an application of positive psychology in the organizational context. Positive psychology has its roots in humanistic psychology, which is concerned with human flourishing. In the late 1990s, Martin Seligman, one of the founders of positive psychology, suggested that psychology had focused for too long and too excessively on what was wrong with people (negative psychology). He therefore argued that psychologists should more rigorously study what was right with people.

Positive organizational scholars took up the task and study human flourishing in organizational contexts. Scholars like Fred Luthans, Jane Dutton, Kim Cameron, and many others attempt to find ways of designing work settings so that they emphasize people's strengths. Their ambition is to determine which organizational practices help people be their best selves and be at their best with each other. They have examined a number of concepts that were previously considered mostly irrelevant for management research, such as compassion, forgiveness, empathy, mindfulness, and consciousness. These concepts can rarely be measured quantitatively, even though many types of psychometric scales can be developed. Nevertheless, research has shown that practices that protect human dignity have significant effects on organizational performance.

Challenges of and Opportunities for Shifting Within Economism

Measurement is a primary challenge when moving toward research that considers the protection of dignity and the promotion of dignity. By its nature, dignity cannot be priced, and attributing quantitative measures to dignity-related phenomena may be challenging. Moreover, the act of quantifying dignity-related aspects might feed into a professional and practical mindlessness that involves putting prices on elements that fundamentally evade the exchange logic. In addition, many dignity development practices will require longitudinal studies or qualitative research approaches, which are more time-consuming, less appealing, and less prevalent.

The underlying complexities of human nature form a secondary conceptual challenge. Building models of human behavior that reflect more recent scientific insight requires some form of reductionism. Again, the work of Paul Lawrence and the model of human nature presented in Chapter 3 may be helpful.[9]

Overarching research question:	Pathway 1: Dignity-related research questions:	
How can organizational practices be transformed to protect and promote human dignity and ultimately achieve well-being and flourishing?	What do the categories of dignity mean for organizational practice: • Dignity as a category for all that is intrinsically valuable? • Human dignity as an unconditional intrinsic value? • Human dignity as a conditional, earned value?	
	Bounded economism RQ: Which organizational practices protect human dignity while creating wealth? Potential research foci: • Violations/protections of human rights • Engagement of four independent drives • Mechanisms that evade exchange logic (integrity, compassion, emotions, mindfulness, trust, etc.)	*Enlightened economism* RQ: Which organizational practices promote human dignity while creating wealth? Potential research foci: • Human Development (e.g., advancing 4 drives, increasing consciousness) • Human Responsibilities • Human Capabilities
	Research method: Empiricism	Research method: Empiricism

FIGURE 7.2: Integrating dignity into management research – Pathway 1

The pragmatic benefit of transitioning toward *Bounded Economism* and *Enlightened Economism* is that the epistemological requirements for such theorizing fall within the dominant understanding of science as empiricism. It is possible for all aspects relating to dignity protection, as well as dignity promotion, to be quantified and, wherever possible, priced (quasi-priced). Such a transition would allow for a convincing presentation of how these aspects affect wealth creation, financial performance, or firm performance. It would also avoid a normative debate on the purpose of the firm, and could better legitimize management research.

PATHWAY 2: SHIFTING TOWARD WELL-BEING AS AN OUTCOME

Directly exploring the effects of organizational practices on well-being (see Figure 7.3) is another way of focusing research on how to ensure better lives and better organizations. Many leading economists and psychologist have suggested that we need to focus our research more directly on increases in well-being as a measure of success.[10] Management research at large has not yet done so. Therefore, the question "What exactly is well-being and how can you organize for it?" is another important area for humanistic management research.

Shifting toward well-being as an outcome requires many more conceptual debates. One of the main debates needs to focus on whether well-being should be understood as hedonistic or eudaimonic; whether well-being denotes pleasure and momentary enjoyment, or whether it is based on human flourishing in the longer term. Chapter 5 argues that the field should have a strong preference for a eudaimonic understanding, but more research and debate are needed. Another necessary debate centers on whether well-being should be understood as health, or primarily as life-satisfaction.[11] A third debate focuses on whether well-being is a state or a trait, which fundamentally influences the debate on whether and in which way organizational practice can influence well-being. All of these questions can probably be resolved, but require dedicated research efforts.

Questions of empirical assessment emanate from these conceptual questions. While it may be possible to assess hedonic well-being by measuring pleasure in the moment via surveys, brain scans, or blood pressure, it is more difficult to measure eudaimonic well-being as long-term flourishing. Similarly, a number of established medical measures can assess health, but life satisfaction is mostly based on subjective assessments. A number of compound indexes have been proposed for the individual level. The application of such measures at the organizational level remains a very important field of research.*

Martha Nussbaum and Amartya Sen present another perspective on assessing well-being.[12] Rather than focusing on outcome measures, they propose that researchers assess processes, such as stakeholder dialogues. Dierksmeier labels this approach "procedural humanism": A form of interaction and discourse that allows voices to be heard and does not impose any preconceived goals.[13] Accordingly, research should assess these procedural approaches, because they can more effective yield appraisals of well-being. Additional research is definitely needed to establish more clarity.

Shifting Toward Bounded Humanism

To shift management research to *Bounded Humanism*, the overarching research question becomes: "Which organizational practices protect human dignity while creating well-being?" Again, the Universal Declaration of Human Rights could be a point of departure when outlining research questions for such research. A study of the effects of human rights violations on individual, group, or organizational well-being, which could occur at the employee, customer, or any other stakeholder level, would be valuable. Further research could build on an expanded understanding of human nature, including the role of emotions, compassion, and the need for purpose in stakeholder well-being. Questions

---

* The Humanistic Management Network is collaborating with the OECD and other partners to close this gap.

about the ways human agency, including mindfulness, entrepreneurial activity, and character, can affect stakeholder well-being are another example of relevant research. As the former president of the Academy of Management Don Hambrick stated, management researchers should take responsibility for improving the management of all institutions, not only firms.[14] As such, *Bounded Humanism* research could actively include the study of all types of organizations.

Another area of particular relevance concerns the role of performance and well-being. While the study of the impact of well-being on performance is representative of the economistic archetypes, research in the *Bounded Humanistic* archetype could explore the inverse relationship: "How does performance affect the well-being of a number of stakeholders?" "Is there a linear relationship between performance and well-being, or a curvilinear relationship, such as an inverted U-shape?" In other words, would low performance and over-performance (measured in financial terms) cause low levels of perceived dignity and well-being?

A related area concerns the question of operating logic. While the "business case" logic dominates economistic archetypes, humanistic archetypes operate under the logic of an "impact case." "How can organizations impact well-being and therefore assess effectiveness and efficiency?" We are already aware of some of these effects, but more systematic research would be beneficial.

Example: Transitioning Corporate Governance Research

The field of corporate governance provides an example of how management research can shift from an economistic perspective to a humanistic perspective. As discussed in Chapter 4, the differing paradigms influence the way researchers look at organizations and their purpose. These paradigms also inform what they study and recommend as better governance practices.

As mentioned in Chapter 4, corporate governance research is currently biased toward *Pure Economism*. By building on homo economicus/ REMM assumptions, agency theory has become the most influential theory for the study of corporate governance. One of the main focal points of corporate governance research relates to how governance structures, mechanisms, and processes can ensure firm performance. Since agency theory assumes that principals (owners) and agents (managers) will behave antagonistically (which may be accurate), the research focuses strongly on who sits on the board of directors to control management. The main thrust of such research therefore explores who controls the managers (agents) and the means (i.e., stock options) they employ to ensure that the interest of the owners (principals) are safeguarded; that is, they will make more money.

Owing to the dominance of empiricism, research usually identifies a quantifiable input measure, a number of control measures, and looks for the effects on performance (mostly by using a regression analysis). In order to use such statistical analysis, researchers spend significant effort to identify board composition, board size, board members' diversity, nationality and gender, or the number of independent directors. They increasingly use sophisticated statistical analyses to explore the respective effects on firm performance, concluding that an xyz board composition is better or worse than another.

Such research is, of course, limited in a number of ways. First, researchers have to limit themselves to those organizations that release relevant data. Such information is mostly provided by publicly listed organizations. As a consequence, the results suffer from selection bias, because the majority of organizations in the world are small and not publicly listed; if they follow different approaches to governance this will be missed. Second, the focus on boards of directors assumes as a given traditional hierarchies in which control is best exercised from the top down. While this organizational form is relevant, other organizational forms of are systematically neglected. Third, the focus on the interaction between boards and managers limits studies to conflicts between shareholders and managers, although many other stakeholders are relevant for good corporate governance. Fourth, the resulting recommendations may be limited to, for example, the widespread use of stock options, or the best governance codes. Stock options were once considered a silver bullet for managing the agency problem. The argument was that if managers are compensated according to a company's market value, their interests are aligned with those of the shareholders. This argument was refuted when managers quickly found ways to manipulate market values and share prices, thus exacerbating the agency problem.

Other recommendations stemming from the economistic perspective, such as the reliance on independent or non-executive directors to better control managers, are, at the very least, questionable. In the wake of all the recent governance failures, from Enron to Lehman Brothers, scholars have concluded that management's cunning ways swayed directors too easily.[15] In the economistic logic, the introduction of "independent" directors should lead to better control of management's wayward ways. However, Shann Turnbull and others find that independent directors have very little knowledge of the organization, and therefore cannot pose the critical questions required to control the organization effectively. What appears logical from the economistic perspective, in which managers are largely viewed as opportunists, has led to structures that resemble a cat-and-mouse game in which the cat (i.e., management) always ends up with the upper hand. In his prolific research, Turnbull highlights other corporate governance paradoxes, such as the deleterious effects of "good governance" standards, which multiply agency conflicts via self-fulfilling prophecies.[16]

Humanistic perspectives on corporate governance help address some of these shortcomings. Adopting a different understanding of human nature (not only as amoral opportunists) allows us to study alternative approaches to dealing with governance problems. Stewardship theory, for example, builds on the social and moral nature of human beings, i.e., assumes that people want to contribute positively and constructively to a better organization. This shift in perspective can provide fundamentally different insights into good governance practices.

A central insight stemming from the humanistic perspective relates to the relevance and importance of trust and trustworthiness.

The trustworthiness of managers is obviously difficult to measure. Still, it is worth exploring why some organizations are resilient during crises, and how management and directors work together – rather than against each other – to ensure organizational success. For example, research has found that mutual trust between stakeholders and management is vital, because this enhances the exchange of critical information.[17] While there is some knowledge on how to build such trust, much more research is needed. Research might, for example, focus on the selection of trustworthy managers throughout the organization. A central question is how to detect psychopaths and prevent them from reaching positions of power. Such research will most likely not be possible by means of the traditional statistical regression model, but can be case-based, or make use of multiple narrative approaches.

To address other corporate governance shortcomings, research needs to focus on alternative governance structures. Rather than focusing on board composition, such research should identify the best support structure to enable managers to promote organizational and well-being-related goals. In research with Shann Turnbull, modeling approaches based on cybernetics were used to understand the processes that ensure better organizational outcomes (financial and well-being-related).[18] This research uses insights from across the natural sciences, and models governance structures that imitate those in nature (such as the brain).

These insights show, for example, that it is sensible to include multiple stakeholders in the governance process, not only directors, managers, and shareholders. Having employees, customers, investors, suppliers, and civil society actors involved in the governance process increases diversity and mimics what biologists call "edge-abundance." Edge-abundance is the effect that nature creates when two or more systems, such as a river and an ocean, come together.[19] At these edges, the potential for critical information to flow is very high. For example, it is possible to gather evidence from external stakeholders, such as brokers, who know that "many mortgage customers cannot afford their payments." It was exactly this increased information flow that protected some banks during the 2008 financial crisis.[20]

Shann Turnbull has long advocated multiple boards. This would provide the governance process with a better support structure than the unitary board system prevalent in Anglo-Saxon countries, or the two-tiered board systems found in continental Europe. He draws on cybernetics and neuroscience to suggest that hierarchical structures are less resilient than systems of parallel checks and balances.[21] This framework has long been implemented to govern nations. Montesquieu famously argued that three separate government branches (the executive, legislative, and judiciary), which check and balance one another, provide better governance than a unitary structure, i.e., a monarchy.[22] Interestingly, such structures mirror the arrangements of the brain, which does not have a central command structure, but has parallel checks and balances.[23]

Such insights are difficult to develop when researchers try to fit their work into the dominant perspective and rarely question its basic assumptions. Owing to an unholy alliance of research paradigm and methodology, most corporate governance research still views traditional board structures as a given. The onus is therefore on humanistic management research to showcase the relevance of other perspectives. Currently, such proof can only be delivered via case studies of organizations that defy the dominant economistic logic and whose governance systems humanistic scholars have examined, highlighting their relevance.

The John Lewis Partnership serves as an instructive example. The John Lewis Partnership is one of the largest UK retailers, running major department stores and supermarkets that its 69,000 employees own and control.[24] Its organizational objective is to promote the happiness of its partners. It does so by following the checks and balances system, and modeling its boards along executive, legislative, and judicial functions. Employees are "partners," and elect their representatives. The company involves all its employees in the governance process by means of Committees of Communication and

Registrars. These bodies allow any employee to provide the Branch Heads, Branch Councils, Central Council, Executive Committee, Board of Directors, and the Trustees with feedback. The employees directly or indirectly elect or appoint all such officers.[25]

Similarly, the customers of the cooperative Raiffeisen bank in Switzerland are included in its governance structure, which allows them to provide the management with feedback.[26] When the management incurs risks that are not well understood in the organization, customers can voice their concerns directly with the controlling board members. This approach allowed many smaller banks, credit unions, and savings associations to survive the 2008 financial turmoil.

Further evidence of the efficacy of more humanistic governance models can also be seen in the cooperative networks of Mondragón, a group of manufacturing and retail companies based in Spain.[27] Mondragón's 60,000 workers are also the owners of the more than 150 firms that constitute the network. Each of these 150 cooperatives has five separate boards: a supervisory board, a management board, a social council, a workers council, and many work units. The twelve super-ordinate organizing groups are similarly governed, with several independent boards fulfilling different functional tasks. Studies have reported that these firms have achieved unparalleled performance and resiliency in both good and bad times over many years.[28]

These types of organizations are rarely included in traditional economistic research, either because they are not publicly traded, because there are too few of them, or because they are too difficult to access. Another reason for the relative neglect by researchers of cooperative structures may also lie in these organizations' missing "fit" with the dominant economistic paradigm. Given the current crises in corporate governance, it might be time that alternative approaches are explored.

Shifting Toward Pure Humanism

To shift management research to *Pure Humanism*, the overarching research question becomes: "Which organizational practices promote dignity and achieve higher well-being?" Research in this area focuses on the earned, conditional aspects of dignity, like human development and character development. In this archetype, research might, for example, employ the capability development approach promoted by Amartya Sen and Martha Nussbaum.[29] The transition from *Bounded Humanism* to *Pure Humanism* can be achieved through the merging of a human rights perspective with a human responsibility focus. Research can establish the kind of responsibilities associated with certain human rights in the context of organizations in order to produce higher levels of stakeholder well-being. Research can also examine how such responsibilities should be developed.

As stated before, Martha Nussbaum's list of basic capabilities can serve as an empirical starting point for this research. Her catalog includes: (1) life; (2) bodily health; (3) bodily integrity; (4) the full engagement of senses, imagination, and thought; (5) the ability to express emotions; (6) the ability to use practical reason; (7) the ability to affiliate with others; (8) being concerned about and living in harmony with animals, plants, and the natural world; (9) the ability to engage in play; and (10) the ability to exercise political and material control over one's environment. These points span various levels of analysis, including the individual, the group, and the organization, as well as culture and society at large.

Research questions relate to the development of capabilities, as well as their effectiveness and efficiency in terms of improving well-being. The central question determines which practices enhance responsible behavior so that human welfare is ultimately advanced. Such research could be conducted empirically in social enterprises, NGOs, or B-corporations.

Example: From Corporate Strategy to Social Entrepreneurship
Michael Porter is considered one of today's most influential management researchers. As stated on his webpage, "Michael Porter is the founder of the modern strategy field and one of the world's most influential thinkers on management and competitiveness." He credits

his formal training in economics with providing the main insights for his work on competitive strategy. While he has dedicated most of his career to understanding competition and corporate strategy, he has in recent years discovered the power of collaboration.[30] He highlights the field of social entrepreneurship as an excellent example of collaboration, and credits social entrepreneurs with inspiring novel forms of strategy. In an article Michael Porter wrote with his colleague Mark Kramer, they suggest that corporations should examine the practice of social entrepreneurship more closely.[31] They argue that corporations can increase their legitimacy if they engage in the creation of well-being or "shared value creation."

The field of social entrepreneurship represents qualities of *Pure Humanism*. Social entrepreneurs find solutions to large and chronic global problems and aim to create well-being. Muhammad Yunus, one of the leading social entrepreneurs known for developing microfinance for deprived communities, suggests that there are two types of people and two types of organizations. The first category represents people who want to make money, and want to work for businesses that make money; the second type of people want to do good to others, and want to work for businesses that serve humanity.[32] When Yunus started his organization, Grameen Bank, the concept of social entrepreneurship was still in its infancy. Bill Drayton popularized the label in the 1980s[33], when he and his colleagues at Ashoka identified people who create large system changes, like Yunus. Drayton used "social" as a descriptor, because most "entrepreneurship" only seemed to capture the activities of people who want to make money. He described social entrepreneurs as people who solve the biggest social problems by entrepreneurial means. Their relentless pursuit of social change is one of the main ways of identifying them. Drayton suggests that social entrepreneurs cannot rest until they have fundamentally transformed society to eradicate a social problem. Muhammad Yunus, for example, talks about a society in which we have poverty museums, because he believes that humanity can get rid of poverty just like it eradicated polio. All descriptions of social entrepreneurs fundamentally challenge economistic assumptions about human nature. These dedicated human beings develop organizing practices that respect human dignity at its core, and are very resourceful in their endeavor to bring social change about in order to create well-being.

Countering the inadequacy of the economistic research paradigm, social entrepreneurship is becoming a respectable field of humanistic management research. Over the past decade, more researchers have started examining the emergence of social entrepreneurship. Much of the research draws on in-depth case analysis. Some researchers are also trying to abstract from case studies and build theory. New journals have emerged to capture this research and to support the institutionalization of the field.

Challenges and Opportunities

Measurement is a primary challenge for management research that embraces well-being as an outcome variable. Similar to dignity, well-being is a multifaceted concept. The outcome variable of management research may have to be reduced to measurable units, especially if the main research methodology is empirical. Finding such measures calls for concerted efforts and interdisciplinary collaboration.

More broadly, research in the *Bounded Humanism* and *Pure Humanism* archetypes involves challenges relating to theory building, because, in most cases, conceptual and possibly even qualitative case study research need to be conducted before embarking on more traditional quantitative research. Quantitative research could, however, be conducted within nonprofit organizations, social enterprises, for-benefit organizations, or public agencies.

Bounded Humanism and *Pure Humanism* research clearly challenges the epistemological bandwidth of traditional management research. A significant amount of conceptual research will is required to build theories, and include normatively engaged theorizing, as well as qualitative and anthropological research. Such research can help avoid oversimplification of both dignity and well-being, although these research approaches are unusual in the current management field.

Overarching research question: How can organizational practices be transformed to protect and promote human dignity and ultimately achieve well-being and flourishing?	Pathway 2 Well-being-related research questions: What exactly is well-being and how can one organize for it? How can well-being be assessed?	
	Bounded humanism Which organizational practices protect human dignity while creating well-being? Potential research foci: <ul><li>Violations/protection of human rights</li><li>Engagement of the four independent drives</li><li>Mechanisms that evade exchange logic (compassion, emotions, mindfulness, trust,etc.)</li></ul> Research method: Pluralistic (narratives, case studies, experiments, observation)	*Pure humanism* Which organizational practices promote human dignity while creating well-being? Potential research foci: <ul><li>Human development (e.g. advancing the fourdrives, increasing consciousness)</li><li>Human responsibilities</li><li>Human capabilities</li></ul> Research method: Pluralistic (narratives, case studies, experiments, observation)

FIGURE 7.3: Pathway 2 – Shifting management research toward well-being

Finally, research in *Humanism* poses an additional challenge regarding a required reengagement with ethics and the normative side of research. Those who consider science's prevailing paradigms objective, and who advocate value-free exploration, may find this suggestion problematic. McCloskey's suggestion to renew our understanding of social science as creation of narratives (rhetoric) may be helpful in this process.[34] Such a perspective could allow the development of shared global values that support the universalist notions of humanism. Such normative quests rarely form part of management research, but may open fruitful research avenues. The renowned theologian Hans Kueng's work on a global ethos, which elaborates the common values that connect the major religious cultures, may be of assistance in this regard.[35]

Different Approaches to Research

Noted management scholar Ed Freeman and his colleague David Newkirk argue that traditional management research faces three problems: the problem of research, the normative problem, and the

problem of the use of knowledge. The problem of research is connected to the dominance of positivism. The normative problem is
related to the understanding of management research as an objective,
amoral science. The problem of the use of knowledge is linked to a
false sense of certainty that positivistic research creates. Freeman and
Newkirk argue that what they call the "separation thesis," or the
"separation fallacy," lies at the heart of the issue, which is most
clearly evidenced in "the exclusion of ethics from business judgments
but generalizable as a duality between the worlds of management and
the humanities."[36]

Humanistic management reunites ethics and business judgment,
as well as management and the humanities. Consequently, research
methods that are useful to ethics, business ethics, and the humanities
are also helpful to management research. Humanistic management
research clearly requires a pluralism of research approaches. This
pluralism requires openness to different forms of knowledge and knowledge creation. Such an epistemological openness requires methodologies beyond empiricism. In traditional management circles, these
methodologies are often met with skepticism: "But this is not really
research." This form of epistemological openness is, however, required
when inviting various disciplines to come together.

Epistemological openness also requires a debate on normative
stances within social sciences and a priori knowledge, i.e., assumptions
regarding human nature. In the shift described in this book, the a priori
assumption that human beings are solely utility maximizers has been
replaced by the a priori assumption that human beings are endowed
with dignity that needs to be protected. It is assumed that the foundational aspiration of human beings is a eudaimonic type of well-being or
flourishing rather than mere wealth. Research suggests that an increasing number of people, including researchers from many disciplines
within the humanities, social sciences, and natural sciences, find these
assumptions an acceptable baseline, yet to some research traditions,
ethics and normative stances are considered "unscientific." The overarching question for humanistic management research of "How can

organizational practices be transformed to protect and promote human dignity, and ultimately achieve well-being and flourishing?" can be explored by employing differing methodologies, including statistical analysis and formal modeling. Before typical theory-testing methodology can be applied, however, we need much more conceptual research and a focus on theory development and theory building. Such conceptual work can be based on various disciplines, including theology, religion, philosophy, as well as literary theory. Freeman and Newkirk label such conceptual work "narrative theory." They suggest that "much can be learned from literary theory, narrative ethics, and other sources in the humanities where the scholarship of creative human activities consists largely of developing narratives that make sense of the outcome."[37] They also state that:

> We simply cannot blindly accept the dominant narrative of business and business schools, based on false positivism and the separation fallacy it encourages. Our challenge is to create rich new narratives that are ripe with human possibility and responsibility, that show us better ways to engage in value creation and trade.[38]

Sandra Waddock shares a similar perspective and argues for scholars to become healers or, as she says, "shamans."[39] They should set out to understand the problems, find cures, and help disseminate them. This type of research lends itself far more to clinical-style, case-based research. Telling stories about instances in which certain global and social problems were successfully addressed is critical for humanistic management research.

The fine arts informs another form of humanistic management research. Freeman and Newkirk point out that much can be learned from observing and engaging in creative performance.[40] By understanding art, music, theatre, or dance, we can gain further insights into human experience and flourishing. Such research will have to be rather personalized, subjective, and context-dependent, but can be critical for illuminating creative performances, which lie at the core of better organizing practices.

While the above list is clearly not exhaustive, the point is that that the transformation toward more humanistic management research requires foundational shifts, regarding not only *what* is studied but *how* it is studied. The transition also challenges the purpose of scientific research: To simply produce information or knowledge or to, ultimately, produce wisdom? In this sense, humanistic management aims to become philosophical in the original sense of the word, an ally of wisdom.

CONCLUDING REMARKS

This chapter suggests ways in which the humanistic paradigm can help transform management research. A first pathway focuses on bringing the notion of dignity (back) into management research. A second pathway focuses on the creation of well-being as an outcome of organizing practices. To illustrate how this transition has happened, or could happen, generic research questions were outlined and examples provided. These examples showcase how management research can contribute more directly to improving lives and addressing the various crises humanity faces. While some researchers shoulder this task, many more researchers are needed to understand organizing practices that can fully protect human dignity and promote well-being.

NOTES

1 Cited from Freeman, R.E. and D. Newkirk (2011). "Business school research: Some preliminary suggestions." W. Amann, M. Pirson, C. Diercksmeier, E. v. Kimakowitz and H. Spitzeck, eds. *Business Schools under Fire*. London; New York, Palgrave Macmillan. 278.

2 Freeman and Newkirk. "Business school research: Some preliminary suggestions."

3 Jensen, M. C. (2002). "Value maximization, stakeholder theory and the corporate objective function." *Business Ethics Quarterly*, 12(2), 235–257.

4 Margolis, J. D. (1997). Dignity in the balance: Philosophical and practical dimensions of promoting ethics in organizations, Harvard University. Ph.D;

Margolis, J. D. (2001). "Responsibility in organizational context." *Business Ethics Quarterly*, 11(3), 431–454.

5 Pirson, M., K. Martin and B. Parmar (2016). "Public trust in business and its determinants." *Business & Society*, 0007650316647950; Pirson, M. (2007). *Facing the Trust Gap: How Organizations Can Measure and Manage Stakeholder Trust*. St. Gallen, University of St. Gallen; Pirson, M., K. Martin and B. Parmar (2013). "Formation of stakeholder trust in business and the role of personal values." *Journal of Business Ethics*, 1–20, doi:10.1007/s10551-015-2839-2.

6 Jensen, M. C. (2009). "Integrity: Without it nothing works." *Rotman Magazine: The Magazine of the Rotman School of Management*, 99(2009), 16–20.

7 Nussbaum, M. (2003). "Capabilities as fundamental entitlements: Sen and social justice." *Feminist Economics*, 9(2–3), 33–59.

8 Nussbaum, M. (2011). *Creating Capabilities – The Human Development Approach*. New York, Belknap.

9 Lawrence, P. (2010). *Driven to Lead: Good, Bad, and Misguided Leadership*, San Fransisco, Jossey-Bass.

10 Fleurbaey, M. (2009). "Beyond GDP: The quest for a measure of social welfare." *Journal of Economic Literature*, 47(4), 1029–1075; Stiglitz, J. (2013). *The Price of Inequality*. New York, W.W. Norton; Sachs, J. b. J. (2005). *The End of Poverty: Economic Possibilities for Our Time*. New York, Penguin Group.

11 Kahn, R. L., and F. T. Juster (2002). "Well-being: Concepts and measures." *Journal of Social Issues*, 58(4), 627–644.

12 Nussbaum, M. (2011). *Creating Capabilities – The Human Development Approach*. New York, Belknap.

13 Dierksmeier, C. (2011). "Kant's humanist ethics." *Humanistic Ethics in the Age of Globality*, 79–93. London; New York, Palgrave Macmillan.

14 Hambrick, D. (1994). "What if the academy actually mattered?" *Academy of Management Review*, 19(1), 11–16.

15 Kirkpatrick, G. (2009). "The corporate governance lessons from the financial crisis." *OECD Journal: Financial Market Trends*, 2009(1), 61–87; Turnbull, S. (2002). *A New Way to Govern – Organizations and Society after Enron*. London, New Economics Foundation.

16 Turnbull, S. (2012). "The limitations of corporate governance best practices." *The Sage Handbook of Corporate Governance*. T. Clarke

and D. Branson, eds., chapter 19. London; Thousand Oaks, CA, Sage, 428–449.

17 Pirson, M. (2007). *Facing the Trust Gap: How Organizations Can Measure and Manage Stakeholder Trust*. St. Gallen, University of St. Gallen.

18 Pirson, M., and S. Turnbull (2015). "The future of corporate governance: Network governance-a lesson from the financial crisis." *Human Systems Management*, 34(1), 81–89.

19 See http://fieldguide.capitalinstitute.org/edge-effect-abundance.html.

20 Pirson, M. and S. Turnbull (2011). "Corporate governance, risk management, and the financial crisis: an information processing view." *Corporate Governance: An International Review*, 19(5), 459–470.

21 Turnbull, S. (1997). "Stakeholder governance: A cybernetic and property rights analysis." *Corporate Governance: An International Review*, 5(1), 11–23.

22 De Montesquieu, C. (1989). *Montesquieu: The Spirit of the Laws*. Cambridge, Cambridge University Press.

23 Lawrence, P. (2007). "Organizational logic - Institutionalizing wisdom in organizations." *Handbook of Organizational and Managerial Wisdom*. E. H. Kessler and J. R. Bailey, eds. chapter 3. Thousand Oaks, CA, Sage Publications.

24 www.johnlewispartnership.co.uk/about/our-constitution.html (accessed May 23, 2016).

25 www.johnlewispartnership.co.uk/about/our-constitution.html (accessed May 23, 2016).

26 Eckart, M. (2005). *Cooperative Governance: Cooperative Direction and Control as a Competitive Advantage*. St. Gallen, University of St. Gallen.

27 Turnbull, S. (1995). "Innovations in corporate governance: The mondragón experience." *Corporate Governance: An International Review*, 3(3), 167–180.

28 Thomas, H. and C. Logan (1982). *Mondragón: An Economic Analysis*. London, George Allen and Unwin; Pirson, M. and S. Turnbull (2011). "Toward a more humanistic governance model: Network governance structures." *Journal of Business Ethics*, 99(1), 101–114.

29 Nussbaum, M. (2011). *Creating Capabilities – The Human Development Approach*. Cambridge, MA, Belknap.

30 Roger Martin, a long-time collaborator of Michael Porter, suggests that Michael Porter has been moved by humanistic impulses all along and that my treatment here may be seen as dismissive. I am hoping it can be seen as illustrative on how the humanistic perspective can enrich our perspective on organizations and organizing. I do not intend to pass value judgments.

31 Porter, M., and M. R. Kramer (2011). "Creating shared value." *Harvard Business Review*, 89(1/2), 62–77.

32 Yunus, M. (2008). "Social entrepreneurs are the solution." *Humanism in Business: Perspectives on the Development of a Responsible Business Society*. W. Amann, M. Pirson, C. Diercksmeier, E. v. Kimakowitz and H. Spitzeck, eds. Cambridge, Cambridge University Press.

33 I have been told that the terms social entrepreneur and social entrepreneurship were used first in the literature in 1953 by H. Bowen on his book *Social Responsibilities of the Businessman*.

34 McCloskey, D. (1998). *The Rhetoric of Economics*. Madison, WI, University of Wisconsin Press.

35 Kueng, H. (1997). "A global ethic in an age of globalization." *Business Ethics Quarterly*, 7(3), 17–32.

36 Freeman and Newkirk. "Business school research."

37 Ibid. 284.

38 Ibid.

39 Waddock, S. (2015). *Intellectual Shamans*. Cambridge, Cambridge University Press.

40 Freeman and Newkirk. "Business school research."

8   Developing Humanistic Management Practice

When Sam Walton started his first store in Arkansas in 1945, he wanted to ensure that his family would have a secure and stable income because he had experienced what it meant growing up poor. In the early 1920s, his family had been forced to abandon their farm in Oklahoma due to a long drought. Later, the Great Depression of the 1930s made it hard for Walton to find stable employment. Growing up, Walton and his brothers all worked to help their family make ends meet, which was common at the time. When the Second World War ended, Walton wanted to help the many families like his own buy goods at everyday low prices. The concept became so successful that he went on to build a chain of stores, known today as Walmart. The company's success can be attributed to the many families who needed a store with a wide variety of products at affordable prices. Sam Walton died in 1992 – the richest man in the United States.

Walmart clearly served a societal purpose by allowing low-income families to afford everyday products. Using market principles and, increasingly, market dominance, Walmart could ask suppliers to bring their costs down. The lower costs were then passed on to the customers. Aiming to generate a profit imposed discipline on the company, while competition made the company focus even more on providing the lowest possible prices. This is a great approach. Who could dispute the many benefits? In many ways, Walmart is a symbol of how the market can work at its best, serving customers by providing products they could not otherwise afford.

How, then, did it happen that this large company, which uses the market so effectively, has become so vilified? According to a 2016 poll by *Fortune* magazine, both conservatives and liberals hate Walmart with a passion. *Fast Company* magazine dedicated several pages to the topic in its January 2003 issue, arguing that "[t]he giant retailer's low prices often come with a high cost. Wal-Mart's relentless pressure can crush the companies it does business with and force them to send jobs overseas."[1] Other observers contend: "Walmart has a long history of evading the law, abusing its workers, and suppressing strikes through illegal means,"[2] or list "10 reasons Wal-Mart is the worst company in America."[3] A best-selling book is titled: *How Walmart Is Destroying America (and The World): And What You Can Do About It.*

Obviously, Walmart is not alone, and many companies have faced a similar backlash. *Fortune,* for example, writes that the only saving grace for Walmart is that conservatives hate some Wall Street banks even more.[4] Articles and books abound with questions about corporate conduct. Published rankings of reputation, trustworthiness, and responsible conduct have proliferated, and generally reveal that the legitimacy of companies such as Wall Street banks and Walmart is under threat. Whether justified or not, these developments reveal the limits of the economistic logic – the logic of the market above all else. Clearly, there are things people value more than low prices and high profits: they value *dignity.*

The following pages provide examples of a number of organizations that have introduced more humanistic management practices by following one of two pathways. The first section, representing Pathway 1, shows organizations that have reinstated dignity in their management practices. The second section, representing Pathway 2, shows organizations that have decided to focus on well-being creation rather than just wealth creation.

PATHWAY I: REINSTATING DIGNITY IN MANAGEMENT PRACTICE

Well-functioning markets have the power to enhance human dignity. Part of the problem with our unexamined adherence to economism is that essentially none of the preconditions for a true free market exist in today's economic transactions. To take several, markets presume equitable access to capital, perfect information on the part of all market actors, no monopolies and that all costs are properly accounted for in any given transaction.

Walmart helps those who cannot shop in expensive outlets enjoy a better life, but it does so at uncounted social cost. Walmart claims that by maximizing its profits, it enhances the well-being of customers, but it does so by externalizing many of its impacts. Clearly, while the market logic is helpful, it cannot be the only logic that advances communities and societies, simply because human beings and their needs are far more complex (as indicated in Chapter 2). Given the many crises humanity faces, market logic alone does not suffice. While markets can help produce wealth and coordinate distribution, they need to be complemented with other social structures, including the state and community. No serious economist would disagree.

The point of this chapter is to show how organizations – not only societies – can embrace more humanistic ways of doing business. Examples of companies that have, in one form or another, reinstated dignity in their organizing logic, show that management can play an important role in redressing market failures.

Moving from Economism to Bounded Economism

Walmart and Environmental Stewardship

Walmart and Wall Street banks are great examples of very successful *economistic* organizations. Nevertheless, their leadership teams pay increasing attention to non-market forces. In their quest to regain legitimacy, for example, Walmart's leadership has been credited with moving from *Pure Economism* to *Bounded Economism*. Lee Scott, CEO of Walmart from 2000 to 2009, was regularly criticized for Walmart's poor environmental impact, labor practices, and overall economic effect. Ryan Scott writes:

> The drumbeat of criticism became so loud that the company took out full-page ads in more than 100 newspapers nationwide, and

CEO Lee Scott made himself available for interviews with all of the major TV news outlets. Nevertheless, the company remained embattled. In April of 2005, Forbes listed Walmart as the No. 1 largest corporation, but noted that it was embroiled in so many controversies that it had "marched itself straight into a management and public relations quagmire."[5]

As so often is the case, a crisis was needed to kick-start a new conversation at Walmart. When Hurricane Katrina hit the Gulf Coast of the United States in August 2005, the only functioning logistics system available was Walmart's. Ryan Scott continues:

> Most impressively, Walmart's superb supply chain management and distribution systems enabled the company to deliver relief supplies to victims where the government could not. The company was amongst the first to deliver critical supplies to first responders and victims and was one of the first to reopen stores in flood zones. Local leaders and the general public sang Walmart's praises at a fever-high pitch, astonished and grateful that the company was able to come to their rescue while federal agencies had let them down.[6]

All of a sudden, communities were grateful, the press positive, and Lee Scott asked his management team: "How can we become what we were during Katrina every day?" That question sparked a number of initiatives, the most notable around environmental stewardship.[7] Shortly after Katrina, Walmart unveiled an ambitious environmental plan to cut down on waste and reduce greenhouse gases. Lee Scott said, "As one of the largest companies in the world, with an expanding global presence, environmental problems are our problems." He added that the world's largest retailer wants to be a "good steward for the environment" and ultimately use only renewable energy sources and produce zero waste. Marking a shift from *Pure Economism* to *Bounded Economism*, environmental stewardship became a code word for protecting that which does not have a price. Lee Scott and his team sought ways to reinstate dignity in the management processes.

While Walmart gets credit for limiting its impact on the environment, many critics think that it still follows an economistic logic when it prioritizes waste reduction and energy saving, as these are the practices that directly result in cost savings. Others criticize Walmart's blindness to human dignity, especially with regard to the treatment of its employees and suppliers.

People's United Bank and the Financial Crisis

Another example of an organization shifting toward *Bounded Economism* is the People's United Bank (PU). Headquartered in New England, PU Bank is one of the largest regional banking organizations, with more than USD 20 billion in assets and about 300 branches across New England and New York. PU Bank is hailed as one of the few publicly listed banks to emerge unscathed from the 2008 financial crisis. Despite being publicly listed and pressured to increase the shareholder value, PU's leadership decided to remain conservative in its approach to banking.

When deregulation of the banking industry occurred during the late 1980s and 1990s, many banks decided to go "economistic." During regulation, banks were basically financial service providers to the traditional economy. After the repeal of the Glass-Steagall Act, which required commercial banking and securities activities to be separate, many commercial banks tried their luck with investment banking. They offered ever more complicated derivate products. These activities led to a very active financial market in which bankers came to be dubbed the "masters of the universe."

PU Bank dabbled in some of these activities, but its leadership decided that there was a limit. One of the limits was reached when none of the senior executives actually understood the financial products they offered. Another limit was reached when the executives could not see the value of such financial products for their customers. While many other banks saw big opportunities to profit, and PU's shareholders pressured its leadership not to miss out, the leadership nevertheless decided to focus on true financial services. The CEO defended his decision, stating that for them to enter the active trading business was hardly in their customers' interest. He referred to the bank's founding in 1842, when PU Bank started as a community bank for the citizens of the town of Bridgeport, CT. At the time, only the wealthy had access to banking services, such as loans and saving accounts. However, PU's founding mission was to offer savings accounts to Bridgeport-area workers, making it the first bank in Western Connecticut to do so.[8] The CEO suggested that their tradition of service required further commitment.

As a result of its service orientation, the bank's leadership never even considered investing in security-backed investments, instead building up its own credit portfolio. PU's foundational principles of thrift, service, and community orientation allowed it to build what investors regard as a rock-solid balance sheet with highest-grade credit quality.[9] While economistic bankers often ridiculed these practices, PU weathered the financial crisis. Consequently, PU's stock price rose during the financial crisis, increasing its revenues and profits substantially.

The Story of Dm

Long before Walmart began restoring dignity to its management process, a similar transition occurred at dm, a German drugstore company. Founded by Goetz Werner in 1973, dm was a traditional, albeit novel, entrant to the drugstore market in Southern Germany. The drugstore concept was new at the time. Previously you could only purchase basic sanitary supplies in supermarkets and buy over-the-counter drugs at pharmacies. The new concept found many customers, and Werner and his colleagues quickly grew dm to more than forty stores. In accordance with the traditional command-and-control style, diverse levels of management were introduced to ensure cost effectiveness. Five years into the company's growth, Goetz Werner felt that something was not right, but could not put his finger on it. He started educating himself, increasingly requiring his senior management to take executive education classes as well.

Management scholars Wolfgang Amann and Shiban Khan describe how, in some of these executive courses, humanistic elements came into play.[10] For example, the staff was asked to use role playing and creative theatre to describe their working conditions. Quite remarkably, they honestly described their superiors as heartless dictators, and portrayed themselves as working their fingers to the bone. When Werner saw this, he knew something needed to change. This was not the kind of organization he wanted to lead. He thought long and hard about how human dignity could be better protected, and introduced a less rigid hierarchy. He also started to focus on dialogue-based leadership, and made sure that all managers moved away from a command-and-control style. Not everyone could work with the new management style, so many left.[11]

The introduction of dialogue-based leadership generated far more valuable information, which allowed dm to manage the stores more effectively than before. Everyone could offer ideas on what would work best. It became obvious that ordinary employees had better insights into customer behavior than the area managers. Consequently, Werner and his colleagues made sure that everyone on the shop floor had more responsibility and decision-making powers. If, for example, a local competitor offered a better price, shop managers could react swiftly. In addition, if the customers in a particular city preferred one product over another, shelf space could be arranged accordingly without first obtaining approval from the regional management.[12]

Despite the introduction of changes that generated greater respect for employee dignity, economic decline raised issues of whether dm's leadership should reconsider. Rather than going back to a more economistic model, Werner decided to make dignity-based concepts even more central. One of the problems he anticipated was what he called "standardization mania." The first changes introduced at dm stated that values were central to its culture. Despite this, as in many other organizations, staff felt obliged to adopt the management's values and approaches.[13] On further reflection, Werner felt that such an approach was undignified and considered it "tutelage." Rather than viewing employees as a "turnover generating resource" that needed to be molded, he wanted to better recognize individuality in the future.

Dm thus instituted processes that reflected individual values differences and endowed everyone with decision-making authority. Rather than having to earn trust through "good" behavior, trust was given and had to be "unearned." Individual initiative was deemed key to making the organization better. However, individual employees were also encouraged to collaborate with colleagues, meaning that no one individual would take a decision independently, but consulted with others about a specific idea. This process allowed self-organization at all the levels. Erich Harsch, the new CEO of dm, observed: "Even though competition is extremely tough, we have no targets for our employees. We trust employees to develop their own entrepreneurial responsibility to advance the company."[14]

According dignity to the employees led to the transference of dignity to the customers. The slogan became: "Here I am human, here is where I shop (Hier bin ich Mensch, hier kaufe ich ein)." As ecological awareness increased, more sustainable products were introduced and marketed. Standard retail marketing gimmicks, like coupons or selective low prices, were discontinued, because customers saw them as manipulative. While this differed radically from standard practices at the time, dm gained significant benefits. In comparison with its competitors – especially the largest group, Schlecker, which went bankrupt in 2012 – customers, employees, and suppliers preferred to work with dm. Dm continues to grow and has been continuously profitable. With more than 50,000 employees, it achieved turnover of over USD 10 billion in 2015.

Walmart, the People's United Bank, and dm illustrate the transformation of organizations that had previously responded to conventional economistic dictates. Crises prompted their leadership to reflect on values beyond the market. In the case of Walmart, its loss of reputation and the crisis in the environment motivated change; in the case of People's United, it realized that its reaction to competitive pressure was counterproductive; and in the case of dm, it chose to treat its employees and customers with respect. In all cases, however, the companies benefited from restoring dignity back to the organizing process, economically and otherwise.

Shifting from Bounded Economism to Enlightened Economism

In the examples given above, the companies moved from *Pure Economism* to *Bounded Economism*. They at first operated in the market and tried to optimize their position with regard to the competition. They aimed to maximize profit and cut costs. They only valued those elements that were priced; all the rest were externalities. Human beings were seen as resources, and concerns for the environment or society only came to the fore when costs and profits were affected.

In the following section, we explore a number of other companies that included dignity in their organizational strategy from the outset (*Bounded Economism*). They do not only value their community and protect the environment but also take an active role in promoting and advancing dignity. They do so by working within the competitive market system, aiming to create wealth. These organizations embrace *Enlightened Economism*, which is sometimes also labeled Conscious Business or Conscious Capitalism.

AES Corporation – Serving People and Society

AES was established by Roger W. Sant and Dennis W. Bakke in Arlington, Virginia in 1981. Initially a consulting company, AES started building power plants. After building its first power plant in 1985 in Texas, AES expanded, initially in the United States, broadening its operations globally in the early 1990s to achieve its mission of "providing electricity worldwide."

While working at the US Department of Energy, Bakke and Sant had both experienced how bureaucracy can stifle the human spirit. As a result, they focused intentionally on creating a workplace that not only protected dignity but advanced personal development. Bakke writes that when he and Sant started conversations about founding a company together, they agreed it had to be fun. Work should bring joy, which was based on four core values:

- **Integrity** means achieving a "wholeness" in which "the things AES people say and do in all parts of the company fit together with truth and consistency." By carefully weighing all factors – ethical concerns, stakeholder interests, and societal needs – AES strives to act with integrity in all of its activities.
- **Fairness** refers to being fair in the company's relations with all its stakeholders, including employees, customers, suppliers, stockholders, governments, and in the communities in which it operates. On the one hand, fairness captures the belief that it is not right to "get the most out of" each negotiation or transaction to the detriment of others. On the other hand, fairness is not necessarily "treating everybody equally," instead it involves treating everybody justly, depending on his or her circumstances.
- **Social responsibility** is based on the belief that AES has a responsibility to be involved in projects that provide social benefits, such as ensuring customers less, a high degree of safety and reliability, increased employment, and a cleaner environment.
- **Having fun** entails providing a work environment in which people can flourish through the use of their gifts and skills. People have fun when they enjoy the work they do through empowerment, participation in decision-making, continuous development, and improvement.

A different, humanistic view of people lies at the core of AES's organizing principles. Rather than suspecting that employees are untrustworthy, greedy, and lazy, AES considers individuals as (1) creative, intelligent, capable of learning and making decisions; (2) trustworthy, responsible—can be held accountable; (3) unique, and deserving respect and special treatment; (4) fallible; (5) oriented toward teamwork, and (6) eager to make a contribution.[15]

Based on this perspective, AES' organizational structure is not unlike that of dm, yet it takes it a couple of steps further. AES utilizes a "honeycomb" system in its organizational structure: A highly decentralized and non-hierarchical organization that minimizes bureaucracy. The honeycomb system of employee management comprises a web of worker families forming small autonomous teams that govern their own affairs. There are no functional departments, such as Finance or HR to support the honeycomb structure. All these functions are managed at the plant level. For example, the plants do their own hiring, and a worker-led committee participates in the allocation of merit-based bonuses. Empowered employees and teams make all the decisions. The few company officers assigned to these functional areas normally act as distant in-house advisors to the plant project management team responsible for a given project, rather than making decisions at the top level. In an interview, Bakke confirms[16]

> that the modern manager is supposed to ask his people for advice and then make a decision. But at AES, each decision is made by a person and a team. Their job is to get advice from me and from anybody else they think it is necessary to get advice from. And then they make the decision. We do that even with the budget. We make very few decisions here (indicating the headquarters office). We affirm decisions.

Accordingly, the leaders mainly serve as chief guardians of the principles, as chief accountability officers inside and outside AES, and as chief encouragers. By giving employees a greater sense of involvement and responsibility for their actions, this eccentric system has led to positive outcomes, including high employee satisfaction, low turnover, and to perceptions of a growth-oriented and very desirable work environment.

In this sense, the organization provides joy at work and through work. Responsibility to all the stakeholders remains paramount, but the company's unique focus on the promotion of employee dignity is central to its business success.

The Saga of Whole Foods and Conscious Capitalism

Whole Foods Market (WFM) is a chain of grocery stores that provides natural foods and organic products to consumers in the United States, Canada, and the United Kingdom. Four twenty-something year-old's, who were able to borrow money from friends and family, founded the chain in Austin, Texas 1980 to take the natural foods industry to a supermarket format.[17] With previous experience in the grocery store industry, John Mackey, Renee Lawson Hardy, Craig Weller, and Mark Skiles experienced great success with the natural products that were part of the new store concept. The initial company success was helped by there being very few natural food supermarkets in the United States at the time.[18]

Unlike other companies, WFM does not operate on a standard, single-sentence mission statement. Instead, the company bases its daily operations on eight fundamental core values:

- We sell the highest quality natural and organic products available.
- We satisfy, delight, and nourish our customers.
- We support team member excellence and happiness.
- We create wealth through profits and growth.
- We serve and support our local and global communities.
- We practice and advance environmental stewardship.
- We create ongoing win-win partnerships with our suppliers.
- We promote the health of our stakeholders through healthy eating education.[19]

Like other aspects of the company, WFM's organizational structure is nonconventional. The company is said to run as a democracy, with John Mackey as the CEO. Employees are treated well, and seen as the source of collective success.

In addition to the company structure and values, WFM distinguishes itself through the products it offers. Whereas the traditional market players like Walmart focus on industrialized food sold in bulk, WFM provides a space for healthy food, and educates its customers about better eating habits. To achieve this, the stores are well staffed with knowledgeable employees dedicated to spreading awareness of the benefits of organic products. Because the stores are focused on healthy eating, they offer products that may be difficult to buy elsewhere, like chia seeds or genetically modified organism (GMO)-free products.

WFM also educates its suppliers and collaborates with them, allowing the company to source the highest quality products. WFM's offering consists of hand-selected products from many different suppliers that meet the exacting quality standards it established. The quality is defined "by evaluating the ingredients, freshness, safety, taste, nutritive value and appearance of all of the products.[20] "By applying its high quality standards, WFM has cultivated a wide array of products ranging from organic produce to pet supplies, and from organic hygiene products to ready-made food.

WFM's success is based on advancing the dignity of its customers and shows that health can be advanced within the traditional profitability framework. Based on this experience, John Mackey and some of his likeminded colleagues started spreading the message of "conscious capitalism," writing a book by that title, to showcase that capitalistic business formats can be good for the world.

ABN Amro Real – Envisioning a New Bank for a New Society

ABN Amro Real, the Brazilian subsidiary of a Dutch financial group, had over two million retail customers and employed more than 17,000 employees in 1998. The Santander group has since bought the bank, but for the purpose of highlighting its transition toward *Enlightened Economism*, we will focus on the time when it was ABN Amro Real.[21]

Fabio C. Barbosa, became the head of ABN Amro Real at a time when many acquisitions were taking place in the banking sector, and competitive pressure was strong. Many banks decided to follow the mainstream economistic approach to banking. Barbosa believed, however, that "there is limited value in succeeding in a country which does not enjoy the same success itself."[22] Despite the competitive landscape and huge societal problems, he aspired to create a new bank – one that could transform society.

Consequently, Barbosa and his colleagues started exploring the *bank of value* concept in 2001. Underlying this new concept was the belief that an ethical approach to business would allow the bank to achieve total customer satisfaction that would, ultimately, benefit all the stakeholders. The group's business model was embedded in the mission statement: "To be an organization renowned for providing outstanding financial services to our clients, achieving sustainable results and the satisfaction of individuals and organizations, who together with us contribute to the evolution of society."[23]

Much cynicism and skepticism had to be overcome to develop a bank focusing on serving society. The leadership energized many employees by tasking them with projects that improved their local communities. Early projects focused on their offices' immediate neighborhood and on simple activities, like tidying them. Next, more structural issues were addressed, such as the quality of and access to education. Among the projects was the Escola Brazil Project, which a group of employees founded and ran.[24] This volunteer program was primarily aimed at improving the quality of public school education in Brazil, and at helping these institutions adopt more sustainable practices. Other projects aimed at strengthening the capability of community service organizations. These projects allowed employees to see how they could contribute to a better society.

Based on these experiences, the bank then examined the kind of products and services it could offer in order to support the advancement of the society. In 2001, the bank created an ethical fund that screened companies in terms of their sustainability performance. The fund outperformed the market, and attracted a lot of attention from competitors, who launched similar products. Encouraged by this success, the bank developed lending criteria for companies they wanted to support and those they wished to avoid. Rather than servicing all companies, the leadership decided to be more selective and support fewer companies, but become a true financial partner, supporting their growth. Among the companies that benefited was DryWash, a Brazilian company founded in 1994 that has revolutionized the cleaning industry.[25] Using Carnaúba wax, which is derived from the Carnaúba palm, an indigenous plant, the company introduced a new method of "washing" cars that does not use water or harmful chemicals, but does remove dirt efficiently from vehicles without damaging their surface. Not only did the bank finance the company's growth; it also helped the company attract other funding sources, like the International Finance Corporation.

The bank's support was not limited to corporate clients. It also helped those at the base of the pyramid. Together with Acción International, an NGO with vast experience in microfinance, ABN Amro Real created a joint venture called Real Microcredito in 2002. It was founded before the Brazilian government started incentivizing microcredit investments, and before Muhammed Yunus won the Nobel Peace Prize.[26] The bank's first micro-lending project was in the Heliópolis favela, the biggest low-income community in São Paulo (Metaonginfo 2002). Those in need were not required to go to the bank itself in order to gain access to these loans: Ten representatives were sent to work in the Heliópolis favela in order to make with contact potential borrowers, while various other volunteers also contributed to making this project successful.

This example demonstrates how a bank can create services that advance the dignity of employees, customers, and society at large. As with the Whole Foods example, the managers became "evangelists" of a sort. ABN Amro Real created spaces where industry and community partners could exchange their knowledge and best practices: "Espaço Real de Prácticas em Sustentabilidade" was a program designed for the public, and supported companies by encouraging them to rethink and redesign their business processes lucratively and innovatively.

ABN Amro's management was clear that none of these practices would have been implemented had there not been a positive financial impact. Not only was the bank profitable, but the employees considered ABN Amro Real a great place to work. ABN Amro grew so successfully that the Santander Group ultimately took it over, pledging to retain its leadership team. The bank's unusually enlightened banking practices impressed even Santander.

While this case study reflects on a time past, it shows how a transition to more enlightened business practice is possible, even in an industry dominated by economism. ABN Amro successfully promoted the dignity of its employees, its customers, and society at large. Given the recent and numerous scandals in traditional banking, this model is a delightful anomaly.

Shifting from Bureaucratic Paternalism to Bounded Humanism

Many organizations such as hospitals are set up to serve the public good. Serving a noble purpose like saving people's lives does not necessarily translate into humanistic organizational practices. Many employees in the public and NGO sector feel that bureaucratic practices constantly violate their dignity. NGO employees frequently see a huge disparity between how poorly they are treated and their employer's lofty organizational goals. A participant in a recent dignity leadership seminar commented that the Catholic service provider for which she worked violated its employees' dignity often. The humanistic management paradigm can help reorient organizations that are traditionally more paternalistic and bureaucratic.

Bringing Vitality to Midwestern Hospital's Billing Group

Prominent management scholar Jane Dutton describes an interesting if unlikely example: The billing department in a hospital transitioning toward a workplace that makes dignity central to its organizing practices.[27] She describes a physician billing department as being responsible for securing accurate and timely reimbursement for claims on behalf of all physicians affiliated with the hospital system. This task typically involves repetitive work that many consider boring. Those doing it suffer doubly, enduring great stress due to the constant time pressure to secure reimbursements quickly. She recounts:

> The physician billing department at Midwest Hospital (hereafter called Midwest Billing) had historically been a lackluster performer in terms of the scorecard measure of the amount of time it took to collect one dollar of reimbursement. In 1998 it took an average of

180 days to collect a dollar of reimbursement, but by 2001, when
we were studying the unit, this period had been drastically reduced
and sustained at a rate of about 60 days – a rate that makes them an
industry leader.[28]

Between 1998 and 2001 something changed. The unit began to thrive,
and the employees were happy to come to work. In fact, so many other
people working in the hospital wanted to work in the unit that there
was a waiting list. According to Dutton and her colleagues, a compassion revolution had occurred, which was attributed to the new
leadership.

Employees were delighted to work in a place that protected
their dignity. Here is what some employees said:

> I for one love working up here. Absolutely. Everybody – Sarah (the
> unit manager) up here has a good heart. It's amazing to me. I came
> from a place that wasn't nearly as friendly, not half as supportive
> and coming up here's it's just amazing.

> You love being there ... and I don't know. I don't think you even
> think about it. When it's this close I don't even think twice about
> "I'm not going to go help with...." You just jump in and do it
> without even thinking you are having an impact or not. Does that
> make sense?

> Nothing is below anybody here. They don't care what it is. They'll
> do it as long as it helps the department get the job done.[29]

In spite of bureaucratic rules, the unit began to work more like a
community that self-organized. As a result, the employees enjoyed
it more and came alive. They talked about their personal growth in
the compassionate environment. Jane Dutton writes:

> Finally, the vitality of the group was expressed through how people
> spontaneously talked about how they had personally grown from
> being a part of the unit. Like a flower in fertile soil, each person
> expressed in her own way how she felt transformed by what she had

experienced at Midwest Billing. ... Here is one told by Lannie, explaining the effects of being a team leader: "I didn't have self-confidence when I first started there. Sarah approached me with being a team leader, and I said, 'Sure, I'll try it.' And then I came to her later and said I didn't want to do it. She gave me a really great pep talk and said, 'Lannie, you can do it. You do know what you are doing and you do have the self-confidence. You just have to believe in yourself.' I have come a long way. I know I have."[30]

Dutton and her colleagues attribute connectedness practices for the change in the unit. They suggest that basic conversational inter-actions in which people felt truly heard had enlivening effects. Similarly, they found that constructive working relationships created spirals of reciprocity that fed zest and vitality. In addition to the improved personal relations, the rather drab cubicle space was decorated with personal items and pictures of the natural environment. Dutton comments: "subtle yet critical reminders that members of Midwest Billing are living, breathing, whole human beings who inhabit this space for a significant portion of their day."[31]

If a cubicle space in a billing department can undergo such a drastic shift, there is no real reason why other organizations should not be able to embrace humanistic management practices.

BracNet – Developing a Country

Many developing nations are shifting away from paternalistic organizing models to more market-based models. BracNet is a venture that showcases how the market can be harnessed to restore dignity and, when it's done right, develop a country.

BracNet is the brainchild of Khalid Quadir. It is designed to bridge the digital divide in his native country of Bangladesh. Many experts, including the renowned economist Joseph Stiglitz, consider closing the digital divide a precondition for higher well-being, because it can help reduce poverty and close the inequity gap.[32] However, despite all the efforts on behalf of governments (see, e.g., the US

Telecommunications Act passed in 1996) and international NGOs (such as the Open Society Institute), the digital divide continues to grow.

A new breed of entrepreneurs, including Khalid Quadir, has taken a different approach. They have applied their managerial skills to address the digital divide problem more systematically. Doing business in Bangladesh is challenging, but Khalid knew that it could be done. Growing up, he had felt that his country was always depicted as on the receiving end, dependent on outside aid and benevolence. Inspired by the need to demonstrate his people's capacity to sustain themselves, he felt that doing business profitably was an act of empowerment in itself, and that when business approaches could promote general well-being, this should be done.[33]

Khalid saw his task as economic and social development work, something that resembles a typical World Bank project. He wanted to demonstrate a new model for development, one that cross-sector collaborations and for-profit opportunities characterized. He argued that if BracNet was only about building a communications infrastructure, the government needed to be in charge. On the other hand, if his only target was to connect the rural population, BracNet should perhaps be a nonprofit organization. He wanted to combine these motives to bring the most advanced technology to some of the most impoverished areas in a financially sustainable way. He explained:

> BracNet has a social component which is a plus, but it is a clear for-profit venture. The idea is to have a viable project for development which is not based on charity or begging, where people from Bangladesh and others meet eye-to-eye not as dependent receivers.[34]

Concerns about financial sustainability also drove the for-profit decision. While he was confident that there was a market in rural areas, he counted on his urban clients to fund expansion into rural areas until these achieved financial sustainability. Pondering his motivations for seeking such a broad market, Khalid explained:

> [W]ith the rural clients the social component enters the scene.
> Building infrastructure and thus developing the country, BracNet
> can also make profit – so it is a double-edge business.[35]

With the backing of BRAC, currently the world's largest NGO and based in Bangladesh, Khalid refined his concept further, to attract not only socially minded investors but also the more traditional members of the investment community. He was able to build a coalition that included BRAC, but also venture capital groups, social impact investors, and even hedge-fund managers. Together, they funded the first round to rollout wireless Internet access in urban areas. The company then successfully financed a second round, which helped them build a rural connection concept.

Khalid created the concept of internet-enabled kiosks to connect the rural population. He aimed to create small ICT centers that local rural entrepreneurs could run. He called these centers 'e-huts': "'E-huts' are little centers in rural areas that can be compared to KINKOs in the US. They provide technological solutions for small businesses and local people."[36] In addition, local e-huts have the power to support various rural communities through e-services. The e-huts provide computer training to all interested parties, which will in turn support e-health, e-agriculture, e-government, e-business, and, above all, e-learning opportunities. BRAC will provide many of these opportunities directly, finding this a convenient way to reach out to even more people. The broadband internet infrastructure will be crucial for bringing higher levels of education, health care, and economic development to poverty-stricken areas.

BracNet is an interesting case study for many telecom companies across the globe keen to explore how good business could be done in developing countries. In 2012, KDDI, the second largest cellular operator in Japan, entered into a partnership with BracNet and bought a controlling stake. It remains to be seen if the humanistic spirit can be kept alive.

PATHWAY 2: SHIFTING TO WELL-BEING AS THE OBJECTIVE FUNCTION

To deal with the number and the scale of global crises requiring action, many organizations are considering the role they can play in solving them. This shifts the focal point of organizing, the objective function, from "how can we solve an economic problem with more social awareness" to "how can we solve a social problem economically." Many scholars argue that a focus on wealth creation may hinder progress when looking for innovative solutions, while focusing on world benefit creation can be more helpful in delivering both. Such innovative solutions have long been pursued by what Bill Drayton calls "social entrepreneurs." In the early 2000s, a group connected to David Cooperrider started a conversation with business leaders about how business could be an agent of world benefit. Various independent efforts across the world have shown that many organizations wish to be a part of the solution: For-benefit corporations have been formed (B-corps), business organizations for the common good are spreading, and enthusiasm is growing for business practice as a vehicle for larger system change.

From Bounded Economism to Bounded Humanism

Unilever – the World's Largest NGO?

In 2009, Paul Polman became CEO of Unilever, one of the largest consumer goods providers in the world. At the time, Unilever had already begun to embrace sustainable business practices. In 2000, it had acquired Ben and Jerry's, an ice-cream company known for its socially conscious business practices, and in 2007 Unilever committed to having all its Lipton Tea products harvested sustainably. Unilever, a conglomerate of food, health, and beauty products, was traded on the public stock exchange and played by market rules. When Polman took over, however, he suspended some of those rules, including quarterly reporting, and refused to give financial analysts' earnings estimates.

Boynton and Barchan reported on his first day in the CEO position in *Forbes Magazine*:[37]

Immediately, the Dutch-born Polman put his shareholders on notice. . . . Unilever, he explained, was now taking a longer view. The CEO went a step further, urging shareholders to put their money somewhere else if they don't "buy into this long-term value-creation model, which is equitable, which is shared, which is sustainable." "I figured I couldn't be fired on my first day," Polman quipped later on.

He added: "I don't have any space for many of these people that really, in the short term, try to basically speculate and make a lot of money." He said his responsibility is to multiple stakeholders, among them, consumers in the developing world and climate-change activists. Regarding shareholders, Polman said, "I'm not just working for them." On that note, he added this zinger – "Slavery was abolished a long time ago.[38]"

He launched an ambitious reorientation to make Unilever a company that provides solutions to global problems. The leadership developed a Sustainable Living Plan that sets out to impact the "well-being of one billion people in the next 5 years."[39]

Again Boynton and Barchan:

Soon after he became CEO, Polman spearheaded the 10-year Unilever Sustainable Living Plan, which seeks to decouple the company's growth from its environmental footprint. The ambitious goals include doubling Unilever's revenue while slashing the footprint by 50%; sourcing 100% of its raw materials sustainably (meaning that the supply chain is managed according to environmental, social, and ethical principles); and helping more than a billion people improve their health and well-being.[40]

Many companies may make such general statements, but as Rick Wartzman of the Drucker Institute comments in *Fortune*[41]:

Unilever . . . rigorously measures and reports its progress against three ambitious goals it aims to reach by 2020: helping more than a billion people across the globe improve their health and well-being; halving the environmental footprint of its products; and sourcing 100% of its agricultural raw materials sustainably while enhancing the livelihoods of those working across its supply chain. What's more, the company has committed to doing all this while doubling the size of its business, to about $100 billion. (Unilever derives nearly 60% of its sales from emerging markets.)[42]

Unilever aims to do so by reengineering its various brands to address social and environmental concerns by finding their true purpose. Ben and Jerry's was one of the first certified B-Corporations, and Polman and his colleagues thought hard about Unilever becoming a for-benefit corporation. So far, they have not found how to do this amid the tangle of international laws, but they are working on it.

Again Rick Wartzman:

> On the ground, these objectives manifest themselves in many ways, like the recent launch of the Toilet Board Coalition, a cross-sector group that is trying to find scalable, market-based solutions to what it calls "the sanitation crisis." Could this Unilever-led effort make a difference in the lives of the 2.5 billion people around the world who lack access to a safe, clean toilet? Quite possibly. Could it also help Unilever sell more bottles of Domestos, its bathroom germ killer? Definitely.

> Using the same logic, Unilever is trying to position Knorr bouillon as a weapon to combat food insecurity; Lifebuoy, a vehicle to promote good hygiene.

> Making this tangible for those on the front lines isn't easy. So, in late 2013, Unilever launched an online "Social Impact Hub" for its 174,000 employees to learn more about its myriad initiatives in this area. Unilever has also augmented its training programs so that

workers at all levels can understand the company's commitment to sustainability and how their own jobs fit in.[43]

The impact so far has been that employees have become very motivated, making Unilever an employer of choice for many graduates. Just how serious the Unilever leadership is about the transition toward *Humanism* can be seen from their statements regarding the role of their institution. Rather than being simply a better business (aka conscious business), they describe their organization as a force that shapes the common good. Kees Kruythoff, CEO of Unilever North America, views himself as working in one of the largest social enterprises, and Paul Polman states that they are working for the largest NGO in the world. Their leadership is attracting a great deal of attention, and they are credited with leading the business community in pushing for a binding climate agreement at the COP 21 talks on climate change in Paris in December 2015. That level of political ambition shows the active role Unilever wishes to take in creating a better world, not only a richer world.

Elon Musk and Tesla Motors

The story of Tesla Motors describes another organization that is shifting toward *Humanism*. Elon Musk, a software engineer, made his fortune by selling his shares in the company Paypal to ebay. With that money, he bought into Tesla Motors, a company that was attempting to build fully electric vehicles. In 2008, Musk took on the role of CEO, and the mission has ever since been to accelerate the advent of sustainable transport.

With this mission and its strategic approach, Tesla Motors accepted one of the biggest global and social challenges confronting humanity – climate change. *New York Times* columnist Tom Friedman suggests that our future will be decided by whether or not we are willing to tackle these massive global challenges. Tesla Motors is hailed as a pioneer in creating a better future for humanity and thus in creating higher levels of well-being.

Elon Musk elaborates on the firm's strategy:

Our mission from day one has been to accelerate the advent of
sustainable transport by bringing compelling mass market electric
cars to market as soon as possible. If we could have done that with
our first product, we would have, but that was simply impossible to
achieve for a startup company that had never built a car and that
had one technology iteration and no economies of scale. Our first
product was going to be expensive no matter what it looked like, so
we decided to build a sports car, as that seemed like it had the best
chance of being competitive with its gasoline alternatives.[44]

He then explains that the revenue from the sales of the sports car and
the expertise gained were critical to the development of the Model S,
as well as future models that would lead to a mass market car. It is
obvious that Musk uses the market as a tool for advancing societal
well-being. He waived all patent rights in the hope that other established car makers would adopt Tesla Motors technologies in order to
further demonstrate how the company is defying traditional market
practices. The ultimate goal is not necessarily to make Tesla Motors
the dominant company, but to solve the problem of carbon-based
transportation.

Musk states:

Tesla Motors was created to accelerate the advent of sustainable
transport. If we clear a path to the creation of compelling electric
vehicles, but then lay intellectual property landmines behind us to
inhibit others, we are acting in a manner contrary to that goal.
Tesla will not initiate patent lawsuits against anyone who, in good
faith, wants to use our technology.[45]

He then explains how he used to think patents were useful, but
started to doubt this assumption.

At Tesla, however, we felt compelled to create patents out of
concern that the big car companies would copy our technology and
then use their massive manufacturing, sales and marketing power

to overwhelm Tesla. We couldn't have been more wrong. The unfortunate reality is the opposite: electric car programs (or programs for any vehicle that doesn't burn hydrocarbons) at the major manufacturers are small to non-existent, constituting an average of far less than 1% of their total vehicle sales.

At best, the large automakers are producing electric cars with limited range in limited volume. Some produce no zero emission cars at all.

Given that annual new vehicle production is approaching 100 million per year and the global fleet is approximately 2 billion cars, it is impossible for Tesla to build electric cars fast enough to address the carbon crisis. By the same token, it means the market is enormous. Our true competition is not the small trickle of non-Tesla electric cars being produced, but rather the enormous flood of gasoline cars pouring out of the world's factories every day.

We believe that Tesla, other companies making electric cars, and the world would all benefit from a common, rapidly-evolving technology platform.[46]

This is an unusual statement for a traditional, competitive-minded market player. In fact, it transcends the logic of competition, even that of conscious competition, and invites collaboration to tackle much larger challenges. Clearly, such behavior builds trust, and many people are willing to support the company despite its lack of profitability. This was highlighted by more than 400,000 people willing to pay a USD 1,000 deposit to reserve the new Model 3 car years ahead of its availability.

No one thought that this level of consumer trust was possible, but it showcases the power of a humanistic approach, with people willing to collaborate and solve large human problems. When organizations sincerely aim to solve problems, and not just make money from them, they will find a ready market for their products and services.

Bounded Humanism to Pure Humanism

There are far fewer organizations that have made the leap to become truly humanistic. As Frederic Laloux suggests, many organizations need to reinvent themselves in order to reach what he calls a "teal level" of consciousness.[47] In this section, a number of examples are provided that illustrate what it means to promote human dignity by organizing for well-being.

Grameen Bank

As mentioned in Chapter 7, Grameen Bank is the result of economist Muhammad Yunus's search for a cure to poverty. When he returned from the United States to a university position in Bangladesh, Yunus felt the urge to apply his knowledge to help his country. The then recently independent Bangladesh was the poorest country in the world. While many traditional colonial institutions were in place, they were not functioning well enough to assure well-being.

Plagued by both government and market failure, Bangladesh lacked a functioning banking sector. Loan sharks, who imposed exorbitant interest rates, and traditional banks, which would not lend to poor people because they had no collateral, kept entrepreneurial people in poverty. After many iterations, Muhammad Yunus pioneered a microfinance business. The business model centered on lending small amounts of money (called micro-loans) primarily to poor women to allow them to earn a living through self-employment. No material collateral was required to apply for a loan; instead, a social form of collateral was required: Borrowers had to organize in groups of five, and each group member needed to repay his or her loan on time, while ensuring that the other group members did the same. The failure of just one borrower to meet a payment jeopardized the entire group's future borrowing opportunities. This model established a delicate dynamic between "peer pressure" and "peer support" among Grameen borrowers, and is credited with the high loan repayment rate of 95 percent. Despite the delicacy of the business model, the bank had signed up 8.35 million members (96 percent were women) in 81,379 Bangladeshi villages by 2011.

In a redesign of its original model, Grameen abolished the "peer pressure" model, and now provides credit without any collateral. The system is based on accountability, mutual trust, creativity, and participation. The ownership structure of Grameen Bank is a stabilizing feature of the business model. Like cooperative banks, the bank's poor borrowers (93–95 percent) largely own it, while a small minority (5–7 percent) remains in government hands.[48] The fact that the people formerly deprived of banking services now own their own bank strengthens their commitment to the bank, and helps explain its success. In this sense, the organizational model strengthens the business model.

When the business model is examined more closely, Grameen Bank provides four types of loans: income-generating loans with a 20 percent interest rate; housing loans with an 8 percent interest rate; higher education loans with a 5 percent interest rate; and a 0 percent interest loan for struggling society members (beggars). Although the latter goes against traditional economic logic, Grameen Bank makes it work from the humanistic perspective (i.e., helps alleviate poverty).[49] Here is how. Each member receives an identity badge with a Grameen Bank logo to let everybody know that this national institution stands behind them (dB). In addition, the members are covered free of charge by life insurance (dD) and loan insurance programs, and existing Grameen groups are encouraged to become their mentors (dC). This form of social support is combined with favorable loan conditions, which only require the repayment of the principal in installments and in keeping with their repayment ability (dA). More than 100,000 beggars have joined the program. Grameen maintains that of the more than USD 20 million disbursed, 80 percent has already been repaid. In addition, roughly 20,000 have abandoned begging and are making a living in a sales profession. Among them, roughly 10,000 beggars have joined Grameen Bank groups as mainstream borrowers.[50]

This program shows that poor people can work themselves out of poverty and become bankable. Muhammad Yunus explains:

> At Grameen Bank, credit is a cost effective weapon to fight poverty and it serves as a catalyst in the overall development of socio-economic conditions of the poor who have been kept outside the banking orbit on the ground that they are poor and hence not bankable.[51]

Using innovative business models, Grameen Bank has shown that business can protect and increasingly advance human dignity to provide higher levels of well-being.

Grameen Danone

Inspired by Grameen's success, Franck Riboud, the Chairman and CEO of Groupe Danone, offered to collaborate with Muhammad Yunus to "do something good."[52] During their initial meeting in October 2005, Riboud told Yunus that Danone had a major presence in the developing markets, and wished to orient its business even more toward serving the very poor. Yunus recalls making Riboud an impulsive offer:

> Your company is a leading producer of nutritious foods. What would you think about creating a joint venture to bring some of your products to the villages of Bangladesh? We could create a company that we own together and call it Grameen Danone. It could manufacture healthful foods that will improve the diet of rural Bangladeshis – especially the children. If the products were sold at a low price, we could make a real difference in the lives of millions of people.[53]

To Yunus's surprise, Riboud agreed. He also agreed to operate the project as a social business enterprise (SBE). Yunus explains:

> It's a business designed to meet a social goal. In this case, the goal is to improve the nutrition of poor families in the villages of Bangladesh.[54] Grameen and Danone each own half of the SBE Grameen Danone.

Danone found eradicating malnutrition attractive, but the approach was completely novel. According to Schneider (2008), Danone management had to completely change its management style in order to do business the Grameen way. Danone's objective and mission had previously been to maximize shareholder value; now profit had to be a condition, a means – no longer the end and no longer the goal.[55]

Having been conceived as a social business, Grameen Danone was free from shareholder pressure for quick returns. However, the project had to be self-supporting to generate funds for its operations. At the same time, maximization of social goals had to be achieved.

The founding documents state:

The mission of Grameen Danone is to reduce poverty through "a unique proximity business model that will provide daily healthy nutrition to the poor." The specific objectives are stated as:

- developing a product that has high nutritional value and is affordable for the poorest individuals,
- to improve the living conditions of the population: jobs, income level, enhancement of the social fabric, and
- to protect the environment and conserve resources, as well as
- to ensure a sustainable economic activity.[56]

According to Yunus, a social business is a business that pays no dividends. It sells products at prices that make it self-sustaining. The owners of the company can recover their investment in the company over a period of time, but no profit is paid to investors in the form of dividends. Instead, any profit made remains in the business, to finance expansion, to create new products or services, and to do the world more good.[57] He emphasizes that Grameen Danone's bottom line is the reduction of malnutrition while not incurring losses.

Such an innovative approach to creating higher levels of well-being through innovative organizational practices is surely fraught with problems. It is, for example, unclear how many further manufacturing plants will actually be implemented. Furthermore, partnerships between traditionally economistic and humanistic organizations are difficult to manage. Danone's shareholders are increasingly skeptical of the social business model. However, no matter how successful this specific project is, the Grameen group as a whole symbolizes the various ways in which organizations are moving toward *Pure Humanism*. By addressing social problems entrepreneurially, they are protecting and promoting dignity, and creating higher levels of well-being.

CONCLUDING REMARKS

Society needs new approaches to organizing. As the examples in this chapter show, many organizations are attempting to respond to the challenges posed. This transition, however, is still at the experimental stage. Many humanistic practices still need to be developed. A pathway needs to be set forth guiding a company in a transition from economistic management to humanistic. The following chapters consider the drivers of innovation (pedagogy) and the facilitators (policy) of humanistic models of organizations.

NOTES

1 www.fastcompany.com/47593/wal-mart-you-dont-know (accessed June 16, 2016).
2 http://themoderatevoice.com/walmart-has-ruthlessly-exploited-its-workers-for-years/ (accessed June 23, 2016).
3 www.salon.com/2015/05/25/10_reasons_wal_mart_is_the_worst_company_in_america_partner/
4 http://fortune.com/2016/06/06/fortune-500-conservatives-liberals-love-hate/
5 www.huffingtonpost.com/ryan-scott/how-hurricane-katrina-cha_b_8043692.html (accessed June 12, 2016).
6 Ibid.
7 Hunter Lovins points out that Lee Scott, and Rob Walton, a Board member, also took an epic journey with Peter Seligmann of Conservation

International, down the Amazon. According to her, Walmart leadership wanted to move much more rigorously toward humanistic practice; investors, however, were not supportive.

8 Gangahar, A. (2012). "People's United Bank." *Banking with Integrity.* H. Spitzeck, M. Pirson and C. Dierksmeier, eds. London, Palgrave MacMillan.

9 Gangahar. "People's United Bank."

10 Amann, W. and S. Khan (2011). "Dialogue-based leadership style as part of humanistic organizational cultures: the case of dm in Germany." *Humanistic Management in Practice.* Houndsmill, Basingstoke, UK, Palgrave Macmillan, 92–102.

11 Amann and Khan. "Dialogue-based leadership style as part of humanistic organizational cultures: the case of dm in Germany." 92–102.

12 Ibid.

13 Dietz and Kracht (2007). Dialogische Unternehmensfuehrung. Grundlagen – Praxis. Fallbeispiel dm-drogerie markt, campus, p. 121.

14 www.dm.de/unternehmen/ueber-uns/zahlen-und-fakten/ (accessed June 23, 2016).

15 Pfeffer, J. (1997). Human resources at AES Corporation: The case of the missing department. Case HR-3; Rodopman, B. (2011). AES Corporation–Serving People and Society. *Humanistic Management in Practice.* Basingstoke, UK; New York, Palgrave Macmillan. 28–41.

16 Sant, R., and D. Bakke (1998). "Organizing for empowerment: an interview with AES's Roger Sant and Dennis Bakke." Interview by Suzy Wetlaufer. *Harvard Business Review,* 77(1), 110–123.

17 Mackey, J., and R. Sisodia (2014). *Conscious Capitalism, with a New Preface by the Authors: Liberating the Heroic Spirit of Business.* Cambridge, MA, Harvard Business Review Press.

18 www.wholefoodsmarket.com/mission-values/core-values (accessed July 3, 2016).

19 Ibid.

20 Ibid.

21 Palacios, P., and M. Pirson (2011). ABN AMRO REAL–A New Bank for a New Society. *Humanistic Management in Practice.* Basingstoke, UK; New York, Palgrave Macmillan, 13–27.

22 Palacios and Pirson. "ABN AMRO REAL–A new bank for a new society." 13–27.

23 Ibid.

24 Ibid.

25 Ibid.

26 Ibid.

27 Dutton, J. E. (2003). "Breathing life into organizational studies." *Journal of Management Inquiry*, **12**(1), 5–19.

28 Dutton. "Breathing life into organizational studies." 5–19.

29 Ibid.

30 Ibid.

31 Ibid.

32 www.digitaldivide.org/dd/digitaldivide.html (accessed February 8, 2009). For a useful assessment of this issue, see the archive of World Development Reports of United Nations Development Programme, http://hdr.undp.org/reports/. Also see International Telecommunications Union's reports on the subject, www.itu.int/ITU-D/digitaldivide).

33 See Ebrahim, A., M. Pirson, P. Mangas. Patrik Brummer and the BracNet Investment, HBS case No 309065.

34 Ibid.

35 Ibid.

36 Ibid.

37 www.forbes.com/sites/andyboynton/2015/07/20/unilevers-paul-polman-ceos-cant-be-slaves-to-shareholders/#22cb060240b5 (accessed July 3, 2016).

38 Ibid.

39 Ibid.

40 Ibid.

41 http://fortune.com/2015/01/07/what-unilever-shares-with-google-and-apple/ (accessed July 3, 2016).

42 Ibid.

43 Ibid.

44 www.teslamotors.com/blog/mission-tesla (accessed July 3, 2016).

45 www.teslamotors.com/blog/all-our-patent-are-belong-you (accessed July 3, 2016).

46 Ibid.

47 Laloux, F. (2015). *Reinventing Organizations*. Belgium, Lannoo Meulenhoff.

48 www.grameen-info.org (accessed July 3, 2016).

49 www.grameen-info.org (accessed May 12, 2016).

50 Ibid.

51 www.grameen-info.org/about-us/

52 John, D. (2010). "Grameen Danone." *Humanistic Management in Action.* E. v. Kimakowitz, M. Pirson, H. Spitzeck, C. Diercksmeier and W. Amann, eds. New York, Palgrave MacMillan.

53 Yunus, M. (2009). "Social entrepreneurs are the solution." *Humanism in Business: Perspectives on the Development of a Responsible Business Society.* H. Spitzeck, M. Pirson, W. Amann, S. Khan and E. von Kimakowitz, eds. Cambridge, Cambridge University Press.

54 Schneider, E. (2008). Muhammad Yunus Recounts Grameen Success Stories, H40 Berlin.

55 John. "Grameen Danone." Schneider, E. (2008). Muhammad Yunus Recounts Grameen Success Stories, H40 Berlin.

56 Ibid.

57 Yunus. "Social entrepreneurs are the solution."

9 Developing Humanistic Management Pedagogy

When you enter my business school, a Jesuit business school, the first thing you see is a trading room. It gives visitors the impression that finance is at the heart of business education and that trading is the most important business skill. Unsurprisingly, the standard business curriculum the school offers is very much focused on finance, accounting, and economics. This is not unique; in fact, its leadership is only emulating the elite schools.

What business students learn matters, because a business degree is the most popular undergraduate degree in the United States and in many other parts of the world.[1] And despite the financial crisis, the global demand for a MBA degree is still increasing.[2] So what are these many business students learning and carrying into the world?

The journalist Rana Foroohar suggests that it is a very economistic worldview:

> With very few exceptions, MBA education today is basically an education in finance, not business – a major distinction. So it's no wonder that business leaders make many of the finance-friendly decisions. MBA programs don't churn out innovators well prepared to cope with a fast-changing world, or leaders who can stand up to the Street and put the long-term health of their company (not to mention their customers) first; they churn out followers who learn how to run firms by the numbers.[3]

Despite the financial crisis's lessons, MBA programs – and especially their finance and accounting classes – have not changed much. Foroohar explains:

> [M]ost top MBA programs in the United States still teach standard "markets know best" efficiency theory and preach that share price is the best representation of a firm's underlying value, glossing over the fact that the markets tend to brutalize firms for long-term investment and reward them for short-term paybacks to investors.

A number of business school deans are acutely aware of this failure and advocate change.[4] Many of them suggest that business programs should teach future business leaders how to achieve long-term success and the elements of good leadership. Despite such insights, most business schools in America aren't doing this.[5] The traditional curriculum suggests that business is an exact science devoid of messy human concerns.

Foroohar remarks:

> Even after the financial crisis, a survey of the world's one hundred top business schools (most of them in the United States) found that only half of all MBA programs make ethics a required course, and only 6 percent deal with issues of sustainability in their core curriculum, despite the fact that a large body of research shows that firms that focus on these issues actually have higher longer-term performance. Instead, students are taught that what matters most is maximizing profits and bolstering a company's share price. It's something they carry straight with them to corporate America.

The business world is increasingly questioning the value of this kind of education. It creates "takers" and not "makers," and supports a psychopathic mindset. In his book *Car Guys vs. Bean Counters* (2011), Bob Lutz, a former vice chairman of GM, argues that MBA education has contributed to the decline of American manufacturing and the American automobile industry.[6] Business leaders in Silicon Valley hesitate to hire MBAs and prefer engineers, because they add "real value." In addition, the typical MBA leadership style, which is top-down, hierarchical, and number-driven, does not work well in start-ups. People there often want to work for a higher purpose than shareholder value maximization.

Again, Rana Foroohar expresses the problem of the economistic mindset:

> Why has business education failed business? Why has it fallen so much in love with finance and the ideas it espouses? It's a problem with deep roots, which have been spreading for decades. It encompasses issues like the rise of neoliberal economic views as a challenge to the postwar threat of socialism. It's about an academic inferiority complex that propelled business educators to try to emulate hard sciences like physics rather than take lessons from biology or the humanities. It dovetails with the growth of computing power that enabled complex financial modeling. The bottom line, though, is that far from empowering business, MBA education has fostered the sort of short-term, balance-sheet-oriented thinking that is threatening the economic competitiveness of the country as a whole. If you wonder why most businesses still think of shareholders as their main priority or treat skilled labor as a cost rather than an asset – or why 80 percent of CEOs surveyed in one study said they'd pass up making an investment that would fuel a decade's worth of innovation if it meant they'd miss a quarter of earnings results – it's because that's exactly what they are being educated to do.

To transition from this economistic mindset, business education needs to reconnect business education with the humanities, with the sciences, and with practice. More than anything, business education needs to become more human and humane. Ideas on how this can be achieved will be outlined in the following pages, employing the same pathways suggested in previous chapters (see Figure 7.1) In the first section, pedagogical approaches are showcased that have restored dignity to management education (Pathway 1). In the second part, pedagogical approaches are considered that embrace the pursuit of well-being (Pathway 2).

RESTORING DIGNITY TO MANAGEMENT EDUCATION

Advancing management education requires a move away from the economistic mind-set that underpins the majority of current programs. Business scholar Heiko Spitzeck argues that there are (at least) four stages of organizational moral development[7]: economistic, compliance, strategic, humanistic. Currently, most programs tacitly suggest that the solution to the many crises we face is beyond the remit of business. This represents Spitzeck's first stage of business school development: "Not our job." In line with pure economistic logic, this stage implies that business schools' job is to teach students about the function of markets: anything that is not priced should not matter. Non-market concerns are dismissed as "soft stuff" and irrelevant. Spitzeck elaborates:

> These business schools' teaching philosophy is based on traditional neo-liberal economics and following the principle of profit maximization. As genuine social and environmental issues are considered irrelevant, business schools in this stage reject or deny their responsibility to educate ... future business leaders about these areas. They simply conceive this not to be their job and position humanistic education in faculties of sociology or environmental sciences.[8]

Awareness is growing that such a stance is not only unhelpful but detrimental to these schools' reputation, and many are trying hard to regain their legitimacy.

From Economism to Bounded Economism

Those business schools attempting to transform their curricula typically apply boundaries to the economistic model. They may introduce mandatory ethics classes, or include aspects of sustainability in the curriculum. They may even offer a class on corporate social responsibility. These are, however, additions to an otherwise unchanged curriculum, representing a form of *Bounded Economism*.

Several initiatives have emerged in the past decade to promote "responsible" business education. The United Nations offers one of the most prominent initiatives. In 2007, the UN Global Compact Office developed the Principles for Responsible Management Education (PRME). In 2011, Manuel Escudero, who was instrumental in the development of these standards, wrote:

> In the academic environment of the 2000s, where the trend of corporate sustainability and social responsibility had entered the classrooms but had yet to become part of the strategic core of business education, there was the need for a global call to facilitate the process of bringing business schools up to the new challenges and opportunities. The Principles for Responsible Management Education represent this call. The Principles for Responsible Management Education (PRME)[9] are a timely global plea for business schools to gradually transform curricula, research and teaching methodologies on the basis of universally recognized values of sustainability, social responsibility and good corporate citizenship.[10]

The principles comprise:[11]

Principle 1 | Purpose: We will develop the capabilities of students to be future generators of sustainable value for business and society at large and to work for an inclusive and sustainable global economy.

Principle 2 | Values: We will incorporate into our academic activities and curricula the values of global social responsibility as portrayed in international initiatives such as the United Nations Global Compact.

Principle 3 | Method: We will create educational frameworks, materials, processes and environments that enable effective learning experiences for responsible leadership.

Principle 4 | Research: We will engage in conceptual and empirical research that advances our understanding about the role, dynamics, and impact of corporations in the creation of sustainable social, environmental and economic value.

Principle 5 | Partnership: We will interact with managers of business corporations to extend our knowledge of their challenges in meeting social and environmental responsibilities and to explore jointly effective approaches to meeting these challenges.

Principle 6 | Dialogue: We will facilitate and support dialog and debate among educators, students, business, government, consumers, media, civil society organizations and other interested groups and stakeholders on critical issues related to global social responsibility and sustainability.

The UN Secretary General, Ban Ki-moon, suggests that: "The Principles for Responsible Management Education have the capacity to take the case for universal values and business into classrooms on every continent."[12]

Clearly, the ambition is to return dignity-based values to business school classrooms around the globe. As of 2016, 650 leading business schools and management-related academic institutions from more than eighty countries across the world have signed these principles. While the UN PRME office is happy that "more than a third of the *Financial Times'* top 100 business schools are signatories to PRME," there is an active debate on the extent to which this is white-washing or genuine progress. The process requires each of the signatories to report on progress, but many have failed to do so. Whereas PRME provides a global network for academic institutions to advance corporate sustainability and social responsibility that could help business schools move away from *Pure Economism*, the data on how many institutions actually take this significant leap are less clear.

Heiko Spitzeck argues that signing up for UN PRME is equal to an organization reaching the next level of moral development. He calls this level: "We adhere to standards."

He writes:

As more and more business schools realize the reputational issues related to responsible, sustainable and humanistic management they move on [to] a compliance and risk management stage. Schools at this stage aim to join or start initiatives which are visible to critics. Until recently more than [600] business schools have joined the United Nation's PRME initiative[13] but only a minority has convincingly reported progress in terms of implementation. Initiatives such as PRME encourage institutions of higher education worldwide to enhance the understanding of the social, ecological and economic linkages of sustainable development. Schools are urged to develop the values, skills and knowledge which enable people of all ages to assume responsibility for creating and enjoying a humane and sustainable future.[14]

The aim of PRME is clearly to facilitate change. The question is, however, what kind of change? As previously mentioned, I work for a Jesuit Business School firmly rooted in Jesuit values, such as caring for the whole person, and educating men and women in service to others. In spite of this, the school only offers a compulsory ethics class at the undergraduate level, an elective for the MBA level. Research shows that even though a large number of business schools have added courses on corporate social responsibility, these courses remain largely elective.[15]

The questionable effect of the rather cosmetic changes taking place can be seen in the potential downsides of ethics classes. While ethics courses ideally help students do "less harm," they can also help students rationalize expedient behavior. Business Ethics scholar Mary Gentile questions the benefit of current business ethics classes.[16] She suggests that typical business ethics classes have focused on *awareness* and *analysis*, but rarely on action. While awareness is necessary, it is not sufficient for the training of ethical business leaders. Similarly, analysis can be helpful, but without a broader context it can have unintended effects.

Gentile explains:

> I remember interviewing a CEO who shared the story of interviewing an MBA graduate for a job. He asked the MBA what he had learned in his Business Ethics course and the individual responded: "Well, I learned all the models of ethical reasoning – deontological, utilitarianism, virtue-based ethics, etc. – and then I learned that whenever you encounter an ethical conflict, you

decide what you want to do and then select the model of ethical reasoning that can best support your decision." Needless to say, this was not likely the intended message of this MBA graduate's ethics professor, but it is an ironic reminder of the limits of this approach.[17]

Despite the good intentions and capabilities of the majority of business ethics teachers, the MBA student's response is unsurprising. While good ethics education is critical, ethics classes in the bounded economism archetype can, at most, try to counteract and limit the dominant paradigm's effects. Students taking business ethics classes therefore leave rather confused, because business ethics contradicts the standard assumptions they get in all of their other classes of economic man as an amoral actor. In the context of the curriculum, students may take thirty classes based on economistic assumptions and then have one class that questions them. Ed Freeman calls this the "schizophrenic effect of the separation thesis."[18]

Despite the introduction of more courses on business ethics, CSR, and sustainability, many schools have a difficult time "walking the talk." Management scholars Andreas Rasche and Dirk Gilbert suggest that there are different operating logics at play: the internal logic that maintains internal legitimacy and the external logic that tries to establish the school's legitimacy in respect of the outside world.[19] These logics are often contradictory and conflicting in ways that cause a decoupling of responsible management education from traditional business school practice. In some schools, for example, research faculty wedded to the economistic archetype (typically those in finance, economics, accounting, or strategy) question the move toward *Bounded Economism*. They find "all the talk about responsible management" nonsensical. On the other hand, where there is strong support within the faculty for change, administrators may fear the detrimental effects of such a move. Business school leaders are often judged according to their school's rankings, which can create a lot of pressure to conform to perceived standards. The pervasive fear is that shifting the content of the curriculum drastically would impact those rankings, and, hence, the perceived quality of the school.

From Bounded to Enlightened Economism

Nevertheless, some schools push the boundaries of the dominant paradigm. A number of schools have been newly created to position sustainability at the core of business education (Bard MBA, Presidio, Bainbridge), and new programs have been created to focus on more ethical business teaching. Kim Cameron of the University of Michigan argues that, given that practices that avoid harm are not the same as practices that lead to doing good, this focus makes sense.

Other scholars suggest that we need different types of ethics courses in which professors reexamine the prevailing understanding of ethics, not as compliance or adherence to standards, but as expressions of personal virtue and character. Courses in personal development should move away from the dominant organization-centric view and fully embrace human-centric perspective. For example, professors inspired by positive organizational scholarship suggest that issues of virtue, compassion, and integrity should be taught in business education. Educational programs should therefore focus on character and virtue development. Many schools provide such personal development under the umbrella of leadership classes.

Novel Course Offerings

Leadership has become a respected field, almost serving as a catch-all for human practices that escape the economistic logic. Harvard professor Rakesh Khurana suggests that the emergence of leadership in business schools is a reaction to the economistic perspective's dominance.[20] For example, in the aftermath of the financial crisis, Harvard Business School's leadership reflected on the various criticisms it had received.[21] To counter some of them, they introduced a new Field Immersion Experiences for Leadership Development (FIELD) course. It is thought to complement the standard case method by providing first year students with "meaningful and numerous opportunities to act like leaders, translating their ideas into practice."[22] After receiving a number of personal development opportunities, students are sent to an emerging country to solve a practical problem.

Here is what the HBS prospectus says:

> FIELD 1 engages small teams in interactive workshops – held in flexible classrooms called "hives" – that reshape how students think, act, and see themselves. Through team feedback and self-reflection throughout the first term, participants deepen their emotional intelligence and develop a growing awareness of their own leadership styles. At the end of the spring term, FIELD 2 immerses student teams in emerging markets, requiring them to develop a new product or service concept for global partner organizations around the world.

Such classes do, of course, provide very valuable insights and learning opportunities far beyond a case study-based class in ethics or corporate social responsibility. It seems a wonderful idea to send young and ambitious students to a developing country to solve problems. Nevertheless, it remains to be seen whether and how HBS students will act more responsibly afterwards.

Other schools have added a number of similar leadership courses to their programs. Some focus on personal awareness and self-reflection, some are activity-based, while others highlight the elements of good leadership through case studies and books, and yet others present a combination thereof. All of these courses aim to facilitate personal development, and, ideally, help advance human dignity.

Shift in Topics

An increasing number of schools offer personal development opportunities in more traditional class formats. Some of the personal development topics relate to values and character, others to the importance of trust, empathy, and mindfulness.

Values Values is an important topic in many organizational behavior classes. Students are presented with a range of instrumental and terminal values, and are called to reflect on their personal values and to assess them. Many students take, for example, the Implicit Association Test (IAT) or the Values-in-Action (VIA) character-strength test. Personal reflection is encouraged on the basis of such outcome tests. Inspired by positive psychology, some teachers are highlighting character traits associated with improving the human condition, such as forgiveness, hope, altruism, gratitude, transcendence, as well as empathy. Discussions on these values and their importance can be an important step toward shifting the student's outlook.

Character In addition to the conversations on values, the notion of character has gained more visibility in the classroom. While character development is difficult to teach, mere attention to the subject can be helpful. Recent books or articles on the value of character are stepping-stones for conversations not previously attempted. For example, "Measuring the Return on Character" is an article that appeared in Harvard Business Review.[23]

The article starts:

> When we hear about unethical executives whose careers and companies have gone down in flames, it's sadly unsurprising. Hubris and greed have a way of catching up with people, who then lose the power and wealth they've so fervently pursued. But is the opposite also true? Do highly principled leaders and their organizations perform especially well?

> They do, according to a new study by KRW International, a Minneapolis-based leadership consultancy. The researchers found that CEOs whose employees gave them high marks for character had an average return on assets of 9.35% over a two-year period. That's nearly five times as much as what those with low character ratings had; their ROA averaged only 1.93%.[24]

The notion of character is presented as a way to outperform others in the business context, and thus provides a legitimate conversation starter for traditional business classes.

Trust The relevance of trust is highlighted in various management courses. Trusted leaders are studied, and students aim to identify practices that lead to trustworthiness. Articles on managing employee trust are read, and in some classes students play "trust games." This can take the form of student pairs leading each other (one blindfolded) in order to understand the importance of trust, or it can be a replication of the trust game economists play, where a pair shares a windfall profit (such as 100 dollars) to understand the consequences of fair and benevolent behavior.

Empathy Empathy is another subject that receives increasing attention. Several classes highlight empathy to help students better understand, for example, the customer they wish to serve. Empathy is viewed as a key component for good product design or good people management. Some of the communication classes on offer are based on empathy and perspective-taking, as are many negotiation exercises. After all, you will obtain better business results if you can bond well with your counterparts and make them feel that you understand where they are coming from.

Mindfulness Some MBA classes provide guided meditation, and have speakers showcasing the relevance of mindfulness. With the topic becoming increasingly popular in the corporate setting, some business schools offer yoga classes and other forms of mindful reflection. Some innovation-oriented classes use mindfulness techniques to come up with creative ideas. Organizational development courses use mindful engagement with jobs to redesign teams. Job crafting and group crafting are other formats that have gained increased attention.

All of these topics are aspects previously neglected in management education. As a rational maximizer, homo economicus would not require values, character, empathy, trust, or mindfulness – only cost-benefit analysis. While these topics and novel courses clearly embrace human dignity, much of the content is presented within an instrumental logic in which personal development serves business success. In addition, the content is often presented within a competitive logic, suggesting that these practices are not valuable in and of themselves, but simply better than others.

James Doty, a successful business man turned neuroscientist and Stanford professor, reflects on the consequences of such teaching:

> The other thing I've noticed, especially here in Silicon Valley, is for the same Type-A people, it also creates a competitiveness about how mindful they are. Somebody in a conversation with me recently said, 'You *know*, this is my third 10-day silent retreat.'[25]

While it is critical that we understand human nature and human relations better – education can provide much-needed insight into better organizing practices – regading human development as a competition in terms of who is more empathetic, more mindful, or has better values, may be counterproductive. Heiko Spitzeck argues that from a moral development perspective, business schools offer enlightened practices most often for their own competitive interests. He labels it that "it differentiates us in the market" stage. According to Spitzeck:

> Some business schools start to address humanistic business education strategically recognizing the demand for this type of education and the possibility for branding. ... While this stage is more advanced in using skills and knowledge to deal with societal challenges, the main philosophy is still economistic and neo-liberal. Of central concern is the profitability for business. There is not a genuine interest in improving the lives of all stakeholders by using business as a tool.[26]

From Bureaucratic Paternalistic to Bounded Humanism

Outside business school education, several school programs aim to improve stakeholders' quality of life such as in public administration, social work or education. All of these programs educate managers.

While these programs are not the focal point of this book, their relevance should be noted. Public administration long ago introduced "new public management" in an attempt to copy private sector management methods and apply them to the public sector.

Peter Beresford writes:

> Modern managerialism is damaging our working lives and the help and support we can offer others. ... It doesn't matter what work you do: shop assistant, social worker, nurse, teacher or civil servant. ... Many jobs are being restructured around the same image, with increasing bureaucratisation, micro-management and loss of independence. The underpinning assumption seems to be that without firm control, none of us will do what we are meant to. Managers, it can seem, are no longer there to bring out the best in workers, but to make sure they do what they are told.[27]

There is a clear need to remedy some of the problems economistic thinking has brought to the public sector, according to Beresford:

> We mostly hear about neoliberalism, the ideology of our age, as unconstrained capitalism committed to cutting costs and jobs. But equally important are its effects on the jobs we still have. It has resulted in what the American sociologist George Ritzer has called the McDonaldisation of society. Here efficiency is understood in terms of standardisation and narrow economic and bureaucratic judgements. One of its principal characteristics is increasing surveillance and control over workers. We have seen its damaging effects across the public sector, from social work, where it was associated with [a number of] organisational failures.[28]

The need for better leadership is visible in the increase in public leadership programs. These programs teach entrepreneurial government, social entrepreneurship, and shared leadership. Clearly, the goal of these programs is to reduce harm to society and to embrace human dignity.

SHIFTING TO WELL-BEING AS OBJECTIVE FUNCTION

The first universities were founded to enhance human well-being and contribute to society. In the humanistic tradition of medieval Europe, knowledge and information were considered essential for a good life. Studying at a university was supposed to lead to higher levels of prudence and wisdom. To this day, universities claim that they want to contribute to society by educating leaders who will change the world in a positive way. The University of Cambridge, for example, states that: "The mission of the University of Cambridge is to contribute to society through the pursuit of education, learning, and research at the highest international levels of excellence."[29]

The focus of university education has been to use the liberal arts to educate citizens to be well-rounded people. Harvard College states: "The mission of Harvard College is to educate the citizens and citizen-leaders for our society. We do this through our commitment to the transformative power of a liberal arts and sciences education."[30]

From the early twentieth century to this day, even business schools have claimed to educate leaders who will contribute to the betterment of society. Wharton, the first American business school, was founded with the mission to produce graduates who would become "pillars of the state, whether in private or in public life."[31] Harvard Business School claims that "We educate leaders who make a difference in the world."[32] They all specify that the difference these leaders make is a positive one that leads to a better society – not a richer society.

Many other schools provide similar mission statements. However, as Rakesh Khurana outlines in his 2007 book *From Higher Aims to Hired Hands: The Social Transformation of American Business Schools and the Unfulfilled Promise of Management as a Profession*, a typical MBA education falls short of these promises.

The suggestion here is that rather than focusing on educating responsible or wise *business* people, the citizen and the change-maker should be the educational role models (see Figure 9.1).

Educational role models	Dignity		
Objective function	Neglect	Protection	Promotion
Wealth	Free agent	Responsible business person	Enlightened/Wise business person
Well-being	Administrator	Citizen	Change-maker/Healer

FIGURE 9.1: Educational role models

From Bounded Economism to Bounded Humanism

Many schools now seek to reintegrate the liberal arts into the business school curriculum. The Aspen Institute started an initiative to encourage business school leaders to work toward this integration with the intended outcome of producing responsible citizens, not just responsible business people.

One of the early participants in this initiative, Rachel Reiser of Boston University, describes the process:

> Each school takes on a pilot project that furthers the integration of liberal arts and business at their campus. . . . We work to infuse ethics themes throughout the curriculum. The first course undergraduate students take is Business, Society and Ethics; our goal is to make sure this class is not the only time students encounter these themes, but rather to make ethics an interwoven part of their studies.[33]

Other schools have pioneered programs that focus on social impact and societal change. At Stanford, for example, former Dean Arjay Miller created the Public Management and Social Innovation Program in 1971, which he saw as a bridge between industry and government. He suggests that business people need to contribute more actively to legislation that supports societal benefits: "Business is the most powerful force in our society, and well educated businessmen will support needed social legislation instead of opposing it."[34]

Business schools are endeavoring to educate citizens and rebuild their programs to serve society more directly, and not just to reduce harm (bounded economism) or enhance wealth creation (enlightened economism). Still, much progress needs to be made to lead to an education that is fully humanistic. Heiko Spitzeck describes humanistic management education as another step in the moral development of business schools. Rather than providing defensive, compliance-oriented, or strategic approaches, he describes the purpose of humanistic management education as: "We want to improve the human quality of life":

> Some business schools adopt a new humanistic paradigm for their education and see business as a tool to improve the human quality of life. ... Business schools at the civil stage, however, represent a new paradigm – a new way of thinking. They see business education as a leverage for human value creation and social transformation. They are the education sector's social businesses with a clear social mission at the heart of their activities. A good manager in their view aims to generate value for humankind, the broadest set of stakeholders possible. Following this humanistic principle these schools teach the necessary societal as well as economic skills to evaluate a business' effectiveness in terms of human value creation. Societal considerations at this stage have an intrinsic worth and are not simply a means to generate economic profit. Graduates know how to measure social, environmental as well as financial impacts and how to balance concerns in favor of all stakeholders involved. ... they are aware of the pitfalls of applying a pure economic mindset to human challenges and know when economic models and evaluations do more harm than good to the relationships with different stakeholders or the human value creation process.[35]

The goal of humanistic management education, thus, should be an increase in human well-being, both individually and at a societal level. To shift toward such an educational outcome requires focusing anew on the student and the role of personal, human agency. Management scholars JC Spender and Jeroen Kraaijenbrink suggest that entrepreneurship and leadership can be a pathway for humanistic management education.

> Against the positivist- and interpretivist-based modes of management education, we argue management should take entrepreneurship and strategic leadership to the core of their activity. Humanizing management education means making agency central.[36]

Making human agency central can have a number of meanings. It may mean that courses become more self-directed by, for example, allowing students to create unique pathways in keeping with their passion and interests. It can also mean that education should be far more interactive; that students should engage in activity-based learning experiences and reflect on their personal experiences. Or it can mean that learning is not limited to particular subjects, but connected to the students' overarching human experience, which includes engaging holistically with arts, crafts, and science not separately.

At the core of such learning experiences is the question: What makes us human and how can we lead a good life? The liberal arts can provide critical insights into this question. For example, the notion of human dignity should inspire courses covering this area. They might start by exploring the various philosophical and theological concepts of and narratives about the purpose of human existence. They can then develop into explorations of what the purpose of one's life could be. An exploration of society's institutions and the current societal problems can complement such personal reflection. In many cases, students will pivot toward working on societal problems that strike a chord with them, for example, unfair trading practices, environmental protection, or child labor.

Another course, or set of courses, could then expose students to the various forms of fairer trade. They can explore these themes through field trips, or run their own fair trade shop on campus. In many ways, such projects require the skills and competencies that business schools can teach. And, if done well, create better citizens.

Towards Pure Humanism

Expanding on the above notions, curricula can be shifted in more drastic ways. Whereas the educational role model in bounded humanism corresponds to the citizen, this becomes the change-maker in the humanistic archetype. Sandra Waddock suggests that business professors should become "shamans" and help educate students to become "healers."[37] In line with this thinking, Ashoka U, founded in 2008 as an outreach program of the leading network of social entrepreneurs founded as an outreach program in 2008, has suggested that universities, not only business schools, should aim to become a "Changemaker Campus."[38] In this network's view, universities were always meant to be catalysts for social change and, in current times of global fragility, everyone needs to be a change-maker. Institutions of higher education can play a critical role in the process.

Ashoka U's key focus is on social innovation as a vehicle to create a better world for everyone. It reports:

> Building on Ashoka's vision for a world where Everyone is a Changemaker, Ashoka U takes an institutional change approach to impact the education of millions of students. We collaborate with colleges and universities to break down barriers to institutional change and foster a campus-wide culture of social innovation.[39]

This suggestion not only helps students and the world at large but universities themselves:

> Ashoka believes the way colleges and universities can stay relevant is to embed Changemaker skills such as empathy, teamwork, leadership and changemaking into their culture and across their curriculum. In a world that is changing faster and faster, students need interdisciplinary, entrepreneurial, and solutions oriented skillsets to succeed.[40]

Since the inception of the program, more than thirty universities across the globe have become Changemaker Campuses. Some of these schools have developed integrated programs for social change that are highly interdisciplinary in nature. One of these Changemaker Campus universities is Glasgow Caledonian University, which defines itself as a university for the Common Good. The president writes:

> This Strategy places active and cooperative effort towards creating a better and fairer world at its heart. This means that as the University for the Common Good we are "doers", harnessing all of the institution's intellectual, social and emotional capital, and working collaboratively with others to deliver social benefit. It means we aim to do this in a way that embraces, and goes beyond, the traditional role of a university in the creation, curation and transfer of knowledge and problem-solving skills. We aim to challenge conventional thinking about how a university should operate.[41]

Muhammad Yunus, one of the early exponents of microfinance, has been appointed chancellor of Glasgow Caledonian University, and brings his experience of and perspective on social business as a vehicle for global change to the programs. The ambitions for this university and other Changemaker Campus programs go far beyond a university's traditional role. In many places, the university is viewed not only as a purveyor of knowledge but as a key driver of social justice and human flourishing.

A possible approach to structuring a social innovation-oriented education is centered on integrating a) people, organizations, and systems, b) reflection and action, and c) liberal arts and business education. A general outline of how this could be done is given below.

Personal Agency – Reflection and Action

Starting with individual students and placing their agency at the core of the learning experience, several curricula focus on personal reflection and discovering personal passions, as well as a set of change-oriented leadership skills. Life plans, built on personal reflection and personal passion, are written in which students map out their life as one of the positive impacts leading to well-being. Positive psychology, philosophy, anthropology, and theology courses are helpful to highlight human agency.

Understanding the System – Building Reflective Capability

To complement individual reflection, some curricula ensure that students have a better understanding of the system in which they live and operate. Understanding the institutions and the social context is critical, and liberal arts classes can contribute in this respect. Courses on political science, sociology, economics, philosophy, and social studies can be very helpful. In addition, a specific focus could be placed on understanding the current economic paradigm and its downsides. By retracing the history of economic thought, more context can be given for the possibility of applying humanistic management.

Building Organizational Capabilities

The traditional skillset that business education provides can be presented in the context of the "passion and change" project with which a student wishes to engage. The overall objective is to equip students with the requisite skills to manage change effectively. This curriculum element often covers all relevant managerial functions, such as strategy, operations/logistics, marketing, finance, organizational behavior, and human resource management, and how these functions relate to higher human well-being. A special module on communication and change management is a keystone element, because these are crucial skills for any change effort to succeed.

Example: The Social Entrepreneurship Collaboratory

Gordon Bloom, a mentor and colleague of mine started a class at Stanford University in 2002, which he called the Social Entrepreneurship Collaboratory (SE Lab). It features many of the aspects of a modern university education that facilitate a humanistic pedagogy for social change, notably a student-centered approach that engages teams across disciplines to work collaboratively and experimentally on social change projects.[42] He explains:

> [The SE lab] provides students with an opportunity to discover and to focus their intelligence, energy, and passion on identifying and confronting social problems of their choice; provides them with a curriculum that integrates theory and practice; introduces them to a broad set of resources supportive of social entrepreneurship; and invites them to co-create a collaborative environment that mentors them in designing and developing solutions and the social change organizations to implement them. By sharing their innovative ideas and approaches to social change, students gain more than the opportunity to develop their individual projects. In many cases they undergo a transformative experience that empowers them to continue their life as a socially entrepreneurial change agent.[43]

Student-Centered Approach

Brittany, at that time a junior in college, was one of the many students attracted to this kind of learning. Her father had been paralyzed in a car accident when she was only fourteen years old. Afterwards, her family struggled to adapt to their new situation. With the help of mentoring by fellow quadriplegics, her father was soon able to live an independent life, and even found a job. When Brittany lived in China seven years later, her host father, also a paraplegic, and his family struggled with similar issues. She was happy to tell him how her father had learned to deal with the challenges of daily life, such as using a fork or putting on socks. She witnessed again how much difference mentoring can make. Her dream was to connect her Chinese host father with her real father to allow them to exchange experiences. This is how the idea for i-bility – an internet-based mentoring platform for people with disabilities – was born.[44]

In another example, Uri, whose great-aunt died in a terrorist attack at a Jerusalem bus stop in 2002, and Hisham, a Palestinian student whose cousin was killed by Israeli troops during a demonstration in Nablus, came to the conclusion that revenge was not a lasting solution to their problems. They sought to improve conditions in the Middle East by addressing the economic roots of terrorism. Based on the premise that the enforced poverty and limited opportunities for Palestinians make terrorism relatively more attractive, they wanted to offer young Palestinian men micro-loans to start businesses. The idea of Jozoor Microfinance (*Jozoor*: "roots" in Arabic) was born.[45]

These three students are just a small sample of students wanting to address the world's problems personally through their actions. They don't wish to wait for another institution to take action, but instead want to put their energy and passion to good use.

Solution-Oriented Approach

Classes at the SE Lab are structured so that the students can work on solutions together, in small teams, but also with the entire class. The main aim is to cut through complexity and arrive at a solution that is scalable.

According to Bill Gates:

> Finding solutions is essential if we want to make the most of our caring. If we have clear and proven answers anytime an organization or individual asks "How can I help?," then we can get action – and we can make sure that none of the caring in the world is wasted. But complexity makes it hard to mark a path of action for everyone who cares – and that makes it hard for their caring to matter.
>
> Cutting through complexity to find a solution runs through four predictable stages: determine a goal, find the highest-leverage approach, discover the ideal technology for that approach, and in the meantime, make the smartest application of the technology that you already have – whether it's something sophisticated, like a drug, or something simpler, like a bednet.[46]

The SE Lab provides a protected environment where students can experiment and test their ideas. Inspired by the Silicon-Valley incubators and design studios, it uses a modular social change planning process to cut through the complexities of social change. The goal of the planning process is to equip student teams with a set of communication materials (including an executive summary, a business plan, presentations, and various pitches to different audiences) so they can clearly share their ideas with future partners, collaborators, donors, and the public at large. This approach allows student teams to create and develop innovative social change projects, thereby making the most of their care for society whilst pursuing their passion.

Collaborative, Directed Process

To participate in the SE Lab, teams must go through a rigorous application process. First they have to apply as a team, submitting a two-three pages project outline. If selected, they work with their team and a group of other teams on the different modules. From then on, students are asked to work on their own projects, addressing crucial questions such as:

1) Why are you doing what you are doing? (Problem and Opportunity statements)
2) What are you doing? (Mission, Vision, Strategy)
3) How are you doing it, and how does it create social value, and provide a solution for the outlined problem? (Business Model, Theory of Change)
4) Who is doing it, and why are they the right people? (Management Team, Advisory Board)
5) Who are you working with (Partners), and with whom are you competing? (Competitors)
6) Where will you focus regionally, and who are the beneficiaries?
7) When will you do what? (Implementation Plan)
8) When will you know that you have succeeded? (Performance Measurement)

The SE Lab setting allows students to have a meaningful outlet and supportive environment in which to develop into more effective social change agents. By harnessing their passion, the program engages them at a very different level than most other courses. The

SE Lab builds on this passion and helps transform students' ideas into an actionable plan, rather than building a plan that sacrifices values, passion, and the desire to make a meaningful impact, an all too common result in venture formation classes that teach simple business planning. The focus on social value generation rather than mere economic value generation allows a very different team dynamic to evolve. This team focus is a very effective approach to collaboration, which is crucial for success. It differs from the approach taken in traditional business planning venture classes. Finally, the focus on application is very distinctive from many traditional classes on case-based entrepreneurship.

A Transformative Change-Maker Experience

Many projects started or were developed in this classroom setting, while others morphed and merged with existing organizations. It is important to note that many projects are never implemented. This does not make the classroom experience less useful. Students often remember a way of approaching a certain opportunity later on, which allows them, as social intrapreneurs, academic social entrepreneurs, or something else, to use their changemaking skills in different contexts.

Many students value the active learning experience, regarding the Lab as a transformative experience:

ARNEL C.: This has been a very wonderful class for me. After 15 years in public service this course has given me a different perspective. This course has given me so much hope that I also feel compelled to be more involved. I am beginning to take on more responsibilities and considered switching careers.

ERIC S.: The Lab had an enormous influence. I actually followed through with my business plan, more or less. We started Unitus Capital, which is similar but even more ambitious. In the past year, we have raised almost $150m for various social enterprises in Asia. The lab was transformatory in that it connected me to a lot of great people, allowed me to refine my idea and gave me quite a bit of confidence and was generally fantastic.

These testimonies illustrate the potential of a course that taps people's passion for social change in a collaborative, action-oriented environment. SE Lab students grow and move forward by reaching goals that they may have been able to envision, but were unable to achieve at the outset, by the end of the semester. The Lab therefore creates an environment in which the students' ideas and project teams can be unleashed and flourish, and gives students the opportunity to create their own path.

By helping students gain confidence in their abilities, educators all over the world can do their bit to make a difference. Positioning the vast possibilities of social entrepreneurship within a university environment will help create the next generation of leaders across many sectors. Building on the example of the SE Lab, many schools could develop this approach further in their endeavor to help students become self-directed change-makers.

CONCLUDING REMARKS

As we have seen, a variety of shifts has already taken place in management education. The most prevalent shifts occur *within* the economistic paradigm. Slowly but surely more schools will see their role as actively encouraging the development of change-makers through management education as a humanistic ideal.

NOTES

1 http://college.usatoday.com/2014/10/26/same-as-it-ever-was-top-10-most-popular-college-majors/ (accessed July 4, 2016).
2 www.visionpointmarketing.com/blog/entry/trends-mba-program-enrollment (accessed July 4, 2016).
3 http://evonomics.com/want-to-kill-your-economy-have-mba-programs/ (accessed June 25, 2016)

4 See for example Roger Martin, former dean of Rotman School of Management or Nitin Nohria, dean of Harvard Business School.

5 There are notable exceptions such as Presidio Graduate School, Bainbridge Graduate Institute or possibly the Bard MBA offerings, which are pioneering sustainable business programs.

6 Lutz, B. (2011). *Car Guys vs. Bean Counters: The Battle for the Soul of American business*. New York, Penguin.

7 Spitzeck, H. (2011). "A developmental model for humanistic management education." W. Amann, M. Pirson, C. Diercksmeier, E. v. Kimakowitz and H. Spitzeck, eds. *Business Schools under Fire: Humanistic Management Education as the Way Forward*. Houndmills, Basingstoke, Palgrave Macmillan. 410–422.

8 Spitzeck. "A developmental model for humanistic management education." 419–425.

9 www.unprme.org (accessed July 4, 2016).

10 Escudero. "The future of management education: a global perspective." *Business Schools under Fire: Humanistic Management Education as the Way Forward*, 293–302.

11 www.unprme.org/about-prme/the-six-principles.php (accessed July 4, 2016)

12 Escudero. "The future of management education: a global perspective." 293.

13 See www.unprme.org/participants/index.php (accessed May 23, 2010).

14 Spitzeck,. "A developmental model for humanistic management education." 419–425. (corrected for English language errors)

15 Rasche, A., D. U. Gilbert and I. Schedel (2013). "Cross-disciplinary ethics education in MBA programs: rhetoric or reality?" *Academy of Management Learning & Education*, **12**(1), 71–85.

16 Gentile, M (2011). "Giving voice to values: a pedagogy for values-driven leadership." *Business Schools under Fire: Humanistic Management Education as the Way Forward*. 227–237.

17 Gentile. "Giving voice to values." 227–237.

18 Freeman. R.E. and Newkirk, D. (2011). "Business school research: Some preliminary suggestions." *Business Schools under Fire*.

19 Rasche, A., and D. U. Gilbert (2015). "Decoupling responsible management education why business schools may not walk their talk." *Journal of Management Inquiry*, **24**(3), 239–252.

20 Khurana, R. (2007). *From Higher Aims to Hired Hands : The Social Transformation of American Business Schools and the Unfulfilled Promise of Management as a Profession.* Princeton, Princeton University Press.

21 Holland, K. (2009). "Is it time to retrain business schools?" *New York Times.* New York. March 12.

22 www.hbs.edu/mba/academic-experience/Pages/the-field-method.aspx (accessed June 17, 2016).

23 https://hbr.org/2015/04/measuring-the-return-on-character (accessed July 5, 2016).

24 Ibid.

25 http://greatergood.berkeley.edu/article/item/what_mindfulness_is_missing

26 Spitzeck. "A developmental model for humanistic management education." 419–425.

27 www.theguardian.com/social-care-network/2014/aug/07/bureaucracy-bad-management-social-work (accessed June 12, 2016).

28 Ibid.

29 www.cam.ac.uk/about-the-university/how-the-university-and-colleges-work/the-universitys-mission-and-core-values (accessed July 4, 2016).

30 https://college.harvard.edu/about/history (accessed June, 23, 2016).

31 www.wharton.upenn.edu/wharton-history/ (accessed July 5, 2016).

32 www.hbs.edu/about/Pages/mission.aspx (accessed July 5, 2016).

33 http://news.richmond.edu/features/article/-/12100/aspen-undergraduate-business-education-consortium–the-aspen-institute-travels-to-richmond.html (accessed May 12, 2016).

34 www.gsb.stanford.edu/stanford-gsb-experience/leadership (accessed May 25, 2016).

35 Spitzeck. "A developmental model for humanistic management education." 419–425. (edited for English language)

36 Spender, J. C., and J. Kraaijenbrink (2011). "Humanizing management education." *Business Schools under Fire: Humanistic Management Education as the Way Forward,* 257–272.

37 Waddock, S. (2015). *Intellectual Shamans,* Cambridge, Cambridge University Press.

38 www.ashokau.org (accessed March 23, 2016).

39 Ibid.

40 Ibid.

41 www.gcu.ac.uk/media/gcalwebv2/universitynews/2020-Strategy-Brochure.pdf (accessed May 27, 2016).

42 Bloom, G. and M. Pirson (2010). "Supporting social change agents through the classroom: the SE lab model (unleashing a rising generation of leading social entrepreneurs: An emerging university pedagogy)." *Journal of Corporate Citizenship*, December 39, 103–112.

43 This section is adapted from Bloom and Pirson. "Supporting social change agents through the classroom: the SE lab model (unleashing a rising generation of leading social entrepreneurs: An emerging university pedagogy)." 103–112.

44 Example adapted from Bloom and Pirson. "Supporting social change agents through the classroom: The SE lab model (unleashing a rising generation of leading social entrepreneurs: An emerging university pedagogy)." 103–112.

45 Ibid.

46 Gates, W. (2007). "Harvard Commencement Speech." Harvard College, Summer 2007.

10 Developing Humanistic Management Policies

Humanistic management represents a paradigm shift and therefore impacts not only the way academics do research, practitioners practice business, and educators teach but also how civil society and the political system create overall support structures. What some call the creation of supportive ecosystems is labeled "policy" in this chapter. Policy includes public policy set by traditional government entities, but also rules, and guidelines, and the relevant associations and institutions that civic-minded actors create. These various initiatives create a larger support system for economic actors, of which a selected number are presented in this chapter.

As outlined in Chapter 1, the capitalist system that prevails in many parts of the world faces many challenges, from climate change to environmental destruction, to poverty and social inequality, to terrorism and renewed political radicalism. Even in those countries heretofore most supportive of free trade and free markets, such as the United States and the United Kingdom, dissatisfaction with "business as usual" has reached new heights. Brexit and the vote for Donald Trump as U.S. President are a result of that. To highlight, Donald Trump and Bernie Sanders, as well as their populist messages to reign in free trade, undermine the idea of "markets above all," a message that has been carried around the world successfully since the fall of the Berlin Wall in 1989.

Often labeled the "Washington Consensus," scholars such as Joseph Stiglitz suggest that there has been a globally coordinated effort to support *Pure Economism* in public policy. Originally representing ten principles to focus the concerted efforts of the World Bank, the IMF, and the US Treasury Department on supporting economic development in Latin America, the term has since become synonymous with neoliberal policies that are indifferent to dignity and well-being. While development economists and public policy experts debate the reality of such far-reaching "consensus," an increasing number of citizens around the globe are protesting against the dominant ideology of economism. Even actors who benefited from the system now distance themselves.

Bruce Watson of the *Guardian* observed in 2014:[1]

> 2013 may well go down as the year in which serious structural problems in the global capitalism game became impossible for even its winners to ignore. It was, after all, the year a factory collapse – blamed on inattention to maintenance standards resulting from the furious pace of manufacturing necessitated by low prices for fast fashion – led [the] Gap and others to work to improve workplace safety in Bangladesh. It was the year the Koch brothers, the billionaire bankrollers of the Tea Party caucus, publicly distanced themselves from the budget-shrinking policies of their creation. And it was the year in which Walmart, the undisputed master of global retailing, admitted that it is facing lower revenues due to income pressures: In other words, the working poor – Walmart's target demographic, which also includes many of its own employees – are being forced to watch their pennies and, consequently, are spending fewer of them at Walmart. If capitalism, as it's currently practiced, is starting to run into fundamental structural problems, the next question is what can replace it.

Many people think it is some form of nationalism or socialism. This backlash can be attributed to the breakdown of the economistic narrative. A life-conducive alternative story still needs to be developed and disseminated. In its absence people resort to old stories of nationalism, which promise to restore dignity for a certain in-group while undermining it for a certain out-group (say Muslims). The humanistic perspective can help ensure dignity for all. That perspective clearly needs more support from existing institutions and new institutions need to be created.

In the following pages, a number of policies are showcased that support more humanistic practices. Once again, we will employ the model developed in previous chapters (see Figure 7.1).

PATHWAY I: RESTORING DIGNITY THROUGH POLICY

One of the most common responses to the question of how to change the system is to fix it from within. The former dean of the Rotman School of Management in Toronto, Roger Martin, writes that much can be done to simply restitute fair play. He presents several examples of currently legal business practices that undermine markets' overall function. A simple way forward would be to prevent such practices by means of the legal system.

High-speed trading, for example, is seen as a perfectly legitimate way for some privileged investors to gain an advantage over the rest of the market by using faster technological connections. To this effect, the New York Stock Exchange opened a trading technology facility in Mahwah, New Jersey in the early 2000s. The space was rented out to any financial market operator willing to pay extra in order to have access to more direct routes to send their trading instructions. Roger Martin writes:

> These firms understood that having their server in close proximity to NYSE servers would create a speed advantage; it would mean that trades from their co-located servers would reach the NYSE servers a few milliseconds faster than trades from servers not in the facility.[2]

Such speed advantages can be crucial for high-frequency traders, because you can systematically game the system in your favor by getting your order to the front of the trading queue. In fact, there is a whole emerging industry based on gaming the market system legally. The company Spread Networks has even invested several hundred million dollars to build an even faster link between the NYSE and the Chicago Board of Trade. Again, Roger Martin:

The link cut transmission time to an estimated 13.3 milliseconds. But that is a proverbial slow boat to China compared to the two microwave networks under construction, which promise to cut the time to 8–9 milliseconds because microwave is more direct than fiber optical cable. Why does all of this infrastructure investment make economic sense? If traders using it can get their orders in a millisecond faster than the hoi polloi, they will have a proverbial license to print money. Even a small technology advantage can translate into billions of dollars in trading profits. It's all part of playing our emergent global economic game.[3]

In a similar fashion, accounting practices can undermine the principles of fairness. Repo 105 is a legal accounting practice that allowed Lehman Brothers to hide its increasing levels of debt. In the lead-up to the financial crisis, it was difficult for outsiders to detect the scope of the problems that Lehman faced. The books looked decent, and rarely was anyone able or willing to scrutinize the footnotes. In addition, a credible accounting firm and a legal advisor approved all the balance sheets.

Roger Martin explains:

> Lehman was able to camouflage its decline by using repurchase agreements, specifically the now-infamous Repo 105 vehicle. Repo 105 is a legitimate accounting technique that allows a firm to classify a short-term loan as a sale. Lehman used these repurchase agreements extensively. At the end of a quarter, Lehman would take out a massive short-term loan (as much $50 billion in the second quarter of 2008), classify it as a sale, and use the loan to pay down its debt. ... This was all perfectly legal – Lehman scrupulously followed the letter of the law regarding Repo 105. Lehman and its advisors were playing the game using all the tools available to them.[4]

Another example of the distortions of the *Pure Economism*/free market model can be seen in analysts' increasing significance. Despite their role as independent observers, they have amassed true influence and power over the performance of stocks. With shareholder value as the typical yardstick for management performance, CEOs of publicly listed companies engage in a weird dance to manage analysts' expectations. Protected by the Safe Harbor rule, CEOs can play the analysts' game that will allow them to come out on top, thus beating estimates so that they increase the share price. As Roger Martin observes,

> Protected by Safe Harbor, CEOs began to spend a lot of their time and energy on providing guidance. And they got really good at it. Before 1995, U.S. publicly-traded companies beat their consensus estimates 50% of the time, as one would expect given the random nature of economic activities. By 1997, they were able to meet or beat consensus estimates an impressive 70% of the time. Such accuracy suggests that CEOs began to use the Safe Harbor Provision and the guidance it allowed to influence or manage expectations down to a level they could beat. Beating guidance became ever more important; regardless of the absolute level of performance, a stock performs better if the company meets or beats analyst earnings expectations.[5]

Such examples show how the current "free market" system is being "gamed" to benefit a few privileged actors. Yet the pervasive rhetoric all too often suggests that government regulation would be bad for the economic system. Avid readers of Friedrich Hayek and Adam Smith know that a functioning legal system is key to functioning markets, but the pure economistic mindset has trouble embracing regulation.

From Pure Economism to Bounded Economism

Limiting the activities of free-riders has been central to functioning market systems. Thinkers from Adam Smith to Friedrich Hayek are very clear that government has a critical role to play in "bounding" the market. The current system is slanted to value price over dignity, and global awareness has reached a point at which appetite for regulation has increased. Ben Heineman writes in Harvard Business Review:[6]

> All companies that operate internationally face a striking dual challenge in dealing with public policy: Nations across the globe enact an ever-changing, ever-expanding array of detailed legislation and regulation to protect workers, consumers, investors, and the public welfare, and these diverse rules shape what companies can and cannot do. Moreover, corporations are not trusted in this era of populist discontent because their role in shaping public policy is often seen as bought by money, shaped by elites, and concerned solely with private not public interests.

Such public mistrust is not unfounded, as the examples above reveal. The problem of traditional regulation, however, is the mismatch between its national reach and the global scope of commercial activities. National regulations may serve as signals, but rarely curb abusive market behavior. Some observers suggest that companies themselves need to take an active role to regulate "corrosive" behavior. Ben Heineman suggests:

> To meet this daunting challenge, corporations need a strategic, forward-looking, and balanced approach to government and public affairs. But many don't have one, instead adopting only defensive, short-term, or narrowly self-interested "government relations" tactics. Too few businesses have sought to make a systemic approach to public policy an important dimension of their global posture. Too few are capable of advancing their private interests in a way that also advances genuine public interests, forging alliances beyond other corporate actors to promote genuine "public goods" – such as public infrastructure – which are necessary for a strong society, a growing economy, and fair competition, and which the market cannot provide.[7]

As mentioned previously, the United Nations Global Compact is an example of an initiative undertaken by corporate actors and public policy institutions. The Global Compact has a global reach and is a clear attempt to return dignity to management. Influenced by the Universal Declaration of Human Rights, the Global Compact is a voluntary collaboration based on the following ten foundational principles:[8]

Human Rights

Principle 1: Businesses should support and respect the protection of internationally proclaimed human rights; and

Principle 2: make sure that they are not complicit in human rights abuses.

Labour

Principle 3: Businesses should uphold the freedom of association and the effective recognition of the right to collective bargaining;

Principle 4: the elimination of all forms of forced and compulsory labour;

Principle 5: the effective abolition of child labour; and

Principle 6: the elimination of discrimination in respect of employment and occupation.

Environment

Principle 7: Businesses should support a precautionary approach to environmental challenges;

Principle 8: undertake initiatives to promote greater environmental responsibility; and

Principle 9: encourage the development and diffusion of environmentally friendly technologies.

Anti-Corruption

Principle 10: Businesses should work against corruption in all its forms, including extortion and bribery.

The Global Compact has been hailed as a milestone in global efforts to curb the effects of *Pure Economism*. Since its inception, other frameworks, such as the Global Reporting Initiative and the Carbon Disclosure project, have gained prominence as vehicles that companies can use to report their impact on dignity-related phenomena, including the environment, human rights, labor conditions, etc. One of the pervasive criticisms of such initiatives has been that companies use these reports as a public relations exercise. Rather than evaluating their conduct seriously, companies are accused of "whitewashing" or "greenwashing."

Despite such criticism, the movement to curb *Pure Economism* has found prominent platforms. In the absence of global regulations, such platforms can influence public opinion and serve as a form of public control. The Global Reporting Initiative and the Carbon Disclosure project are two such attempts to measure those things that escape traditional pricing mechanisms.

> The Global Reporting Initiative is an international independent organization that helps businesses, governments and other organizations understand and communicate the impact of business on critical sustainability issues such as climate change, human rights, corruption and many others. By using the GRI Guidelines, reporting organizations disclose their most critical impacts – be they positive or negative – on the environment, society and the economy. They can generate reliable, relevant and standardized information with which to assess opportunities and risks, and enable more informed decision-making – both within the business and among its stakeholders. G4 is designed to be universally applicable to all organizations of all types and sectors, large and small, across the world.[9]

Such universal applicability and standardization can be seen as a stepping-stone toward the global comparisons of organizations. Such standards-based comparisons can feed into traditional market evaluation, educate consumers, or feed into possible regulatory measures. Bloomberg, the financial data provider, already includes measures for non-market related issues (ESG)[10] and suggests that they can be used as shorthand measures for risk assessment. As a second step, there are moves to make such information relevant for market-based assessments of companies. The Sustainability Accounting Standards Board (SASB), for example, is working to make ESG concerns material to business conduct. As a consequence, measuring dignity-related phenomena will allow for its integration into market-based frameworks, and will ultimately shift market behavior to align more with the public interest. Their website states:[11]

> SASB believes that every investor has the right to material information. SASB democratizes the availability of decision-useful information related to critical aspects of corporate sustainability performance and provides a basis for concerted action by companies, investors, regulators and the public in addressing environmental, social and governance issues.

The Carbon Disclosure project, which motivates companies and cities to disclose their environmental impact based on CO_2 emissions, has pursued a similar route. Based on such disclosure, it is possible to assess the risks related to environmental impacts, which were formerly unknown. Should global regulation be accepted, such information can help observers identify high-risk companies and assess the amount of stranded assets (assets such as coal and oil that may not be used). A second step would be to put a price on carbon. Carbon pricing is a typical example of policy within *Bounded Economism*. A good of intrinsic value, such as the environment, is priced indirectly by measuring carbon emissions. As such, a typical externality is priced in the otherwise unchanged market.

Policy efforts in the context of *Bounded Economism* aim to curb the impact of *Pure Economism*. The main aims are to reestablish fair markets and develop mechanisms to assess externalities. Various efforts have been made to build on global standards in order to oblige market players to assess their risk of violating dignity.

From Bounded to Enlightened Economism

Moving beyond the idea of regulation and the pricing of externalities, many companies advocate policy that will foster enlightened market players. Some leaders of the "Conscious Capitalism" movement stridently advocate a libertarian approach to laissez-faire, suggesting that capitalistic companies will eventually solve any societal problem with the help of conscious consumers. Michael Strong, the co-founder of Conscious Capitalism, Inc., argues that the future belongs to virtuous companies, because of increasing transparency and because consumers in large parts of the world are moving up Maslow's hierarchy of needs.[12] This means that, globally, as consumers become more aware, they increasingly demand better business practices. Over the long term, customers will use the market to reward conscious companies. While some companies will have lapses, overall, the enlightened market ensures that virtue will be rewarded.

Advocates of conscious capitalism also suggest that private actors will provide standards from enlightened self-interest, as Walmart did when it developed supplier certification. Similar industry self-regulation helped the diamond industry establish the Kimberley Process, and helped Whole Foods develop an animal compassion standard. Structural changes are also key to making the best use of the market principles. Michael Strong advocates green tax shifts or property rights solutions to prevent the tragedy of the commons, the problem societies face when public goods such as the environment are overused. In addition to regulatory system changes, the focus of public policy should mainly be on supporting privatization efforts to ensure that enlightened players are not disadvantaged in the market.[13]

Scholars James O'Toole and David Vogel admire the ambition of conscious capitalism, but also have strong reservations.[14] They question the extent to which the current financial market system will support long-term-oriented strategies. They fully support virtuous business conduct, but see it as tied to leaders of organizations. They ask: What happens when the founders of conscious companies leave? They fear that the general business culture will tend to overturn conscious business practices, as happened in the case of companies such as The Body Shop, Ben and Jerry's, or, indeed, Seventh Generation, which fired its founder and CEO Jeffrey Hollender.

Hollender explains:[15]

I was fired 6 months ago after 23 years and I was never allowed to set foot back in the company. I was fired because my view of the role Seventh Generation should play in society fell out of step with the board's view of the role.

How did I fail? How did I get myself fired?

- I didn't institutionalize values in the corporate structure
- I took too much money from the wrong people
- I failed to give enough of the company to the employees who would have protected what we'd built
- I failed to create a truly sustainable brand.

Jen Boynton comments: "Because these elements were not in place, Hollender lost power and was unable to maintain his vision for the company."[16] O'Toole and Vogel question the sustainability of enlightened business practices when not backed up by serious shifts in public and government policy. They suggest that the adherents of conscious capitalism overlook the critical role that government policy needs to play to reconcile corporate and public interests.[17]

Others echo these doubts about the longevity of enlightened business practices. Communitarian commentators, such as Michael Sandel, suggest that a fully marketized society will not lead to a better use of the commons.[18] Despite such criticism, Michael Strong and John Mackey believe that entrepreneurs and conscious capitalists can "solve all the world's problems,"[19] and advocate privatized schools, privatized health care, private courts, and privatized water and energy provision.

From Bureaucratic Paternalism to Bounded Humanism

While conscious capitalists are mostly opposed to coercive regulation and paternalistic command and control solutions, some advocate "conscious" policy by "conscious" governments as being helpful. Others have long suggested that the best humanistic organizing practices should be deployed throughout administrations of all sorts in order to return dignity. Enterprising governments, enterprising NGOs, and citizen-centered public administration are pathways to practices that protect human dignity.

In their 1992 book, *Reinventing Government*, authors David Osborne and Ted Gaebler suggest that public administration needs to undergo a revolution to embrace and protect the notion of human dignity.[20] For that matter, they argue that public administrations:

> 1) steer, not row (or as Mario Cuomo put it, "it is not government's obligation to provide services, but to see that they're provided"[21]); 2) empower communities to solve their own problems rather than simply deliver services; 3) encourage competition rather than monopolies; 4) be driven by missions, rather than rules; 5) be results-oriented by funding outcomes rather than inputs; 6) meet the needs of the customer, not the bureaucracy; 7) concentrate on earning money rather than spending it; 8) invest in preventing problems rather than curing crises; 9) decentralize authority; and 10) solve problems by influencing market forces rather than creating public programs.[22]

Scott London comments:

> Osborne and Gaebler are careful to point out that while much of what is discussed in the book could be summed up under the category of market-oriented government, markets are only half the answer. Markets are impersonal, unforgiving, and, even under the most structured circumstances, inequitable, they point out. As such, they must be coupled with "the warmth and caring of families and neighborhoods and communities." They conclude that entrepreneurial governments must embrace both markets and community as they begin to shift away from administrative bureaucracies.[23]

In a similar fashion, there has been a push to move social sector organizations, including NGOs, to become more socially entrepreneurial. Social entrepreneurship is seen as a way to serve human dignity and embrace the role of both markets and communities.

PATHWAY 2: SHIFTING TO WELL-BEING AS THE OBJECTIVE FUNCTION

One of the major shifts in public policy regarding the economy has been the focus shifting from wealth creation to well-being creation. As stated before, the Organization for Economic Cooperation and Development (OECD) has long measured success by increases in gross national product (GNP) or gross domestic product (GDP). Since its fiftieth anniversary in 2011, the OECD, representing thirty-four of the industrialized countries, such as the United States, Germany, Australia, as well as Turkey, has offered alternative measures of success centered on well-being.

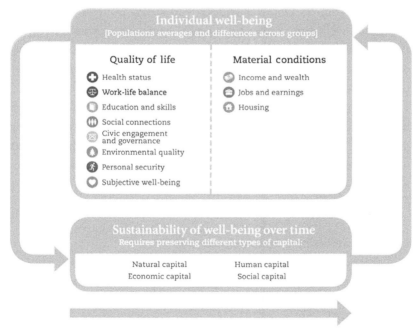

FIGURE 10.1: Well-being concept developed by the OECD

Rather than evaluating progress by an aggregate measure of consumption and investments, the OECD measures well-being as a composite of individual well-being and systemic enablers of well-being. At the individual level, the measure combines the subjective quality of life indicators, as well as the objective material conditions. As such, the measure transcends prior measures and includes not only market-based but also dignity-related phenomena.

From Bounded Economism to Bounded Humanism

Long before the notion of well-being received much attention, scholars had begun to focus on the type of growth that economic policies supported. The conversation on quantitative versus qualitative growth captured the nascent view that many citizens prefer a good life over a materially rich life. More recently, Sandra Waddock and others have advocated thriving rather than growth being the central objective for business organizing. As we saw in Chapter 8, businesses such as Unilever endeavor to assess their organizational impact on well-being rather than profit. To facilitate this transition, the OECD is now working with the Humanistic Management Network and other partners to transfer the concept of well-being measures from the national level to the organizational level.

Such measures are critical in facilitating a shift toward more humanistic organizing practices. Many ideas are currently being developed: adjusting legal structures, establishing investment vehicles, assessing impact, as well as creating new governance structures. Still, a lot more needs to happen to build a supportive ecosystem.

Legal Structures and Impact Standards

The creation and adoption of for-benefit organizational structures in state laws (B-Corps) are some of the most recent policy developments in the United States. B-Lab, the organization behind B-Corps, was founded for those entrepreneurs who want to combine the best of community organizing and market principles. Rather than dwelling on doing less harm (bounded economism), companies can explore how they can contribute to doing more good by means of B-Lab.

Unlike the leaders of Conscious Capitalism, many of the business leaders and entrepreneurs who B-Lab represents did not feel that the current market structure supported their business approach. Much like Jeffrey Hollender, they wished to have a legal vehicle that would ensure the principles of humanistic organizing. B-Corp legal standards allow companies to serve a higher purpose than profit maximization. The B-Corp certification process allows companies to assess ways in which they can increase the well-being of their stakeholders. In addition, B-Lab supports the structuration of a supportive ecosystem for organizations that aspire to be the best *for* the world, not only the best in the world. They do this by:[24]

1) Building a global community of **Certified B Corporations**™ who meet the highest standards of verified, overall social and environmental performance, public transparency, and legal accountability;
2) Promoting **Mission Alignment** using innovative corporate structures like the benefit corporation to align the interests of business with those of society and to help high impact businesses be built to last;
3) Helping tens of thousands of businesses, investors, and institutions **Measure What Matters**, by using the B Impact Assessment and B Analytics to manage their impact – and the impact of the businesses with whom they work – with as much rigor as their profits;
4) Inspiring millions to join the movement through story-telling by B the Change Media.

B-Lab's mission is to transform the mindsets of many people toward a humanistic way of organizing, not only in the United States but increasingly around the globe. In Europe, Economy for the Common Good (ECG) is taking a similar path. Bruce Watson writes:

> The program seeks to address a capitalist system that, in its words, "creates a number of serious problems: unemployment, inequality, poverty, exclusion, hunger, environmental degradation and climate

change". The solution, ECG argues, is an economic system that "places human beings and all living entities at the center of economic activity." To achieve this goal, the ECG proposes an economic system that applies the "standards for human relationships as well as constitutional values" to the economy. In other words, this is an economy that "rewards economic stakeholders for behaving and organizing themselves in a humane, cooperative, ecological and democratic way."[25]

Both initiatives hope to partner government actors to develop a system that treats such companies preferentially, i.e., tax breaks, low interest loans, or preferential public purchasing contracts. Unlike the Conscious Capitalist approach, these actors see value in government and collaboration between public and private actors.

Managing the Commons
In addition to measuring outcomes of organizational activities, adding legal structures, establishing standards, and changing cultures, a critical element in humanistic policy relates to the management of the commons. By definition, the commons are a critical resource without a private owner. In contrast to the economistic approach, which suggests creating quasi-owners of rivers, air, or forests, the humanistic perspective offers another perspective. Rather than only employing market principles, the humanistic approach looks for combinations of community organizing and market principles to avoid the "tragedy of the commons." As stated before, the tragedy of the commons denotes the problem of the over-exploitation of public goods like the environment.

David Sloan Wilson and his colleagues at the Evolution Institute suggest that some of the approaches used by B-Lab can help bring markets and communities together to manage the commons better.[26] Following many of the design principles proposed by Elinor Ostrom (see below), Wilson and colleagues find that B-Corps firms can manage collaboratively, while respecting non-market goods.

Eight Principles for Managing a Commons

1. Define clear group boundaries.
2. Match rules governing use of common goods to local needs and conditions.
3. Ensure that those affected by the rules can participate in modifying the rules.
4. Make sure the rule-making rights of community members are respected by outside authorities.
5. Develop a system, carried out by community members, for monitoring members' behavior.
6. Use graduated sanctions for rule violators.
7. Provide accessible, low-cost means for dispute resolution.
8. Build responsibility for governing the common resource in nested tiers from the lowest level up to the entire interconnected system.[27]

Other scholars are developing ideas about how the commons can be managed better, and focus on non-market goods such as the earth's atmosphere or creativity. Climate activists are pressurizing governments by "reclaiming the sky," thus suggesting that they will confront polluting companies' abuses of the commons. The "Creative Commons" group is also oriented toward confronting abuse. Law professor and co-founder Lawrence Lessig has for some time suggested that creative work should be accessible to the commons and not guarded behind legal firewalls. He and his colleagues have proposed and developed an alternative to "all rights reserved" copyright, so that creators can individually and legally share their work with anyone they want. Lessig claims that economistic content distributors, who act to maintain and strengthen their monopolies of cultural products, such as popular music and popular cinema, dominate modern culture and that Creative Commons can provide alternatives to these restrictions.[28]

Toward Basic Income

Yet another policy emerging from the humanistic perspective relates to unconditional basic incomes (UBI). Rather than having paternalistic bureaucratic systems check and approve social welfare payments, the idea here is that everyone should receive a living stipend to ensure a humane existence. The UBI idea is gaining traction globally, and is supported in a number of circles, whether liberal, communist, or libertarian. Some argue that happiness would increase, because inequality would be reduced. Others say that if people received a basic income, they would focus more on what they are intrinsically motivated to do, which would also increase well-being.

These ideas are being tested as this book is being written. Kira Newman writes:

> The technology investor Y Combinator plans to offer basic income to a group of Americans for five years and study what happens. The Canadian province of Ontario will be designing a basic income pilot as a way to support residents who are struggling in today's labor market. Finland and the Netherlands have committed to basic income experiments that could reach more than 100,000 people, and the nonprofit GiveDirectly is raising $30 million to offer thousands of Kenyans a basic income for up to 15 years.[29]

Clearly, there are questions to be answered regarding UBI's fiscal feasibility. Similarly, many observers question the negative motivational effects that unconditionality can have. While all of these developments are debatable, they show that the humanistic perspective can trigger alternative policy proposals that can help address some of the most urgent crises.

Toward Pure Humanism

Riane Eisler, a long-term proponent of more humanistic organizing practices, applauds many of the prior policy changes, yet suggests that policy needs to be directed toward dignity promotion. She argues that our societal policies need to focus much more on what kind of future our children should have.[30] Such a perspective would restore a consideration of future needs in the decision-making process, and would also prioritize those decisions that affect children positively. This would include a cleaner environment, more support for child care, and support (however provided) for all kinds of care services that can contribute to the flourishing of society through the flourishing of children.

Clearly, the educational system is one of the central institutions well placed to contribute to the flourishing of children. In most countries, the educational system has been developed to provide graduates with job-relevant skills, including the core subjects Science, Technology, Engineering, and Math. However, the original humanist foundations of the liberal arts are often neglected, with many children becoming what the British educationalist Ken Robinson calls "batch products" – mass-produced and standardized human resources.[31] Changing educational policies to support human dignity, develop human agency, and promote a change-making spirit is a critical element. As stated in Chapter 9, there are various actors, including Ashoka, that actively promote such policies. Ashoka works, for example, with K–12 schools in the United States to implement change-maker curricula based on empathy.

In addition to shifts in educational policies, other institutions – including the financial markets – can be transformed. A growing trend in the investment industry is the emergence of "impact investors": people and institutions endeavoring to create well-being by using their money to invest in impact. These investors do not seek to maximize profit (even though some of these investments are profitable), but they also do not want to spend their money according to traditional philanthropic practices.

A group of social impact investors is working together to change the way market actors invest. They are thinking about separate market systems, or separate social stock exchanges (SEEs), where social enterprises, cooperatives, social businesses, and for-benefit corporations can gain access to capital in order to scale their impact. International development scholar Bandini Chhichhia observes: "Social businesses, in their many forms, have been around for a while, but the latest trend seems to be SSEs – trading platforms listing only social businesses. Using SSEs, investors can buy shares in a social business just as investors focused solely on profit would do in the traditional stock market."[32] These investors, however, assess the listed social businesses based on impact. If impact investors want to advance well-being by educating women, for example, they can compare a number of social businesses that advance educational opportunities for girls and then make impact-oriented investments.

A number of these SSEs already exist:

- UK: Social Stock Exchange opened in June 2013. The exchange does not yet facilitate share trading, but instead serves as a directory of companies that have passed a "social impact test;" it also acts as a research service for would-be social impact investors. The great news for social businesses is that it is never too late to get listed on an SSE and get much-needed visibility.
- Canada: Social Venture Connexion opened in September 2013. It presents itself as a "trusted connector," providing social businesses with access to interested impact investors, service providers, high visibility, and a means to value their triple bottom line at affordable prices.
- Singapore: Impact Exchange opened in June 2013 and is the only public SSE. It aims to function similarly to the UK SSE by providing information about valued social businesses, and impact investing funds. Interestingly, it also includes nonprofits, which can issue debt securities such as bonds, on its list of issuers.
- South Africa: SASIX was the second global SSE. It opened in June 2006 in an attempt to provide vital finance to unknown social businesses. It operates like a conventional social stock exchange and offers ethical investors a platform to buy shares in social projects according to two classifications: sector and province.[33]

While these are only small pilot projects, they showcase the move toward more humanistic institutional systems. Many more initiatives will be needed to fully unleash the potential of humanistic organizing, yet there are many good reasons to believe that there are true alternatives to the currently dominant economistic paradigm.

CONCLUDING REMARKS

Clearly, the current societal environment calls for new approaches to policy. The humanistic paradigm can guide such policy, whether in the more traditional form of public policy and government regulation, or as public-private collaborations to promote the common good. The creation of a supportive institutional ecosystem is critical to advance enlightened, humanistic practices in the future. Ideally this conversation can be advanced across the various societal actors, including businesses, NGOs, public administrations, media outlets, and universities. The current challenges require more cross-sectoral collaboration than ever before.

NOTES

1 www.theguardian.com/sustainable-business/values-led-business-morals-economy-common-good (accessed July 6, 2016).
2 Martin, R. L. (2014). "The gaming of games and the principle of principles." *From Capitalistic to Humanistic Business*, Basingstoke, Palgrave Macmillan, 13–24.
3 Martin. "Gaming of games and the principle of principles." 13–24.
4 Ibid.
5 Ibid.
6 https://hbr.org/2016/04/corporations-need-a-better-approach-to-public-policy (accessed July 6, 2016).
7 Ibid.
8 www.ungc.org (accessed July 6, 2016).
9 www.globalreporting.org/information/about-gri/Pages/default.aspx (accessed July 6, 2016).
10 ESG stands for Environmental, Social and Governance related concerns
11 www.sasb.org/sasb/ (accessed July 6, 2016).
12 Strong, M. (2011). "What are the limits to conscious capitalism?" *California Management Review*, **53**(3), 109–117; Mackey, J. (2011). "What conscious capitalism really is: A response to James O'Toole and David Vogel's 'two and a half cheers for conscious capitalism'." *California Management Review*, **53**(3), 83–90.
13 Ibid.
14 O'Toole, J., and D. Vogel (2011). "Two and a half cheers for conscious capitalism." *California Management Review*, **53**(3), 60–76.
15 www.triplepundit.com/2011/06/jeffrey-hollender-seventh-generation-fired/# (accessed July 6, 2016).

16 Ibid.

17 O'Toole and Vogel, "Two and a half cheers for conscious capitalism." 60–76.

18 Sandel, M. J. (2012). *What Money Can't Buy: The Moral Limits of Markets*. New York, Macmillan.

19 Strong. "What are the limits to conscious capitalism?" 109–117; Mackey, "What conscious capitalism really is: a response to James O'Toole and David Vogel's 'two and a half cheers for conscious capitalism'." 83–90.

20 Osborne, D., and T. Gaebler (1992). *Reinventing Government: How the Entrepreneurial Spirit Is Transforming Government*. Reading, MA, Adison Wesley Public Comp.

21 Cited from www.scottlondon.com/reviews/osborne.html (accessed July 6, 2016).

22 Ibid.

23 Ibid.

24 www.bcorporation.net/what-are-b-corps/about-b-lab (accessed July 6, 2016).

25 www.theguardian.com/sustainable-business/values-led-business-morals-economy-common-good (accessed July 6, 2016).

26 https://evolution-institute.org/wp-content/uploads/2016/01/EI-Report-Doing-Well-By-Doing-Good.pdf (accessed July 6, 2016).

27 Ostrom, E. (2009). "Design principles of robust property-rights institutions: what have we learned?" *Property Rights and Land Policies*. K. Gregory Ingram, Yu-Hung Hong, eds. Cambridge, MA, Lincoln Institute of Land Policy.

28 www.theregister.co.uk/2004/06/15/german_creative_commons/ (accessed July 6, 2016).

29 www.yesmagazine.org/happiness/would-unconditional-basic-income-make-us-happier-20160614 (accessed July 6, 2016).

30 Eisler, R. (2014). "Roadmap to a new economics: beyond capitalism and socialism – economics as if children and their future actually mattered." *From Capitalistic to Humanistic Business*. Basingstoke, UK, Palgrave Macmillan, 97–118.

31 Robinson, K. (2010). "Changing education paradigms." *RSA Animate, The Royal Society of Arts, London*, http://www.youtube.com/watch.

32 http://ssir.org/articles/entry/the_rise_of_social_stock_exchanges (accessed July 7, 2016).

33 Ibid.

Concluding Remarks

Speaking to the global elite gathered at the World Economic Forum in Davos in 2001, former UN Secretary General Kofi Annan said, "If we cannot make globalization work for all, in the end it will work for none."[1] Globalization has not worked well because it facilitated unfettered capitalism, in which the powerful could violate human dignity without much repercussion. The resurgence of nationalist and socialist political movements indicates the extent to which globalization has not promoted the well-being humans aspired to. As a consequence, the Western, liberal democratic world order is threatened and nearing its end.

At its inception, that order had been supported by a new economic narrative. In the wake of World War II, a few men gathered in Mont Pelerin, a village in Switzerland, to create a new way of thinking about economics because they cherished freedom and dignity. Ludwig von Mises and Friedrich von Hayek felt the urge to create an intellectual paradigm that would guard against the temptations of collectivism and nationalism. With the experience of Nazi Germany and the threat of the Soviet Union, they worked to create the intellectual foundations of what became neoliberalism. They were afraid of collectivist economic policy and feared the potential for dictatorship. In the early 1960s, the group, now called the Mont Pelerin Society, split and pursued a much more economistic narrative with Milton Friedman as its figurehead. Dignity was not relevant anymore, and freedom was viewed as the opportunity to maximize options. That narrative received a further boost when the US Chamber of Commerce helped create new institutions including think tanks, and media outlets that pushed politicians like Ronald Reagan and Margaret Thatcher into power.[2]

While the economistic version of this narrative (neoliberalism) is increasingly losing legitimacy, the need for an economic narrative that protects dignity and freedom is more relevant than ever.

The story of who we are as people and what we aspire to needs to be seriously rethought.[3] To bring about a better world, we need to manage and organize ourselves and our organizations better. The preceding pages were a call for renewed dedication to understand and practice more humane forms of management. A lot of practices need to be reinvented, tested, distributed, and scaled up to successfully confront the challenges humanity is facing at this point. A lot more people need to work on solving these problems, collaboratively. We need to bring together our best minds, our best hands, and our best hearts to counter the corrosive stories about how we should organize.

The Humanistic Management Network and the newly founded Humanistic Management Association provides a space for those that wish to contribute to better solutions. The association provides spaces for communities of practice that work around how to put humanistic management into practice. The association provides space for cross-sectoral dialogues with academics, practitioners, policy makers, and media representatives through various conference formats. I encourage you to check out our webpage at: www.humanisticmanagement.international.

For those that wish to learn more and dig deeper into specific aspects of humanistic management, I invite you to check out our Humanism in Business book series, our online journal on the Social Science Research Network and our journal, the *Humanistic Management Journal*.

In case you feel yourself moved to write, the journal editors are happy to receive further contributions toward humanistic management ideas.[4] Please find the editorial statement below:

> The humanistic management journal focuses on research that specifically focuses on the **protection of human dignity** and the **promotion of human well-being** within the context of organizing.

Work within the above paradigmatic pillars can focus on the individual, group, organizational, systemic, and philosophical levels. The journal encourages contributions from various disciplinary perspectives representing the consilience of knowledge (e.g. from psychology, sociology, economics, cybernetics, physics, evolutionary biology, anthropology etc...) as well as interdisciplinary and transdisciplinary contributions are encouraged. In similar fashion, perspectives from academia, practice and public policy are encouraged.

The Humanistic Management Journal spans disparate fields including business ethics, environmental sustainability, social responsibility and management studies, in a humanistic research paradigm. It is a venue for thought leaders from academia, practice and public policy

- interested in a life-conducive economic system
- that embrace an Aristotelian conception of organizing/management aiming at "eudaimonia" also reflected in Amartya Sen and Martha Nussbaum's work.
- that follow the trend in humanistic management toward social entrepreneurship and cooperative capitalism
- that view the planetary boundaries as driver of innovation for authentic and sustainable human flourishing
- that consider the possibility of a Global ethos based on universal values (e.g. Hans Kuengs Global Ethic)
- work in the areas of management including but not limited to governance, strategy, flourishing, happiness, social innovation, empowerment, common good creation etc.

You are also invited to explore other ways to partner with the Humanistic Management Association.

Other than the Humanistic Management Association, there are many other groups and networks that work on similar ideas. I would invite all to collaborate more effectively to bring about much needed change. The Leading for Well-Being initiative is an attempt to bring many of the thought and action leaders from academia, practice, policy, faith groups, civil society and media together to develop strategies and theories of change that can help us create and disseminate practices that protect dignity and promote well-being. Please be in touch if you are interested: info@humanisticmanagement.international.

NOTES

1 www.un.org/press/en/2001/sgsm7692.doc.htm
2 Lovins, L. H. (2016). "Needed: A better story." *Humanistic Management Journal*, **1**(1), 75–90.
3 Waddock, S. (2016). "Foundational memes for a new narrative about the role of business in society." *Humanistic Management Journal*, **1**(1), 91–105.
4 Pirson, M. (2016). "Editorial: Welcome to the Humanistic Management Journal." *Humanistic Management Journal* **1**(1), 1–7.

Index